OTTO LASKE

Recent Titles in
Contributions to the Study of Music and Dance

OTTO LASKE

Navigating New
Musical Horizons

Edited by
JERRY TABOR

Contributions to the Study of Music and Dance, Number 53

GREENWOOD PRESS
Westport, Connecticut • London

Library of Congress Cataloging-in-Publication Data

Otto Laske : navigating new musical horizons / edited by Jerry Tabor.
p. cm.—(Contributions to the study of music and dance,
ISSN 0193–9041 ; no. 53)
Includes bibliographical references and index.
ISBN 0–313–30632–X (alk. paper)
1. Computer composition. 2. Musicology. I. Laske, Otto E. (Otto
Ernst), 1936– . II. Tabor, Jerry. III. Series.
ML74.083 1999
780′.92—dc21   98–42709   12-6-99 doo

British Library Cataloguing in Publication Data is available.

Library of Congress Catalog Card Number: 98–42709
ISBN: 0–313–30632–X
ISSN: 0193–9041

First published in 1999

Greenwood Press, 88 Post Road West, Westport, CT 06881
An imprint of Greenwood Publishing Group, Inc.
www.greenwood.com

Printed in the United States of America

The paper used in this book complies with the
Permanent Paper Standard issued by the National
Information Standards Organization (Z39.48–1984).

10 9 8 7 6 5 4 3 2 1

Copyright Acknowledgment

The editor and publisher gratefully acknowledge permission for the following.

Chapter 8, "A Composer's Cognitive Musicology," is revised and reprinted from N. Schüler
(1995). *Erkenntnistheorie, Musikwissenschaft, Künstliche Intelligenz und der Prozeß. Ein Gespräch
mit Otto Laske.* Axel-Dietrich-Verlag. © Nico Schüler.

for Glenna

Contents

PART III: COMPOSITION AND COGNITIVE MUSICOLOGY IN PRACTICE

Illustrations

Acknowledgments

I would like to thank Otto Laske for his tireless assistance, sacrifices, and advice during the preparation of the manuscript. He and his work have become a significant influence on my own compositional processes and research interests. The lasting friendship we have gained as a result of this project is most highly valued. I am thankful to Thomas DeLio for introducing me to Otto and functioning as an insightful mentor throughout the project. My wife, Glenna, who is also a supportive friend, has been more patient and helpful in the process of producing this book than I could have hoped. The incomparable support provided by others in my family—in particular my mother and father and Gregg, Sharon, Bret, Debbie, Nic, and Michelle—is also greatly appreciated. Thanks go to my good friends and artistic inspirations Scott McCoy, Christopher Shultis, Stuart Saunders Smith, Silvia Smith, Thomas Licata, John Bartlit, Daniel Ward, Craig McClelland, and Douglas Nottingham as well as the music faculty and staff of Salisbury State University. Thanks to each of the illustrious contributors who agreed to dedicate their time and energy to writing such intriguing chapters in Otto's honor. Their patience while awaiting publication of their work is most appreciated. I wish to give my thanks to each of the various editors at Greenwood Press who were excellent and understanding advisors throughout the production process. Finally, I thank God for this opportunity to produce a book on one of the most important figures in contemporary music.

Introduction

AIM AND SIGNIFICANCE OF THE BOOK

Since 1964 Otto Laske has published more than 110 different essays and produced sixty-five compositions, nearly all of which challenge established norms in the field of music (see "Bibliography"). Thanks to his significant experience in many diverse fields such as music, psychology, computer science, artificial intelligence, linguistics, and philosophy, Laske has been able to stretch, and very often cross, musical boundaries. The impracticality of circumscribing Laske's broad body of work in one volume will become increasingly clear to the reader. Consequently, the aim of *Otto Laske: Navigating New Musical Horizons* is to provide an overview of Laske's musical thinking as expressed in his original compositions, published lectures, articles, and books. Insightful chapters by an international cast of scholars (see "About the Editor and Contributors") from such disciplines as composition, music theory, cognitive and computational musicology, and computer science enable the reader to gain a greater appreciation of Laske's lasting contributions to music. It is hoped that the chapters in this book will inspire others to further examine this musician's exciting research and creative activities.

The publication of *Otto Laske: Navigating New Musical Horizons* may be considered significant for two reasons. First, it outlines the rapidly changing environment that exists in the areas of music composition and research. Computer-based technologies are increasingly emerging as a necessity for both domains. Reflecting this dependence is an interdisciplinary point of view that has taken hold recently, one that is imbued by ethnographic considerations of the musical experience, research in perception and brain functions, the design of computer-based neural networks that emulate musical activities performed by humans, and inquiries into the psychological composition of artists. Contributors to this book aptly point out and detail why our understanding of musical cognition has changed to such an extent that traditional conceptions of music creation and research are rapidly being replaced by entirely new methodologies. Another reason this book is valuable is that it sheds light on the work of an influential pioneer in both computer music composition and cognitive musicological research. It demonstrates that Laske has been at the helm of innovation in these fields for more than twenty-five years and that his ideas provide a framework within which such innovation can be understood and implemented with remarkable clarity and success. Chapters in the book explore Laske's unique conception of composition as informed by his ideas known as composition theory, a branch of cognitive musicology that is changing fundamental ways in which composers create. His scientific understanding of the compositional process has, for the first time, made it possible to systematically formalize computer-assisted and computer-synthesized music. Laske's own research provides a practical venue in which to investigate cognitive musicology and composition theory—two domains that, until now, have never been addressed in one volume.

Otto Laske: Navigating New Musical Horizons has broad appeal because of its interdisciplinary content which is intended to engage readers from artificial intelligence, psychology and other cognitive sciences, music, computer science, and philosophy. It functions as an overview for initiates in these fields, but offers intriguing and detailed explorations for experienced professionals. Composers will find this book informative as it helps them to better understand the structure of their own creative processes and their potential for compositional investigations. Many of the aforementioned developments seen in recent music research and composition in America and Europe—two continents in which Laske's work is well known—are clearly represented in the book and are placed in a historical context. For this reason, it is an ideal reader for many types of college-level courses in computer music composition and history, cognitive musicology, and cognitive sciences in general at both undergraduate and graduate levels. And since this volume is one of the first of its type to speak to such wide-sweeping and comprehensive innovations, it should prove to be of interest for many years to come.

OVERVIEW OF THE CONTENTS

The book is organized into three parts that, collectively, provide a well-rounded survey of Laske's ideas. Included are an introductory chapter on Laske's education and professional background with a comprehensive overview of the linkages between his research and compositions, nine chapters that detail Laske's far-reaching impact on musical thinking, a translated and revised interview with Laske (originally published in German), one of each of Laske's groundbreaking articles and lectures (the latter of which has remained unpublished for inclusion in this book), and a selected bibliography of Laske's writings and compositions.

Part I, "Composition and Composition Theory," consists of chapters that give particular attention to the *process* of composing with computers, as well as the contextual meaning of sounds to those who compose electroacoustic music. In "Sonology: A Questionable Science Revisited" (chapter 1), Barry Truax reveals the impact of Laske's ideas concerning the meaning of sound through the historical, compositional, and environmental contexts in which people interact with sounds every day. Having been present at the Institute of Sonology in Utrecht when Laske began formulating his theories, Truax provides the reader with a firsthand look at why Laske's research was fundamental to the work of the World Soundscape Project (an environmental sound research group based at Simon Fraser University in British Columbia, Canada). The author draws parallels between society's efforts to make sense of the infinite number of sounds produced in our environments and the similar process undertaken by tape music composers. He comes to the startling conclusion that computer music may be functioning as the interface between human/environmental relationships and that musical competence, which is based upon abstract relationships in sound, may not be much more than "a specialized version of environmental sound competence." Michael Hamman's "Structure as Performance: Cognitive Musicology and the Objectification of Compositional Procedure" (chapter 2) investigates aspects of Laske's theoretical work as it relates to the use of computers in composition and sound synthesis. Taking Laske's procedural view of creating, Hamman considers compositions and sounds in light of the processes that created them, as well as the environment and goals that give rise to such processes. Hamman states, "In this context, an artifact traces a process in which the 'inner' becomes the 'outer.' Computers contribute enormously to this process since they effectively 'objectify' the processes that are otherwise internal." Such a perspective on the relationship of human/computer interaction in artistic creation is a significant thread linking much of Laske's work in cognitive science and composition theory. In "PROJECT 1: On the Analysis and Interpretation of PR1 Tables" (chapter 3), Gottfried Michael Koenig, himself a pioneer of computer music, explains early developments in his important composition program called PROJECT 1. He also provides an enlightening composition-theoretical view of Laske's continued interest in using PROJECT 1 for research. By drawing on several of Laske's informative writings, Koenig explains how the concept behind PROJECT 1 facilitated Laske's innovative thinking about music. Following this theoretical discussion are Koenig's own notated musical examples and descriptions that exhibit the way this compositional tool functions.

Part II, "Cognitive Musicology," incorporates four chapters that tie together several main threads that run through Laske's writings on (cognitive) musicology. The attempt to understand the process, or the "doing" of music is the motivation behind most of Laske's research, as discussed in chapter 4, entitled "A Brief Overview of Otto Laske's Work." Joel Chadabe articulates Laske's evolving perspective of doing music (i.e., performing musical tasks such as composing, analyzing, listening) by recounting the historical odyssey of Laske's investigations. Also shown is how Laske's empirical research into musical thinking led him to study psychology, a field in which he is now a practicing clinician. This chapter, written by a composer, addresses issues relevant to composition and cognitive musicology and therefore serves as an apt transition between the first two parts of the book. "Portrait of an Extraterrestrian" (chapter 5), by Bernard Bel, explores two fundamental concepts in Laske's musicological investigations—competence and performance. These concepts (borrowed from Chomskyan linguistics and then modified) are fleshed out with extraordinary clarity, then filtered through a computer scientific perspective as experienced by the author. Task environment and the artist's "alter ego" are discussed within the context of competence and performance and help explain the far-reaching ramifications of Laske's ideas. In chapter 6, "Adequacy Criteria for Models of Musical Cognition," Marc Leman expounds on the philosophy, history, and future of how models that test theories of music perception and cognition are evaluated and justified. He takes the position that the change in research paradigms seen in the last three decades in musicology implies a change in model adequacy criteria, making traditional musicological approaches no longer acceptable to many researchers. The energy and logic with which Leman describes, then challenges musical conventions (using references to Laske's work) reconstructs for the reader the invigorating environment of ideas causing one of the most profound revolutions in music history, cognitive musicology. For decades, Laske has been proposing changes to the methodology of musicological investigation by calling for the use of computers to test postulated music theories and models. In his intriguing essay, "Modeling Musical Thinking" (chapter 7), Jukka Louhivuori describes his own experience of building music theories and models based on his ethnographic study of Finnish spiritual folk songs. Challenges he faced in testing his hypotheses about this orally transmitted (and therefore memory dependent) music are tied to the need for using artificial neural networks in the research of musical processes. In the 1980s, Laske recognized this direction as having the most potential. Results of these learning-capable computer models are startlingly successful and have been published in various periodicals throughout Europe and America. Louhivuori's understanding of the implementation of still more comprehensive artificial neural network models is apparent in this discussion of his own and Laske's research. Perhaps even more remarkable are his convincing predictions of what such systems have in store for the future of cognitive musicology, thereby demonstrating Laske's foresight.

Part III, "Composition and Cognitive Musicology in Practice," contains writings by Laske himself, an interview with Laske, and a brief chapter by his longtime friend, Curtis Roads, that outlines the role Laske has taken in supporting technology in the arts. These chapters provide the reader with a fascinating look at how Laske's research is put into practice. "A Composer's Musicology" (chapter 8), an interview conducted in 1992 by Nico Schüler, is a revision and translation of the original 1995 transcription published in German (distributed by Verlag und Vertrieb Axel Dietrich). Many of Laske's controversial views regarding traditional musicology, composition, and the future direction of music are revealed here for the first time. This candid discussion provides the reader with Laske's own linkages between his creative work and research, often within the context of reminiscences of life in Europe and the United States. Perhaps most intriguing about this interview is the way in which Laske's uninhibited challenges to traditional views of music are mounted with a convincing combination of logic and soul not often found in academia. Informed by research in psychology and the cognitive sciences, Laske's essay, "*Furies and Voices*: Composition-Theoretical Observations" (chapter 9), explores his own process of composing his 1990 tape piece entitled *Furies and Voices*. Laske refers to the artist's alter ego by explaining that an objectification of knowledge in the form of computer programs takes place to manage certain portions of the compositional process the mind does not (or cannot) accomplish. Applying many other concepts that embody his approach, Laske formulates a historical and scientific argument concerning the misunderstood aesthetics and origins of computer music composition in general. (This chapter is a revised reprint from *Readings in Computer-Generated Music*, Denis Baggi, ed. [Los Alamito, CA: IEEE Computer Society Press, 1992], pp. 181–196.) "Creating Music as an Articulation of Prelinguistic Senses of Self" (chapter 10), a lecture whose content is published here for the first time, consists of Laske's extraordinary ideas about the artistic process as formulated after conducting ethnographic research on the childhood and adolescence of living musicians, poets, and visual artists. Laske postulates that art making "is an attempt to articulate prelinguistic senses of self, or modes of experience already mastered in infancy." Providing support for his convincing findings are his interpretations and expansions of research by other important psychologists. These concepts are seamlessly woven into Laske's perspective on music composition and, in particular, tape music. "The Newcomp Experiment" (chapter 11), by Curtis Roads, provides a rare glimpse into Laske's diverse artistic life. Here, the author shares insights into the impetus and organization of the important New England Computer Arts Association (Newcomp), of which Laske was cofounder and later, artistic director. Roads discusses the organization's interdisciplinary thrust—which is consistent with Laske's creative and research interests—and Laske's skill in maintaining such an organization in the face of arts funding cuts throughout the 1980s.

Finally, an extensive bibliography is provided to help the reader gain perspective on Laske's prolific career in the arts and sciences. (It should be noted that Laske has published dozens of articles in areas unrelated to the arts that are not included here.) The list is broken up into categories of primary importance, articulating the diverse, yet focused, interests Laske maintained for over a quarter of a century. The bibliography cites all of Laske's major publications, compositions, and, as a point of interest to the reader, many of his unpublished writings in English and German. Laske's career as a published poet is also well represented in the bibliography.

A Pioneer in Composition and Research

Jerry Tabor

For nearly thirty years Otto Laske (b. 1936) has been influential as a composer, musicologist, and cognitive scientist. Perhaps this can be attributed to his broad training in these and other disciplines. His insights into musical activities come from a variety of sources such as linguistics, psychology, artificial intelligence, computer science, and philosophy. The creative and comprehensive manner in which Laske has been able to bridge such diverse disciplines is extraordinary. Traversing these bridges is indeed a fascinating exploration of what it means to be a musician of Laske's caliber. This chapter will introduce this composer/researcher's ideas by presenting an overview of his educational and professional background and the major influences seen throughout his body of work. Since these elements are all so closely linked to Laske's own compositional endeavors, a survey of his compositions will also be presented, engendering a reflection on the various technologies that are the strand holding his work together.

EDUCATIONAL AND PROFESSIONAL DIVERSITY

A brief overview of Laske's education and professional background conveys the vigor and breadth with which he has gained an understanding of the arts. After having spent much of his childhood in Bremen, Northern Germany, where he attended a social science high school, he studied Latin and Greek at the Goethe-Schule in 1957 and then entered Goethe University where he studied sociology and empirical social research. Laske further diversified when he began studying critical theory under Theodore Adorno and pursued advanced studies in musicology, English and American literature, and the history of science, especially Islamic and Chinese sciences. While completing his Ph.D. in philosophy, Laske also studied piano at Hoch's Conservatory (now Hindemith Conservatory) and composition with Konrad Lechner at the Akademie für Tonkunst, Darmstadt, Germany. He had opportunities many young composers idealize when he took summer school courses at Darmstadt with a variety of leading composers from Europe and America. Among them were Milton Babbitt, Earl Brown, Pierre Boulez, Lejaren Hiller, Gottfried Michael Koenig, György Ligeti, and Karlheinz Stockhausen.

Laske was awarded a Fulbright in 1966 to attend the New England Conservatory of Music in Boston. There, he continued his studies in music theory with the esteemed Robert Cogan and composition with Robert Ceely and Avram David. He had mainly come to America to learn about computer music (after having heard a lecture on the subject given by Gottfried Michael Koenig in 1964), but because of the greater availability of synthesizer technology at the time, he instead worked in studios at Brandeis University (Waltham, Massachusetts) and McGill University (Montréal, Canada). Nevertheless, following this period, he was most prolific in vocal and acoustic instrumental genres producing over a dozen compositions.

The time span of 1970 to 1975 proved to be most valuable with regard to Laske's development as a composer of computer music. He became a resident composer and researcher at the Institute voor Sonologie (Institute of Sonology), Rijksuniversiteit te Utrecht, The Netherlands. There he taught courses on topics such as Piaget's genetic epistemology and Herbert Simon's theory of problem solving as well as psycholinguistics. Adding to this already impressive list were courses in Chomskyan linguistics and Pierre Schaeffer's sonology. He also worked in the institute's electronic and computer music studio, one of the largest and most advanced in the world at the time. During this period, he finished his entire *Structures* series of compositions (twelve tape pieces composed using *musique concrète* techniques, voltage control synthesis, and digital synthesis), a comprehensive milestone in the history of electronic and computer music. This time was also fertile for developments in cognitive research in music (cognitive musicology). Laske and Barry Truax (then a postgraduate scholar at the institute) conducted research in problem solving during elementary compositional performance tasks using unformed electroacoustic sounds. To facilitate this research, Laske and Truax designed OBSERVER, computer software that functions as a compositional partner and allows for the tracking into protocols of the musical creative processes of children, ages seven through twelve (Laske 1992a).

In 1975 Laske returned to the United States to expand upon the research he had been conducting in Utrecht. He received a two-year fellowship to pursue postdoctoral studies at Carnegie-Mellon University in Pittsburgh, Pennsylvania. His work there (still impacting his current research interests) included the study of psychology with Herbert Simon (noted researcher of human problem solving and its applications to artificial intelligence), research on the theory of melody composition, and the coding of OBSERVER protocols in PSG[1] for the purpose of computer simulation of the compositional process. As assistant professor of music at the University of Illinois in 1977, Laske had occasion to study MUSIC 360 (by Barry Vercoe of Massachusetts Institute of Technology [MIT]) with John Melby. Upon moving to Boston the following year, he seized the opportunity to study computer languages at Boston University, and he soon turned his full attention to MUSIC 360 and SSSP (Structured Sound Synthesis Project, by William Buxton [Buxton et al. 1978]). Laske's work with the latter program yielded his fascinating composition for tape and dancer, *Terpsichore* (1980).

In the 1980s, Laske cofounded Newcomp (together with Curtis Roads—see chapter 11 in this volume) in order to promote computer art in the Boston area. His eagerness to understand more about software design and artificial intelligence and their benefit for music making led him to work in the computer and (after 1985) expert system industry. Through his work as senior scientist at Arthur D. Little, Inc., in Cambridge, Massachusetts, and as knowledge management consultant in Europe, he was able to touch base with his very early training in the social sciences, especially sociology (1952–1958), and to develop a consulting style focused on knowledge acquisition for expert systems. This work led to an increasing interest in issues of human resources management in corporate organizations. Feeling that he knew too little about what makes people "tick," specifically adult development, Laske began a study of developmental psychology at Harvard (1992–95) and clinical psychology (1995–1999). As a Psy.D., he intends to take his therapy work into organizations as a corporate therapist and to pursue his neuropsychological interests by working in traumatic brain injury and related rehabilitation fields. For Laske, these endeavors are necessary developmental steps that complement his long-standing work with computers.

COGNITIVE SCIENCE INFLUENCES

This cursory glance at Laske's education and professional experience conveys a broad base of influences that found their way into his creative and research activities. Even more concrete a representation is the bibliography of his work found in the back of this volume. But a discussion of the ways in which these diverse disciplines are reflected in Laske's research would prove extremely fruitful.

Early on, Noam Chomsky's notions of generative grammar, a branch of linguistics, had a profound impact on Laske's musical thinking. Three important linguistic issues visible in Laske's writings are the idea of structuring linguistic performances through rules (generative grammar), the contrast of deep versus surface structure, and the distinction between competence, performance, and task environment. A generative grammar is concerned with giving an accurate formulation of the rules that generate and interrelate the surface and deep structures needed to convey meaning within a language (Chomsky 1969:7). As early as 1973, Laske became interested in programmed grammars that comprise rule sequences for actions rather than for their product. In his critique of grammar applications in music, he emphasized the need to study the performance and task environment context in which grammars function. This perspective led him to place primary emphasis on understanding the processes required to create music. Within twentieth-century music, there has occurred what Laske calls a paradigm shift in compositional processes from model-based to rule-based approaches to composition. The former is dependent upon an abstract conception of existing musical works achieved through analysis. The analyst in this situation is the composer who may study his/her own, or someone else's works. A model-based approach requires a stylized implementation of what has been learned from existing compositions. An example of this is someone who, through analysis of Debussy's music, composes a neoimpressionistic piece on the basis of Debussy's *Prelude to Afternoon of a Faun*. Rule-based composition, in contrast, involves the creator in choosing his/her processes to conform with the musical idea. This requires the analysis of previously used compositional processes or a stipulation of processes not used before, rather than an analysis of already existing music (Laske 1989:48). Rule-based composition "makes him [the composer] an expert in virtual music, his processes being as virtual as the music they generate" (ibid.). Laske clarifies the paradigm shift by stating:

> What is at issue here is the difference between compositional paradigms based on *existing* music, and those based on *virtual* music. The history of using rules in composition is an ancient one. However, rule-based composition in the present specific sense came into its own only through electronic music (e.g., Koenig's *Essay,* Peters, 1956), at the same time reinforced by computer programs (e.g., Xenakis' ST 10 [1955]). Although one might maintain that twentieth-century composers have adopted rule-based composition ever since Schoenberg (about 1919), it was not before 1955 that rule-based composition emerged as a paradigm. (op. cit.:56)

Just as rules evolve as a linguist begins to better understand how a particular sentence structure is generated, rules change as a composer's understanding of the musical goal increases through working with materials. On the other hand, a goal could change as other possibilities are discovered. It is necessary to note that in the most successful rule-based compositions, the rules are never generated without the composer's complete understanding of what will be achieved. Without such an understanding, rules are often poorly formulated because the composer is unaware of the possible results and/or problems the rules may generate. Negligence in this regard is often brushed over in the name of indeterminacy when, in fact, true indeterminacy is planned by structures whose rules are shaped to take into account all the possibilities of that structure.[2]

The second mentioned influence on Laske's work is Chomsky's conception of deep structure. Chomsky himself credits the universal grammarians of the seventeenth, eighteenth, and nineteenth centuries for the development and initial use of the concept of deep structure, "which reflects the basic properties of thought and conception" (Chomsky 1969:5). He further explains that such a notion of deep structure assumes that languages differ very little on the deep level though they may greatly vary on the "less interesting level of surface structure" (ibid.). On these grounds, Chomsky asserts the importance of understanding the relationship between surface and deep structures and, therefore, the need for rules modeling the understanding of such relationships. Chomsky calls these rules grammatical transformations, conveying the idea that deep structure is a base, or starting point, and the transformations of that base eventually become the surface structure we hear or read as a sentence (Allen and Van Buren 1971:101). A very simple example of this process is given in *Syntactic Structures* (Chomsky 1957:27) by showing that each level is rewritten until the surface structure of a common sentence is achieved. Figure 0.1 is a slightly modified configuration.

In this representation of language, one can see a similarity to Heinrich Schenker's conception of musical deep structure where the surface of the composition is an elaboration and articulation of the same principles seen on the deepest level. More recently, composers such as Iannis Xenakis have defined deep structure as an outside-time aspect of musical architectures. For example, in his piece *Nomos Alpha* (1965)[3] for solo cello (Xenakis 1967), materials are selected and fashioned to articulate aspects of a few specific mathematical groups chosen at the outset. Manipulations are performed on the groups that are regenerated into new forms. Xenakis performs these same procedures on musical materials yielding new sound combinations. Given the fact that the focus is on the actual manipulation of the numbers *within a group* rather than the numbers themselves, they are treated as abstractions that can be applied independently to many parameters of sound: dynamics, duration, density, nature of timbre, nature of gesture, etc. Deep structure is seen here as a set of outside-time operations that governs the transformation of given starting sounds toward the surface structures we hear. Xenakis first recognized the possibility of creating new sounds by using group theory, then formulated the abstract rules to achieve the desired goal. Thus, *Nomos Alpha* is an example of rule-based composition where the largest level is first determined based on a desired goal; then, the surface levels are obtained by working in a top-down fashion (as in Figure 0.1).

Xenakis' ST (for stochastic) series computer programs are used to assist the composer by allowing him/her to stipulate the large-scale characteristics of a composition (deep structure). The computer is then permitted to generate the surface structures by using rules written into the programs. The composer can define the overall density by using three parameters: instrument, event start time, and event duration. The first two are closely linked by the number of desired

Figure 0.1
Transformations of a sentence from its deepest structure to its surface

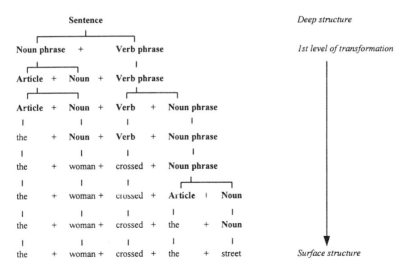

density levels defined by alternative orchestrations and event start times. On the deepest level, the relationship between the degree of density and the number of orchestrations can be specified (Laske 1982:17). This program takes the most abstract, outside-time aspects of the composition (its underpinnings) and generates the surface structures, which are heard in time. The top-down compositional design features described here attracted Laske to the ST10 program with which he composed his solo flute piece entitled *Fluctuations* (1982).

Laske himself has made considerable use of G. M. Koenig's 1969 PROJECT 1 program (see chapter 3 in this volume), which allows the composer to specify the overall evolution (deep structure) of certain musical parameters over time. Laske refers to PROJECT 1, and Koenig's more recent program, PROJECT 2, as "a first step toward an AI [artificial intelligence] view of composition" (Laske 1981:54). In the former program, the composer has interpretive control over the tonal definition, registration, and sequence of events, their relative duration (and/or silence), the total number of events (and thus length of sections), and a random number seed to distinguish variants of a resulting score. The program uses these parameters in computing a data list (see Figure 3.1) that needs to be interpreted by the composer, who follows self-imposed rules while representing data in notation. Because the data could be interpreted in a number of ways, by using any set of rules, Laske considers the raw data a deep structure, while interpretations of that structure underlie the generation of surface structures. This closely parallels Chomsky's notion of deep and surface structures as seen in this quotation:

The deep structure of a sentence is the abstract underlying form which determines the meaning of the sentence. . . . The surface structure of a sentence is the actual organization of the physical signal into phrases of varying size, into words of various categories, with certain particles, inflections, arrangement, and so on. The fundamental assumption of the universal grammarians was that languages scarcely differ at the level of deep structure—which reflects the basic properties of thought and conception—but that they may vary widely at the . . . level of surface structure. (Chomsky 1969:4–5)

Laske created many of his instrumental and tape works in the 1980s using PROJECT 1. He gives in-depth explanations of his own compositional processes that make use of such top-down design approaches in articles such as "Toward an Epistemology of Composition" (Laske 1991) and "*Furies and Voices*: Composition-Theoretical Observations" (Laske 1992b, and chapter 10 in this volume).[4]

Chomsky influenced not only Laske's compositional work but also his musicological research. Laske embraced one of the most profound notions brought to light by Chomsky, that is, the distinction between competence ("what a speaker of a language knows implicitly" [Chomsky 1966a:9]) and performance (what a speaker does, or the manifestation of competence in the form of language use, [ibid.]). Chomsky himself describes competence as "a system of rules that relate signals to semantic interpretations of these signals" (ibid.). The speaker is usually unaware of such rules being implemented. Chomsky believes that since this is the case, there may exist an intrinsic knowledge of underlying linguistic structure (grammar) that leads to a speaker/listener's ability to understand an arbitrary sentence of his/her language and to respond with an appropriate sentence in any given situation. Chomsky conjectured in a 1965 lecture that "highly abstract and highly specific principles of organization are characteristic of all human languages, are intrinsic rather than acquired, play a central role in perception as well as in production of sentences, and provide the basis for the creative aspect of language use" (Chomsky 1966b:49). While a speaker's "principles of organization" are his/her competence, the improvisatory abilities of a speaker, or the "creative aspect of language use" represent his/her performance. The former facilitates the latter. Having the knowledge base of competence gives the speaker the ability to produce (perform) new sentences that are easily comprehended by others, even if these sentences do not physically resemble familiar ones (Chomsky 1966a:10).

In direct correlation with Chomsky, Laske explains competence as what a musician knows implicitly, while performance is what a musician does with the knowledge (Laske 1993a[5]). He recognizes, however, that the musician must be trained, and that knowledge of music is apparently not "hard wired" in the brain as knowledge of language seems to be.[6] The numerous tasks (performances) for which musicians use their competence include composing, analyzing, performing on an instrument, conducting, listening etc.(op. cit.:217). Here Laske extends the notions of deep and surface structure to another semantic level, where the competence may be the same for each task (task-independent knowledge), but different tasks may require a different manifestation (performance) of that competence (Laske 1979:134). Though these concepts are identical to Chomsky's, Laske distinguishes his view of competence and performance in music in one regard: he observes a need for a control structure to empirically test the ways knowledge is actually used in performance (Laske 1988:262).

While many aspects of Chomskyan linguistics proved to be useful in Laske's composition and research, the work of important figures in the field of psychology has also had an extraordinary impact. Laske saw music research potential in techniques used by Allan Newell and Herbert Simon in the study of human problem solving at Carnegie-Mellon University. Rather than relying on statistical data concerned with groups of people in a population, as many psychologists had been doing in the 1950s and 1960s, Newell and Simon thought it more appropriate to conduct empirical studies with individuals (Newell and Simon 1972:10). They felt that after having studied many individuals, they could more accurately define the commonalities in human behavior. Laske has done empirical research in creativity of children and mature artists in much the same way, preferring qualitative to quantitative research (Laske 1977, 1979, 1984a; chapter 10 in this volume).

While focusing on the individual, Newell and Simon recognized the extent to which humans adapt to a given task, thereby effecting, that is, structuring behavior. Such adaptation reveals a great deal of information about the observed person as well as the task environment that person creates. Newell and Simon define the task environment as "an environment coupled with a goal, problem, or task—the one for which the motivation of the subject is assumed" (Newell and

Simon 1972:55). They found that behaviors are demanded by a given situation and that a subject's "behavior tells more about the task environment than about him. We learn about the subject only that he is in fact motivated toward the goal, and that he is in fact capable of discovering and executing the behavior called for by the situation" (op. cit.:53). The researchers acknowledge that determining a theory of human problem solving is difficult given that "the shaping influence of the task environment seems to make the specifics of the problem solver's internal structure almost irrelevant" (op. cit.:788). Laske also recognizes the influence of the task environment when musicians perform musical tasks, particularly with regard to composing with computers (see chapter 9 in this volume). The task environment constitutes the hardware, software, and the composer's understanding of these and musical elements. In addition, Laske describes the computer as an "alter ego" that embodies portions of the artist's knowledge in the form of software, allowing the composer to complete tasks in ways impossible before computers were available. Laske asserts that computerized task environments shape the behavior of composers in new ways (Laske 1975, 1977, 1988, 1990; chapter 9 in this volume).

Laske has made use of computers in music research much as Newell and Simon have in psychology—to track observed behaviors so they can later be simulated by computer programs, which embody the procedures (rules) necessary to produce a given behavior. From Newell's and Simon's point of view, the human is an information processing system, as are computers. By writing computer programs that simulate human thinking, programs become precise symbolic models. In this way, specific knowledge pertaining to behavior can be implemented in symbolic form (Newell and Simon 1972:5). Laske gives interesting, in-depth demonstrations of these issues as they relate to music in such articles as "Can We Formalize and Program Musical Knowledge?" (Laske 1988) and "Toward a Theory of Musical Cognition" (Laske 1975).

Investigations in artificial intelligence as well as creativity theories have had profound effects on Laske's research directions. Marvin Minsky at MIT, another researcher of artificial intelligence, came to believe that the mind is a "society" made up of agglomerations of mini-experts, or agents, each of which takes on a subtask that works toward reaching the goal described as the main task (Minsky 1985). Large numbers of mini-experts are necessary even for very simple tasks such as stacking toy blocks. Laske makes use of the concept of mini-experts to understand the processes of artists while they use their domain competence. This facilitates dealing with knowledge concretely because the programs created both reveal what is understood about the process being emulated and provide symbolic models for the behavior that can be observed and maintained. Laske discusses and demonstrates agents and programs as models in articles such as Laske 1984b, 1986, 1990, but also addresses mini-experts in interactive situations where some experts become automated by computer (Laske 1990). In a compositional situation, computers are the artist's "objective" alter ego because the artist has programmed and set his/her knowledge in an object (i.e., a program).

In recent decades, creativity has become a widely studied and documented aspect of human behavior. A point Laske makes in this regard is that given all the available research, one can no longer assume one knows what creativity is

(Laske 1993b:6). Examples of widely accepted research in the field include Howard Gardner's theory of multiple intelligences (Gardner 1983), Robert Sternberg's triarchic theory of human intelligence (Sternberg 1985), and Margaret Boden's notions of personal creativity (individual life history) and historic creativity (effected by the historical and cultural situation in which one lives) (Boden 1990). Laske (1993b), agreeing with Howard (Howard 1982), states that one needs a theory of domain competence if one is to find a theory of creativity, making necessary a dialectic separation of the two. Once each is understood in its own right, their interaction can be properly assessed.

In line with a contemporary understanding of creativity and its relationship to competence, Laske has felt the necessity, since 1972 (Laske 1972), to establish a new approach to music theory that is consistent with more precise, scientific approaches to theories found in other disciplines. Traditionally, analyses of individual compositions serve as theories of music. However, Laske holds that such activity actually leads to theories of musical creativity (not of music in general). Even the study of classes of compositions establishes little toward a theory of music. Rather, it conveys a theory of competence (but only for a certain type of compositional task). To establish a true theory of music, Laske has proposed replacing traditional analyses of artifacts with the formulation of computer programs that simulate human behaviors during musical tasks of all kinds (e.g., composition, performance, analysis and listening). He believes that after having gained an understanding of the use of knowledge in different musical task performances, perhaps a general theory of music competence (thus a theory of music) can be established. Such a theory of competence will then facilitate work on a theory of musical creativity.

AN EXPERIMENTAL COMPOSER

Two things that have remained constant throughout Laske's over thirty-year compositional life are his intense aural imagination and his keen sense of structure. This pairing is no doubt tied to his expertise in observing the creative process—including his own; but it is also a strong indication that he understands his role as the inspired partner in his task environment. Laske's compositional output is as varied and qualitative as his writing about music (see "Bibliography": Compositions). He has explored many instrumental and vocal combinations, though he has never attempted to compose for tape with acoustic instruments or voice. (His use of computer technology together with acoustic instruments is, to date, only for the purposes of automation in the process of composing.) His tape music is also full of variety and reflects many different technological explorations. Thus, perhaps the most practical way to view Laske's work is to consider separately those compositions created (a) without computers and (b) with computers, and breaking down the latter category into stages by software/hardware the composer has utilized. Interestingly, this approach renders a virtual chronological overview of his work, each stage representing the newest technologies. It should be noted that much of the information provided here about Laske's compositions was learned during conversations with the composer over the last few years, or through observation and analysis. When a different source is referenced, it will be cited.

Precomputer Compositions

Laske's precomputer compositions (1964–1972) can be placed into five distinct subcategories:

1. a cappella
2. voices and instruments
3. instrumental
4. musique concrète and electronic music
5. compositions involving a "virtual computer," in Laske's words

The early a cappella works have rarely been performed, partly because of their technical demands and the nontraditional and detailed performance practices employed. A fine representative of these works is Laske's 1968 composition *Kyrie Eleison*, first prize winner in the 1969 Gaudeamus Festival (Bilthoven, The Netherlands). In this work for thirty-six single voices (several of whom are treated as soloists), Laske makes use of unconventional rhythms and wide skips in conjunction with dense clusters. Furthermore, there are several moments in which at least seventeen different vocal lines articulate as many different rhythms simultaneously. Traits also found in Laske's later computer-assisted music, such as the gradual displacement of grouped melodic lines toward a scattered chaotic state—one might think of the visual effect of falling and shattering glass as a metaphor—are already taking shape in these early works. Other compositions of this genre include his *Tristis Est Anima Mea* (SATB, 1968) and *Quatre Fascinants* (three altos and three tenors, 1971, revised 1992).

Laske's pieces for voice and instruments from this period are five in number. One of these represents his only purely graphic musical score: *Incantation* (1967), for a sizable ensemble including two sopranos, alto, tenor, two choirs, brass, viola, and percussion. (His other two graphic scores are for choreography alone.) Only *Song* (1965) is for voice and piano. The others are for duets, trios, or slightly larger chamber ensembles, such as mezzo soprano and string quartet (*Voices of Night* [1985]).

Of Laske's four *musique concrète* works, three (*I*, *II*, and *VII*) are from his exciting *Structures* series, composed from 1970 to 1975. *Structure VII* (*De Profundis*, 1974, revised 1990), is an impressive work that incorporates various sixty-cycle hum-like analog sounds (heard at nearly all pitch levels) combined with processed vocal sounds manipulated in various ways to result in a contrapuntal texture. It is striking that the vocal sounds in this sixteen-minute work have similarities to those found in Laske's more recent work, *Treelink* (1992)—a piece composed with Symbolic Sound Corporation's real-time, object-oriented, computer-based KYMA System. The one *musique concrète* work composed later than *Structure VII* is *Message to the Messiah* (1978, revised 1991). This work utilizes masterfully manipulated taped sounds produced by the Buchla synthesizer.

Looking forward to what will become Laske's unshakable compositional approach are what he refers to as his "virtual computer" works: *Piano Piece No. 1* (1967), and *Piano Piece No. 2* (1969). Following the influence of early Stockhausen, these works were composed with computer-informed thinking (as Laske puts it)—a top-down or goal-driven approach where the goal is used to start the generative process. This rule-based approach at the time yielded works that reflected the kind of music Laske would compose much later in his career; and they are surprisingly fresh even today.

A Beginning Dialog with Computers

Aside from the four *musique concrète* works, every composition Laske produced after 1970 required a computer in the creative process. Important points in the chronology of these works reflect Laske's interaction with various computer systems of different capabilities. In all cases he thought of the computer as the artist's alter ego (Laske 1990), which was reflective of what he had found in his musicological research. Laske concluded that computer programs are, in effect, objectifications of the composer's knowledge. When some of the mind's mini-experts are automated, the society of mind is reorganized, yielding results not possible without such approaches (op. cit.:53). As Laske's research reveals, the computer and any programs utilized with it are not merely tools but a habitat, that is, a task environment yielding external memory in partnership with the composer. This environment provides the *point of origin* of the composer's problem posing activities (op. cit.:55).

Vital to Laske's use of computers for composition was the rich collegial and technical environment in which he found himself from 1970 to 1975 at the Institute of Sonology in Utrecht. Here, he composed his *Structures* series. These works were initially produced for concerts at the Geertekerk (in Utrecht) and the Museum of Modern Art (in Amsterdam). But much more important is the fact that they helped him realize the impact of the task environment on the outcome of compositional explorations. *Structure III* (1972) and *VI* (1974) are electronic music (i.e., works composed using voltage control synthesis—no tape manipulation or computers). *Structure IV* (1973), *V* (1973), *VIII* (1975), and *IX* (1975) are all computer music, composed with the groundbreaking POD (Poisson distribution) interactive composition system created by Laske's Institute colleague, Barry Truax. Making use of distortion synthesis (frequency modulation) and Koenig's concept of *tendency masks*—large-scale designs used to control distributions of various parameters (see chapters 1 and 10 in this volume)—Laske was unencumbered to develop his compositional forms entirely by ear. Allowing the computer to take care of the sound synthesis, his typical procedure was to create quadraphonic sound segments and later mix them by ear. Laske revised several of the works in the *Structures* series nearly twenty years later, when he felt adequately distanced from the initial process of composing them. Being able to better see "what is and is not important in the music [he] wanted to do justice to the original intent by eliminating redundancies."

PROJECT 1 in Tape and Instrumental Music

The late seventies were a time for study and discovery. They led Laske to one of the most significant and pivotal points in his compositional career. He began using Koenig's PROJECT 1 program to automate certain elements of the compositional process. This rule-based, interpretive approach came to be such an important creative factor for Laske that throughout the 1980s all but two of his works were produced with PROJECT 1, including instrumental and solo tape venues! Even today, Laske feels this program is one of the most "congenial to his way of thinking." (Formal features of the works discussed here will not be detailed since PROJECT 1's generative traits are discussed by Koenig himself in chapter 3 of this volume.)

Laske's tape compositions of this period, though made with Koenig's program, reveal yet another interesting sequential layer of technological experiments. *Terpsichore* (1980) was realized with William Buxton's SSSP (Structured Sound Synthesis Project, Buxton et al. 1978), but was based on PROJECT 1 output data. SSSP had a dynamic graphical interface for music synthesis and editing that used conventional notation (Buxton et al. 1979). This fact is revealing when considering *Terpsichore*'s relatively precise use of pitch along with its diverse timbral palette. Given this notation-based method of synthesis, PROJECT 1 was ideal for generating the initial score data.

Voie Lactée (1984) and *La Forêt Enchantée* (1987) represent quite a new direction for Laske's work, one that he would try to return to for years to come. These compositions were produced using the real-time synthesis capabilities of the DMX-1000 Signal Processing Computer (see Wallraff 1979). Controlled by a general purpose master computer, this external number cruncher was a 16-bit minicomputer specifically designed for digital audio signal processing. It was driven by the MUSIC-1000 software, which was similar to Max Mathew's MUSIC V and MIT's MUSIC 11, except that it synthesized sound in real time (Digital Music Systems, Inc. 1981). (It turned out to be a faster version of Barry Vercoe's MUSIC 360, the precursor to CSOUND.) Laske interpreted PROJECT 1 score tables to generate MUSIC-1000 score files for *Voie Lactée* and *La Forêt Enchantée* and drew from a catalogue of his own predeveloped instruments and orchestras as from a traditional orchestral palette. Thus, the works share similar traits; but since each was composed from a different PROJECT 1 score table (and realized by Laske's interpretation of that score table), they each have very distinct gestural attributes. Revealing the process by which they were composed, these works maintain an ensemble-like quality—gestures and phrases are passed among a multitude of timbres as though orchestrated for an electronic orchestra. This approach is a precursor to the one often used today with the MIDI workstation, with which many composers create and listen to their music. However, Laske's process acknowledges the paramount significance of working in the computerized environment; and rather than using it as a tool to imitate something not accessible to him such as an ensemble of performers, he allows it to function as a habitat that has as great an influence on his choice of sound and structure as his own creativity.

Because of its similarities with MUSIC-1000, Laske found himself working with CSOUND in the late 1980s and early 1990s. He created two compositions with CSOUND in conjunction with PROJECT 1 that demonstrate remarkable programming skills, compositional design prowess, and determination. *In Memory* (1988, revised 1991) and *Hallucination* (1991) share many characteristics with *Voie Lactée* and *La Forêt Enchantée* because their programming environments were so similar. Yet, the later two works seem to project a more advanced level of mastery when compared to works composed only a few years earlier. Laske's structural and sound design decisions of this time seem to mesh into a unity and sonic intensity rarely matched by composers of tape music. Nonetheless, Laske felt that CSOUND was too arduous a program and that it lacked the real-time capabilities he had grown to appreciate. And after all this time, he still had not found a system with the design flexibilities present in Truax's POD system.

While Laske composed a great deal of tape music with PROJECT 1, he also composed many fascinating instrumental works. One of the finest chamber ensemble compositions of the latter half of the twentieth century is his *Perturbations* (1979). Composed for flute, clarinet, violin, viola, cello, piano, and two percussion, this thirteen-minute composition embodies Laske's sense of balance in gesture, orchestration, and expressive energy. The eight performers seem to meld together into one as the melodic and rhythmic lines pass through the ensemble, each line eventually scattering into a multitude of individual fragments.

Laske expanded the functionality of PROJECT 1 by designing (in collaboration with his graduate student Don Cantor) a new program, PRECOMP, to help generate, analyze, and interpret PROJECT 1 score tables. PRECOMP fully embodies PROJECT 1; but it has a graphical user interface in which score definitions are entered, whereas Koenig's program alone showed only command lines that prompted the user to enter data. (It should be noted that presently there are many versions of PROJECT 1, including those for WINDOWS, which utilize a graphic user interface.) PRECOMP also creates various types of graphs of the score table so that visualizing parametric activities within the music is possible. This feature facilitates a way to see natural musical breakpoints in the score table, thus helping musical interpretation to be better informed. (A program designed to compute breakpoints as a function of composer stipulated rules is still not implemented, nor is a program that was designed to transform score tables into CSOUND-like note lists. For more on the computation of score table breakpoints, see Laske, 1992a.) Laske's compositions *Immersion* (1987), for saxophone, and *Match* (1989), for piano, were created with PRECOMP (see Laske 1990, 1991). *Immersion* is a highly expressive work that very sensitively explores the musical and technical capabilities of the saxophone. It is composed of surprisingly smooth melodic lines seamlessly embellished by timbral shifts, trills, registral shifts, and rapid groups of notes that somehow hide the usual abruptness of dramatic range changes of the kind found in this work. To fully appreciate this composition's artistry, it is important to not only look at the score but to hear a performance of it. Laske also used PRECOMP to compose the open-form score of *Match*, whose twelve sections can be freely combined by performers, using one or two pianos. There are relatively loud bursts of chords throughout that are linked by subtle and disjunct, yet narrow, rapidly moving melodic lines. Full of surprises and dynamic variation, this exciting work is beautifully conceived and, when played accurately, keeps the listener on seat's edge throughout.

The PODX System

A remarkable change in direction in Laske's compositions occurred at the end of the 1980s when he was introduced to Barry Truax's PODX system (Truax 1985). This system had the flexibility of POD but now synthesized polyphonic sound in real time through the DMX-1000. By the time Laske began using this software for his composition *Furies and Voices* (1990), several synthesis algorithms were supported including those needed for granular synthesis (the type used in this work). In the real-time context of PODX, tendency masks were used to layer control structures for various parameters and made it possible to instantaneously change and hear design choices. In *Furies and Voices*, Laske finally had an environment in which he could merge all three types of rule-based composition: stipulative (he stipulated rules for generating designs); interpretive (he manually intervened in a computer realization of his designs); and improvisational (he formulated rules within which intervening could take place).[7] The interplay between these methods of composing makes this one of Laske's most exciting tape compositions. It can be heard on the "Electro Acoustic Music VI" CD from Neuma Records, along with works by other important composers such as Jean-Claude Risset, Thomas DeLio, and Agostino Di Scipio.

The KYMA System

In 1989, Laske established his own computer-based studio. Such programs as PROJECT 1 and CSOUND were to play a prominent role in this creative environment. But, after his computer was accidentally (and serendipitously) destroyed, he purchased the KYMA System, created by Carla Scaletti and Kurt Hebel. This decision was partly the result of his growing disinterest in the arduous task of programming CSOUND score and orchestra files, but also of Laske's change in compositional interests that paralleled his long career as a poet. KYMA allows the user to sample sounds (e.g. speech) directly to the hard disk and work with them in multiple ways in software. But more important, it would seem, was the real-time interaction KYMA offered (for which Laske longed since his work with the PODX system) with its object-oriented programming capabilities. Laske's musicological and compositional realizations were often based in graphic representations of structure; so KYMA seemed to be the ideal system.

Although the KYMA System has gone through enormous changes in the last decade, it is indeed similar to PODX in that it is comprised of software (controlled by a general purpose personal computer) that drives an external signal processor (called the Capybara). Its graphical, object-oriented programming environment allows the composer to design abstract structures representing any level of a composition (Laske 1993b:12–13) and assign it to an icon. These icons, in addition to graphs that can be generated of any sound on the hard disk, act as visual aids to concepts not easily verbalized (ibid.). Of further significance to Laske is the fact that these capabilities paralleled those of the PRECOMP program he and Cantor expended so much energy developing. Musical elements of any type (timbre, filters, events, movements) can be identified by a single icon, which can then be chained to other icons in various ways—as in tree diagrams—to represent different structural levels. Thus, icons function as kinds of subprograms that may be opened and easily edited, allowing the composer to hear the results instantaneously. (One might find parallels between these subprograms in this environment and Minsky's mini-experts.) Reinforcing Laske's idea that task environments influence compositional output is his 1992 work *Treelink*. In this fascinating work, he utilized the power of the KYMA System to create complex tree diagrams that combined processed spoken text and synthesized sounds. He organized and edited many examples of these elements according to levels of intelligibility through dynamic high-level filters; and the process is remarkably audible in the music. Adding to the intriguing sound of the work is Laske's reading of his own poem of the same title (from his collection *Becoming What I See* [1996]). Laske has suggested that "the expression of this poem that most closely reflects his intentions is not its written or spoken form, but the hybrid realization heard [on the "Electro Acoustic Music V" CD (Neuma Records)] which combines a digitally processed reading of the text with a variety of synthesized sounds" (Tabor 1998). A kind of sequel to *Treelink* is Laske's *TwinSister* (1995); the same sonic elements and procedures are involved in this work. But as a clinical psychologist, Laske began to realize how large a role biography plays in one's understanding of the world. Thus, in *TwinSister*, Laske tries to articulate the biographical elements of his World War II-torn experience as a child with his twin sister, Helga. The work captures memories for Laske such as the faded sounds of the Chopin mazurkas his sister practiced in the blue-painted living room of their childhood home. Through readings of Laske's German poem, *Twin Sister*, and its paraphrased English translation, the composer balances the contrast between the forcefulness of the German language and the understated clarity of the English language. This is an exciting composition in which Laske intuitively relies on his mastery of materials but concentrates on composing a quasi-autobiographical sketch, enhanced by quotes from *Voie Lactée*, *La Forêt Enchantée*, and *Voices of Night* (1985).

CONCLUSION

As an innovative and methodical researcher Laske is a pioneer in a new domain of inquiry into musical activity. His focus on the process of doing music enriches traditional musicology by incorporating a better understanding of how musicians use their domain competence. Laske recognizes that while the historical aspects of music are a necessary factor in an appreciation of the musical experience, so too are the processes individuals initiate to investigate such a history, to analyze, compose, or listen to music. While his cognitive musicology moves quickly forward toward new understandings, Laske's foundational work in the field has made an indelible impact on music research. Further, his present investigations into the imprint psychological issues have on doing music will undoubtedly contribute to our present understanding of music making.

It is likely that one of the reasons Laske's research has had such an impact on theoretical discourse is that he is himself an impressive participant in the musical creative process. He is as careful a composer as he is a researcher; and he understands his own processes—better than most composers understand their own—because of his expertise in composition theory and other areas of cognitive musicology. His unique aural imagination and his strong sense of structure have produced compositions that will assuredly become treasures, both in the electroacoustic and the acoustic repertoire. If his current work in progress is any indication, there are many more important compositions to come. There is at least one indelible truth his music and research teach us: that walking the thin line between doing music and investigating that doing—without getting stuck on one side of the line or the other—produces an extraordinary musician. Indeed, Laske may be one of the greatest of our century.

NOTES

1. Production System Generator (PSG) is a procedural (process oriented) language invented by Allen Newell and Herbert Simon. Since it is designed for the purpose of simulating human processes, Laske used it to replicate actions documented by OBSERVER's protocols in hopes that it would eventually allow him to replicate the results of the observed subjects. This first procedural language, however, was unwieldy and temporally not fine-grained enough. Eventually, PSG was developed by Newell into a newer procedural language called SOAR.

2. For example, John Cage's *Variations II* (1961) allows for the determination of every structural level and musical parameter by means of measurement between the given physical symbols. Cage's understanding of indeterminacy and the ramifications of structuring it allowed him to eliminate structural holes that could engender interpretational uncertainty.

3. For more on *Nomos Alpha* see Thomas DeLio's "The Dialectics of Structure and Materials," in Contiguous *Lines: Issues and Ideas in the Music of the '60's and '70's*, T. DeLio, ed. (Lanham, MD: University Press of America, 1985). Also see Xenakis, Iannis, *Formalized Music: Thought and Mathematics in Composition* (Stuyvesant, NY: Pendragon Press, 1992).

4. Laske (1991) discusses several approaches to composition and addresses at considerable length his piano composition *Match* (1989). In this volume (chapter 9) the composer discusses the process of making *Furies and Voices* (1990) for tape.

5. This is a summary of Laske's early writings.

6. For this reason, Laske compares musical competence to poetic language competence, rejecting such a comparison with spoken language.

7. See chapter 9 of this volume.

REFERENCES

Allen, J., and P. Van Buren (1971). *Chomsky: Selected Readings.* London: Oxford University Press.

Boden, M. (1990). *Creative Mind.* New York: Basic Books.

Buxton, W., E. Fogels, G. Federkow, L. Sasaki, and K. Smith (1978). "An Introduction to the SSSP Digital Synthesizer." *Computer Music Journal* 2(4):29–38.

Buxton, W., R. Sniderman, W. Reeves, S. Patel, and R. Baecker (1979). "The Evolution of the SSSP Score Editing Tools." *Computer Music Journal* 3(4):14–25.

Chomsky, N. (1957). *Syntactic Structures.* The Hague: Mouton.

Chomsky, N. (1966a). *Topics in the Theory of Generative Grammar.* The Hague: Mouton.

Chomsky, N. (1966b). "Linguistic Theory." In R. Mead, Jr., ed. *Language Teaching: Broader Contexts.* Middlebury, VT: Northeast Conference on the Teaching of Foreign Languages.

Chomsky, N. (1969). "The Current Scene in Linguistics: Present Directions." In D. Reible and S. Schane, eds. *Modern Studies in English.* Englewood Cliffs, NJ: Prentice-Hall, pp. 3–12.

Digital Music Systems, Inc. (1981). *MUSIC-1000 Manual, Version 1.0.* Boston, MA.

Gardner, H. (1983). *Frames of Mind.* New York: Basic Books.

Howard, V. (1982). *Artistry: The Work of Artists.* Cambridge, MA: Hackett.

Laske, O. (1972). *On Problems of a Performance Model for Music.* Utrecht, The Netherlands: Institute of Sonology.

Laske, O. (1975). "Toward a Theory of Musical Cognition." *Interface* 4(2):147–208.

Laske, O. (1977). *Music, Memory and Thought: Explorations in Cognitive Musicology.* Ann Arbor, MI: University Research Press.

Laske, O. (1979). "On Problems of Verification in Music Theory." *College Music Symposium* 19(2):129–139.

Laske, O. (1981). "Composition Theory in Koenig's Project One and Project Two." *Computer Music Journal* 5(4):54–65.

Laske, O. (1982). "A Definition of Computer Music." *Feedback Papers* 27–28:8–24. Cologne, Germany: Feedback Studio Köln.

Laske, O. (1984a). "Keith: A Rule System for Making Music-Analytical Discoveries." In M. Baroni and L. Callegari, eds., *Proceedings of 1982 International Conference on Musical Grammars and Computer Analysis.* Florence, Italy: Leo S. Olschki, pp. 165–200.

Laske, O. (1984b). "Understanding Listening Procedurally." *Sonus* (5)1:61–71.

Laske, O. (1986). "Toward a Computational Theory of Musical Listening." In F. Vandamme, J. Broeckx, and H. Sabbe, eds. *Proceedings of the 1983 International Conference on Music, Reason, and Emotion.* In *Communication and Cognition.* 18(4):363–392.

Laske, O. (1988). "Can We Formalize and Program Musical Knowledge?: An Inquiry into the Focus and Scope of Cognitive Musicology." In M. Boroda, ed. *Musikometrika 1.* Bochum, Germany: Studienverlag N. Brockmeyer, pp. 257–280.

Laske, O. (1989). "Composition Theory: An Enrichment of Music Theory." *Interface* 18(1–2):45–49.

Laske, O. (1990). "The Computer as the Artist's Alter Ego." *Leonardo* (23)1:53–66.

Laske, O. (1991). "Toward an Epistemology of Composition." *Interface* 20(3–4):235–269.

Laske, O. (1992a). "The OBSERVER Tradition of Knowledge Acquisition." In M. Balaban, K. Ebcioglu, and O. Laske, eds. *Understanding Music with AI*. Menlo Park, CA: AAAI Press, pp. 258–289.

Laske, O. (1992b). "Furies and Voices: Composition-Theoretical Observations." In Baggi, D., ed. *Readings in Computer-Generated Music*. Los Alamitos, CA: IEEE Press, pp. 181–197.

Laske, O. (1993a). "A Search for a Theory of Musicality." *Languages of Design* 1(3):209–228.

Laske, O. (1993b). "Mindware and Software: Can They Meet?: Observations on AI and the Arts." *Proceedings of the International Workshop on Knowledge Technology in the Arts*. Osaka, Japan, pp. 1–18.

Laske, O. (1994). "Creating Music as an Articulation of Pre-Linguistic Senses of Self." Invited lecture, Conference on "Technology and the Composer." Bibliothèque Nationale de Luxembourg, and University of Maryland at College Park, MD. [Chapter 10 of this volume.]

Minsky, M. (1985). *Society of Mind*. New York: Simon and Schuster.

Newell, A., and H. Simon (1972). *Human Problem Solving*. Englewood Cliffs, NJ: Prentice-Hall.

Sternberg, R. (1985). *Beyond IQ: A Triarchic Theory of Human Intelligence*. New York: Cambridge University Press.

Tabor, J. (1998). "Electro Acoustic Music V." *Computer Music Journal* 22(1):75–77.

Truax, B. (1985). "The PODX System: Interactive Compositional Software for the DMX-1000." *Computer Music Journal* 9(1):29–38.

Wallraff, D. (1979). "The DMX-1000 Signal Processing Computer." *Computer Music Journal* 3(4):44–49.

Xenakis, I. (1967). *Nomos Alpha*. New York: Boosey and Hawkes.

Part I

Composition and Composition Theory

1

Sonology:
A Questionable Science Revisited
Barry Truax

> Music theory is here seen as a discipline whose object, method, and scope are still undefined.
>
> —Otto Laske
> *Tutorial Notes, Institute of Sonology, 1972*

It has been twenty-five years since Otto Laske threw down this challenge to the prevailing order of theoretical discussion about music and proposed the alternative—a "generative" theory of music, within which a "sonological theory of perception" figured centrally. Further in his notes, he defined sonology as "a science of sound structures susceptible to a semantic interpretation" and as "a theory of sound structures that carry a meaning and hence are musical." I will leave it to other, possibly future, commentators to chart the influence that Laske's ideas have had on music theory, and instead offer a more personal account, first of the environment in which these ideas were launched, and second of the profound influence they have had on both my intellectual and creative work in electroacoustic music and acoustic communication.

I have deliberately quoted from Laske's unpublished tutorial notes (from 1972), rather than the formal publication to which it led (Laske 1975)[1] in order to recapture some of the flavor of the situation at the Institute of Sonology in Utrecht during the early 1970s where I found myself as a postgraduate student on a two-year study period. Nostalgia aside, I believe that the particular nexus of technical and intellectual elements that existed there at that time was unique and possibly prophetic for the turbulent period of digitization that was about to be unleashed, first on the highly developed analog studios of Europe and North America, and later on the consumer public in general. Given that we have not yet emerged from the chaotic period of growth of the digital era to a mature state where its impact can be properly assessed, it may be useful to return to one of the microcosms where that future was plotted, the Institute of Sonology.

In an unassuming three-story building on one of Utrecht's smaller canal streets (the Plompetorengracht), was assembled on the ground floor a suite of analog electronic and tape studios, all with highly sophisticated, customized equipment for sound synthesis, voltage control, and signal processing. Another room contained the newly purchased PDP-15 minicomputer, complete with 12-bit digital-to-analog converters, for which software had to be written from the ground up, as it were. The teaching faculty included Gottfried Michael Koenig for composition theory and programming; Stan Tempelaars for acoustics, psychoacoustics and signal processing; Frits Weiland for the history of electronic music; Luctor Ponse and Jaap Vink for studio technique; Greta Vermeulen for programming and computer composition; Werner Kaegi for phonetics and logic; and, in a small office on the top floor, Otto Laske who conducted a seminar in music theory from an interdisciplinary perspective. A steady stream of international students and visiting composers from around the world were either working for short periods in the studios or following the annual courses given by the faculty. Visiting lecturers, often from the United States (Chowning, Dodge, Beauchamp, and others), brought news of recent developments in computer music. The stage was set for the birth of a "brave new world" of electroacoustic music under the novel banner of the term sonology.

And what was meant by sonology? Laske offered the most theoretically profound definition, though one that was not necessarily agreed upon by everyone at the Institute. It arose out of a critique of conventional music theory and musicology which, as he wrote in the "Avant-Propos" of his *Introduction to a Generative Theory of Music* (Laske 1973), "has been kept enslaved by its acceptance of things—works and/or scores—as the true object of inquiry without ever giving account of the competence . . . which is at the bottom of all musical production." At this point, Laske had been greatly influenced by Saussure and Chomsky, particularly in putting the emphasis on the tacit knowledge, or competence, which made possible all manifestations of musical activity, whether listening, performing or composing. He sought to explicate the generative principle, essentially sets of rules, which allowed musicians to make sense not only of existing musical structures, but also of novel structures that had not been encountered before—hence the notion of creativity.

In short, Laske never asked what is music but, instead, what is musical? Music was to be understood as the result of mental activity—process not artifact. A central distinction, following Chomsky, was between competence and performance—grammar and strategies, knowledge at rest and knowledge in action. Three components of the grammar, taken from Charles Morris's Theory of Signs, were the syntactic, semantic, and sonological levels with the syntactic level essentially linking the other two. According to this theory, sounds become meaningful through the ways in which they are perceived to be structured. This model stood in contrast to the conventional emphasis on syntax in music theory based on instrumental music analysis where timbre could either be assumed or ignored. Already in the electronic music of the 1950s and 1960s it could be seen that composers were elevating sonic design, even if sometimes crudely modeled, to a role of central importance in that music—a trend that the techniques of conventional music theory were incapable of following or explicating.

Given that the main attraction for me of the electronic music studio lay in its ability, even necessity, to create sound directly, the emphasis Laske placed on sonological thinking was compelling. Many of the sounds we were creating in the analog studio seemed absolutely novel, and their variations limitless. Yet how were we, let alone other listeners, to make sense of this exploding universe of sonic possibility? Even the classical acoustic and psychoacoustic models seemed to apply best to the relatively orderly, contained world of speech and musical instruments and offered few guidelines to the complex, often noisy or hard-edged and textured sounds that emanated so readily from the studio equipment at our disposal. Perhaps the intuitions we were developing in shaping this material were being guided by sonological competence of a generative nature, since clearly many of these sounds had never been heard before.

However, the critical element in this situation, the one that would eventually transform the world of electroacoustic music, was the computer. At first, its presence was a mere curiosity, and from a sonic point of view, its output seemed trivial. Limited to software synthesis (digital synthesis hardware was to come later), it could only produce monophonic streams of sound. Moreover, the synthesis models available were simplistic, such as fixed waveforms, amplitude modulation, and the like. Fortunately, Chowning's visit early in 1973 brought me into contact with the technique of frequency modulation and its sonically more dynamic output (Chowning 1973). As a result, my first computer music composition (a quadraphonic tape solo subtitled "The Journey to the Gods" that was part of the larger cycle of the *Gilgamesh Tapes* designed to accompany a piece of music theater) was almost entirely realized with real-time FM synthesis in the summer of 1973. It was a piece whose stochastic structures and timbral organization were literally inconceivable in the analog studio. The journey into the digital domain had begun, and by this point, the computer had become a compositional necessity.

SYSTEMS FOR COMPUTER MUSIC SYNTHESIS AND COMPOSITION AT UTRECHT

Although more lifelike than the other synthesis methods available at the time (Kaegi's VOSIM system migrated to the computer later), FM synthesis still sounded artificial and in some senses, simpler or purer than the sounds typical of the analog studio. In the intervening years that have seen digital synthesis almost completely replace its analog counterparts, we have also witnessed, in my opinion, an ambiguous division of digital sound production practice. The mainstream approach, largely based on wavetable techniques, has continued to produce sonically simplified sounds that imitate instrumental models but lack their corporeality. To compensate for this deficiency, generous amounts of processing, usually based on time delays (e.g., reverb, chorusing, phasing, feedback), are added to enrich the sound quality and make it palatable. (I am not referring to sample-based synthesis methods, which offer a curiously hybrid approach to the problem.) The minority of synthesis specialists who still wish to move beyond the instrumental model and explore the uncharted territory first opened up by analog techniques, have either refined their control of synthesis parameters to an amazing degree (something that is inherently impossible with commercial synthesizers) or have moved to synthesis models that are no longer based on oscillators and wavetables. Among the most successful of these alternative models to date, in my opinion, are granular synthesis and physical modeling or waveguide approaches (De Poli et al. 1991). Both of these classes of techniques seem to have the potential of creating the sense of volume (i.e., perceived magnitude) and physicality associated with acoustic sounds, without necessarily being restricted to imitating real-world examples.

Another alternative was developed at the Institute of Sonology, possibly with the unstated intent of preserving the open-endedness of the analog experience, namely "nonstandard" synthesis methods such as Koenig's SSP system and Paul Berg's PILE language, two of the most noteworthy examples (Koenig 1980). They are termed nonstandard because they are based on no known acoustic principle or parameter, but rather on basic microlevel data manipulations—expressed either as amplitude/time sequences or in the logical form of machine language operations that result in such sequences. In more colloquial parlance, these approaches continued what has been called the "hard edge Utrecht school" of electronic music, known for its abrasive sound quality and uncompromising compositional structures. (I recall one composer at the Institute who rather proudly claimed that no one had ever been able to sit through the entire length of one of his pieces, and I for one was not about to disprove him.) Although the "noise," in Jacques Attali's sense (Attali 1985), of these pieces has sporadically continued to flourish through connections to punk rock, grunge music, and various forms of "postmodern" deconstructionism, they can also be seen as a continuation of the analog tradition which, by being based on the manipulation of voltages rather than specifically acoustic models, had announced an unbounded world of machine-generated sonological structures.

The importance for Laske of digital sound synthesis was not necessarily its sonic appeal, but rather its ability to create precisely defined neutral sounds, that is, those not predefined as musical through instrumental production. Secondly, the computer's ability to manipulate symbols facilitates the modeling of grammatical rules at all levels. And finally, the user/program environment provides an efficient empirical testing situation for observing musical behavior in action, the trace of which (the protocol) can later be analyzed. In short, musical behavior can be modeled, simulated, and tested within a controlled computer environment, making music theory (perhaps for the first time) subject to empirical verification. The single-user minicomputer system, equipped with real-time digital synthesis capability, no matter how primitive in its limitations, offered the technical facility for such work to be carried out. The computer could be used, not as a sophisticated number cruncher for analyzing artifacts such as scores or acoustic signals, but as an environment for testing musical and sonological behavior.

For me, the possibility of using the computer inspired my development of software for interactive composition and sound synthesis, namely the POD4, POD5, and POD6 programs (Truax 1973), later called the POD system (Truax 1977), and the PODX system (Truax 1985) when the microprogrammable DMX-

1000 was added to provide real-time polyphonic synthesis. These programs were examples of one of two approaches that were inspired by Koenig and Laske, namely programs for automated composition and for computer-assisted composition. In the automated approach, such as Koenig's PR1 and PR2 (PROJECT 1 and PROJECT 2), the composer defined rules for organizing compositional data (Koenig 1970). PR1 allowed no significant user input, whereas PR2 provided the opportunity for the user to input various data lists, selection choices, and parameter hierarchies. The output was then transcribed into whatever musical score representation the composer had in mind. Later, some sound synthesis capability was added. In one of Koenig's characteristically succinct formulations of the essential nature of this kind of algorithmic approach, the compositional problem was described as "given the rules, find the music" (Koenig 1980). This concept is in striking contrast to the dominant model of computer composition often embraced by MUSIC V or CSOUND users in which the task becomes, given the music, find the correct numerical specification (the detailed score and orchestra) for the program to realize the piece.

Laske, who was later to publish one of the most lucid analyses of Koenig's software (Laske 1981), regarded this algorithmic approach as an example of the generative theory in which neutral (i.e., task-independent) compositional rules were formulated and tested by users working on specific compositional tasks. It represented a specific kind of interaction between two bodies of musical knowledge, one externalized in the form of programs and the other embodied internally in the composer's cognitive processes in dealing with the program's output. However, the interaction as an actual process involved the user rerunning the program with modified input, or else, in the case of the program's author, rewriting the software to extend or optimize its rules.

My own approach differed mainly in the communicational model implied by the software (Truax 1976). The two bodies of knowledge were to interact on a more ongoing, step-by-step basis during the compositional process. Using a top-down approach (when structural parameters are specified by the user, and details are worked out algorithmically by the software), I was able to allow the user to begin with only a general sketch of the compositional idea—the duration, average density of events, and at least one of Koenig's *tendency masks* (see Figure 1.1) applied to the frequency-time field—and let a Poisson distribution calculate the specific score. The user's other main task was to define a repertory of sound objects (collections of synthesis parameters which, luckily with FM, were a few powerful variables) and to map them onto the events in the score. Aided by real-time synthesis, the result of the initial compositional idea could be heard quickly and its well-formedness assessed. That is, it was hoped that the program's output would stimulate the composer's imagination to suggest how the musical structure might be extended, refined, and optimized.

In Laske's terminology, such interactive models of composition demonstrate a dialogue between the composer's musical competence and performance strategies. Moreover, experience with the software can be channeled back into future software development as musical knowledge in the form of the composer's needs and ideas is transferred to the programmed knowledge base (Truax 1986, 1991).

Figure 1.1
Control structures for the POD system showing tendency masks for object selection, frequency selection, and density variation

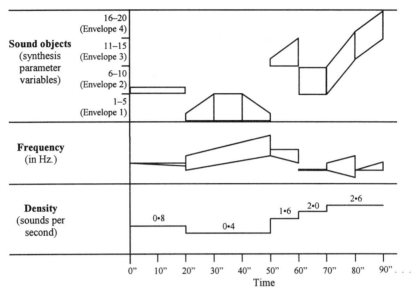

Source: Truax, B. (1976). "A Communicational Approach to Computer Sound Programming." *Journal of Music Theory* 20(2):275. © Yale University Department of Music. Used with permission.

The POD system has proved to be one of the few systems that has survived the perils of hardware obsolescence for more than twenty years in order to allow compositional experience to guide its development. It seems to be one of the exceptions that prove the rule that software development in the digital era lags behind hardware "advances" and seldom occurs in an environment that allows users' ideas to be incorporated into its evolution.

LASKE'S SONOLOGICAL THEORY

In 1972, Laske presented two important papers at the Institute concerning his concept of sonology, later to become the second and third chapters of his *Introduction to a Generative Theory of Music.* The first of these, "Some Postulations Concerning a Sonological Theory of Perception," outlines the theoretical implications of musical perception in terms of sonological competence and strategies for listening. It also outlines an acquisition model for musical competence, a theory that could prove extremely valuable in designing strategies for music education. Following Piaget and Vygotsky, Laske sketches a model of learning in which "sounds saturated with sense" become progressively differentiated into identifiable meanings, at first referential, and subsequently nonreferential and specifically musical. All of this "thinking in sound," with its Piaget-style levels of increasing abstraction, proceeds hand in hand with sound making on the part of the child. It is the progressive ability to create, perceive and understand syntactic structures that allows the child to relate the sonological features of sounds to specific semantic interpretations. Anything that fosters the development of this competence is the proper subject of music education, as further developed by Laske (1976) in "Toward a Theory of Musical Instruction" as well as *Music, Memory and Thought* (Laske 1977).

On May 4, 1972, Laske presented the second of these papers entitled "Is Sonology a Science of the Artificial?" He had been inspired by Herbert Simon's classic set of lectures to engineers, *The Sciences of the Artificial* (Simon 1969). In these lectures Simon makes the basic distinction between the sciences of the real, such as the natural sciences (which describe the way things are), and the sciences of the artificial (the design sciences, which describe how things ought to be, that is, how functionally designed artifacts achieve a dynamic equilibrium with their environment). This classic distinction between the static, measurable object or signal, and the designed artifact dynamically functioning in relation to its environment, though originally intended to illustrate the key difference between the pure and applied sciences, was actually an argument for a systems approach as a cognitive paradigm. Laske seized on the formulation as a cogent metaphor to distinguish sonology from acoustics.

Acoustics and its related disciplines, as sciences of the real, characteristically treat musical artifacts as signals to be analyzed, synthesized, and transmitted to "receivers" who process these signals according to psychoacoustic principles. Laske declared this "scientific" view of sonology to be incomplete, because it ignored music as a performed activity, and faulty because it excluded the cognitive imperatives of sonological design. He also understood that Simon's concept of engineering, as a design science for functional artifacts in the physical world, could equally apply to sonological artifacts designed to achieve cognitive goals within the musical world.

The emphasis of sonology as a science of the artificial is not on taxonomies of physical (or psychophysical) descriptions and measurements, but on goals and functions. However, since it is not a question of one concept to the exclusion of the other, he went on to define the sonological artifact more precisely as "an interface between an inner, perceptual environment and an outer, (psycho-) acoustical environment." Since the inner environment involves decision making and cognitive goals, Laske defined it as a "problem environment," and following the work of writers such as Newell, Simon, and Mesarovic, Laske was to spend the next several years investigating sonology and musical thinking in general as problem-solving activity. His terminology shifted away from the more static, grammar-based generative theory to terms he proposed such as "psychomusicology" and "cognitive musicology." These new definitions were an attempt to divert the traditional discipline of musicology away from its stylistic descriptions of historical artifacts (in order to make it a pseudoscience of the real?) into a direction that would provide a degree of cognitive validity to its conclusions, that is, to make it a science of the artificial. This useful distinction has recently been invoked by Laske again in a discussion of the role of all of the humanities in relation to computer research (Laske 1992). However, it had found its most complete exposition in his landmark book, *Music, Memory and Thought*, which outlined a cognitive approach to musicology and musical learning (Laske 1977).

Laske's distinction between sonology as a science of the real and a science of the artificial can be applied to computer music systems in general, particularly when considered in the manner of the previous section. These programs may be placed along a continuum from computer-realized composition, as in MUSIC N systems (where musical knowledge resides entirely in the composer and the software merely realizes the specifications requested), to computer-composed music, or automated systems (where in the most extreme case, one can imagine the computer embodying all musical knowledge required to produce a work). Actual systems fall between these two extremes, as shown in Figure 1.2, and vary in the amount of knowledge represented in the software system.

In my first article on this subject, I used Newell's notion of the inverse relation of generality and strength in methods of problem solving to describe the systems along this continuum (Truax 1980). Programs represented by the left side of the diagram are more general purpose and, because they embody little musical knowledge, rely most heavily on user-supplied input data. However, they can (theoretically) generate any specifiable output structure. As one moves towards the right of the continuum, more knowledge is embodied in the program, and hence user data gradually falls off as more powerful, but less general, methods are used. More complex results can often be obtained with little input as the powerful strategies of a knowledge base are invoked. Most computer programmers, however, are skeptical of "prejudicing" the generality of a program with this knowledge, more so at a syntactic level than at the synthesis level. On the

Figure 1.2
Variation of user information, program automation, and user interaction

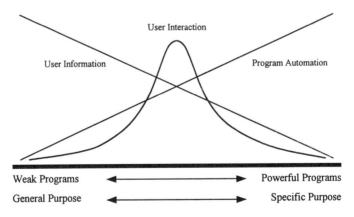

Source: Truax, B. (1980). "The Inverse Relation between Generality and Strength." *Interface* 9(1):51. © Swets & Zeitlinger Publishers. Used with permission.

other hand, I have argued that more powerful strategies allow a user to explore a new musical terrain more efficiently without being burdened by detailed data specification. In Figure 1.2, I suggest that user interaction with the software peaks in the middle of the continuum because of the more equal interplay of user and programmed knowledge.

However, we can also understand this continuum as progressively leading from a concept of music as a science of the real on the left toward a science of the artificial on the right. On the left, the user describes the sonic and musical structure in an objective, usually numerical manner. It is not a process many composers find palatable or cognitively natural, though it has recently become popular again with the CSOUND language that runs at a reasonable speed on the faster microcomputers. As one encounters more interactive systems in the middle of the continuum, one notices that musical thinking increases during one's inter-action with the software. Even relatively nontechnically oriented composers find themselves reacting to partially well-formed sonic structures that stimulate their musical imagination and suggest an optimization process. The procedures provided by the software for altering the output are key to its ability to engage the competence of the user in musical problem solving. Laske has emphasized the importance of procedural knowledge in many of his writings, and it is precisely this knowledge of how to use transforming procedures to reach a musical goal that characterizes the user of an interactive system. In Piaget's sense, this acting upon the musical object in order to understand and design it is the most basic object of play in learning.

Once the user understands at a very deep level the relation between pro-grammed procedures and the structures they produce, this knowledge can be transferred to the software itself, hence the path of development toward the automated end of the continuum. Although the public fears "the machine taking over" in this manner, the more thoughtful humanist hopefully will recognize that the machine only reflects human knowledge that is externally embodied, as it has done in all of humankind's technologies. We have merely advanced from that embodiment as being seen in hardware to its representation in software. When one considers traditional forms of that software, whether in myths, rituals, or the symbolic and written form of the *I Ching*, we realize that even the most current developments are not entirely new or unique. What remains of utmost impor-tance, in fact is indispensable, in all of these "soft" forms is the interaction this externally embodied knowledge provokes with the human mind. Laske has cap-tured some of this role of technology in his description of the computer as "the artist's alter ego" (Laske 1990).

The final stage of my study with Laske at the Institute of Sonology in 1973 involved a collaboration with him on what came to be known as the OBSERVER project. It consisted of a set of programs we created to observe musical thinking in action, particularly as it reflected various developmental stages of competence in children. The musical task was deliberately simple, namely melody creation and alteration, where the subject was given a raw synthesized melody and a se-ries of operators that could be used to alter the parameters of each note. An analysis program classified the input and output melodies according to their rhythmic, harmonic and melic strength based on criteria supplied by Laske that were independent of any specific musical style. This was done so that changes in the melody could be tracked. The stored protocol of recorded actions could then be re-created and analyzed.

The empirical technique neatly bypassed the problems of both verbal expression and instrumental skill, and provided a rare glimpse into musical thinking in action. Admittedly, the subject's internal representations remained implicit; however, the external actions reflected the desired transformation toward a goal state. As Laske observed, "Being at bottom pattern recognition systems, sonological systems develop into problem solvers once they incorporate musical-grammatical postulates. . . . Experimental sonology is thus a science defining and testing pattern recognition systems which can be developed into intelligent perceivers and into musical problem solvers." Even in such a simple task as presented by OBSERVER, we could see even a young child operate on a series of untempered, synthesized tones and shape them into something more coherent—in essence carrying out a primary sonological task.

SOUNDSCAPE STUDIES AND ACOUSTIC COMMUNICATION

In the summer of 1973 I left the Institute of Sonology with several analog tape compositions, my first computer music work, and a radically changed theoretical and practical understanding of the role of the computer in designing and organizing sound and studying its perception. I had been invited by R. Murray Schafer to join the group he had founded called the World Soundscape Project (WSP) in the Department of Communication Studies at Simon Fraser University in Vancouver, a group dedicated to documenting the changing sonic environment and raising listeners' awareness of its importance. At first the contrast with the Institute of Sonology couldn't have seemed greater. Although I sought out a computer with which to recreate my POD system for interactive composition, the work with Schafer was situated in an entirely different set of concerns, what is now called the field of acoustic ecology. However, given the gulf between the esoteric acoustic concerns inside the Institute and the abysmal, traffic-infested soundscape of the city outside, Schafer's call for composers to take responsibility for this neglected aspect of our daily lives was a breath of fresh air.

The events and activities of the WSP group have been described elsewhere (Truax 1984, 1996; Torigoe 1982), but what is striking is the way in which Laske's approach to sonology so aptly applied to the new approach to the soundscape the WSP was trying to formulate. Similar to the dominant musicological paradigm in music, the study of the acoustic environment has been dominated by the methodology of a science of the real, namely acoustical engineering. In that discipline, environmental sound is treated as an artifact to be measured, quantified, and understood only in its measurable effects on humans, the more negative of which are to be controlled. Little seems to be known, except anecdotally, about how listeners perceive, understand, and act upon the sounds in their immediate environment.

The WSP group was involved in 1973 with preparing a document called *The Vancouver Soundscape*, which used various terms such as sound signal, soundmark, and keynote sound (Truax 1974) to identify the prominent and often culturally important sounds of the city, as well as the usually ignored background sounds that provide the aural backdrop to such foreground events. It seemed to me that Schafer was trying to define a taxonomy of functional sonological features rather than purely acoustic descriptions of the environment. In fact, when we came to define "soundscape" more rigorously in the *Handbook for Acoustic Ecology* (Truax 1978) and distinguish it from the "acoustic environment," it was precisely the role of the listener's interpretation of these sounds that made the crucial difference. Although such sounds may be acoustically distinctive, it is the information they convey to the listener that is of primary importance in soundscape studies, and that information comes not only from the observed pattern of and within the sound, but also from the listener's knowledge of its environmental, social, and cultural context. Thus, it is pattern recognition informed not only by syntactic and semantic knowledge but also contextual knowledge.

For instance, the sound signal, such as a horn, whistle, or bell, may encode well-known information about time, danger, or some specific activity. Variations in the sound caused by weather or deviations in production may convey additional information. However, the signal may also provoke associations and memories related to the source with which it is associated, which is often a dominant social institution. Some signals are so unique and have such an important cultural and historical role in the community that they qualify to be called soundmarks, by analogy to landmarks. That is, they go beyond the specific information they convey to symbolize their context, and as such can engender a deep sense of psychological attachment in listeners. Should such sounds disappear or be transformed, a gaping hole would be felt in the community, though perhaps only subconsciously. Schafer describes another set of dominant sounds in the community as "sacred noise" because they escape social proscription through their association with seats of power (Schafer 1977).

A more provocative example of the sonological distinction occurs with Schafer's "keynote" sound, that is, a ubiquitous background sound that forms the perceptual ground to other events. The acoustic approach can only distinguish ambient sounds on the basis of their low intensity level, which is statistically measured as the level exceeded 90 percent of the time. Ambient sounds usually form a perceptual background; however, so can sound signals or other informative sounds if they occur frequently enough and have no urgency for the listener. The sound of waves in a maritime community is cited by Schafer, but in one of the European villages studied by the WSP, the quarter-hour bell seemed to function similarly, a sound signal that would normally attract attention, at least to a visitor. In our technologically controlled indoor environments, the hums of electricity and air conditioning provide the flat line aural background to daily life as a constant reminder of the technological mediation. In other words, what determines the keynote sound cannot be judged by a machine, certainly not a sound level meter, nor can the subtle semantic implications with which it colors our perceptions of foreground events. Just as sonological artifacts are designed to achieve cognitive goals within the musical world, soundscape artifacts achieve analogous goals within the environment.

Similarly, conventional noise studies may be based on the subjective definition of noise as unwanted sound, but their methodology is mainly concerned with assessing the negative effects on those who are exposed to it. Although such effects are serious and the associated risks are important to understand, the effects of noise on the listening process—a person's primary aural interface with an environment—are equally important to study. Here one can observe a wide range of individual reactions based on personal listening habits and contextual experience. For instance, one of the most common phenomena as to what is regarded as noise is the individual's categorization of what constitutes an intrusion. As anyone who has tried to deal with community noise complaints knows, the objective features of the sound, such as intensity level or duration, often play a secondary role to the psychological attitudes towards the sound maker. Residents will object to motorcycles, portable stereos, or even certain human voices, while passively tolerating the louder sounds of garbage trucks, emergency vehicles, or even industrial sounds and aircraft if these are perceived to be a necessary and normal part of the community. What constitutes sonological intrusiveness mainly reflects the listener's understanding of what is part of the community and what is foreign.

A subtler effect of noise on the listening process is the way in which it obscures auditory information, reduces aural definition, and discourages the desire to listen attentively. Although short-term damage may be negligible from these effects, the long-term effect on the listening process, and hence the individual's relationship to the world in general, may be profound. In the attempt to block out unwanted sounds, the listener may start to disregard most sounds in the environment and pay less attention to the details of those that are heard. Since an aural orientation to the environment tends to integrate the listener to the dynamically shifting realities of the world, a weakening of those ties may lead to a feeling of alienation, disconnectedness, and a general sense of meaninglessness. Although noise may be acoustically complex in the physical sense, it is usually perceived as semantically simple, if not entirely meaningless. The cognitive goals it engenders are avoidance or escape, hence a dulling of aural sensibilities and a severing of that link to the environment.

If nature abhors a vacuum, then humans surely abhor the absence of meaning, and thus into the meaninglessness of the contemporary soundscape enter the audio media as a source of pseudoinformation (Truax 1992b). Although such media appear to offer information and entertainment, sociologists, since at least the early 1960s, have noted that the functional roles of "accompaniment" media (i.e., those used as a background to daily activities) are at least equally if not more important (Mendelsohn 1964). Radio, and now frequently television as well, is often used to accompany daily activities, as a way to bracket the day and lubricate social relations by having common experiences to talk about, as well as to influence mood and behavior, a trait that the Muzak Corporation has been exploiting since the 1930s (Cardinell 1948). Whether it is the ubiquitous background music (rapidly becoming foreground music) in public places, the radio or television as accompaniment to daily activities in the home or car, or the

Walkman and portable radios as an accompaniment attached to your person, electroacoustic sound, including a lot of music, is seldom far away. The net effect of all of this imposed sound experience is to turn listening into a consumer activity and sound into a commodity.

The soundscape concept, and Schafer's descriptive approach to it, has continued to prove useful in stimulating aural awareness among those who have come in contact with this work. However, a stronger theoretical model seemed to be needed. Based on the foundation work of the WSP and Laske's notion of sonology, I evolved a communicational model to describe how soundscapes function (Truax 1984). It is intended to provide an alternative to the models of the traditional disciplines that study sound, which are based on concepts of energy transfer and signal processing where the individual is in a passive role of a receiver at the end of a chain of transfers, not unlike the traditional model of musical communication where the message passes from the composer as the source through the medium of the performer to the audience as receiver. In contrast, the communicational model is based on the concept of information exchange. At the center of the acoustic communicational model is the listener because listening is the primary interface where information is exchanged between the individual and the environment. In *Acoustic Communication,* I suggested that instead of listening being the end stage of a series of linear energy transfers from source to listener, we can understand it within a system of information exchange where sound mediates the relation of the listener to the environment. In the traditional soundscape that mediation entwines the listener in a unity with the environment. Hildegard Westerkamp has characterized the relationship as a balance between input and output, impression and expression, listening and soundmaking (Westerkamp 1988, 1990). The information we take in as listeners is balanced by our sound-making activities that in turn shape the environment. Acoustic communication, at its highest level of explanation, documents the coherent relationships to the environment, both individual and social, that sound can create.

CONCLUSION

In his review of *Acoustic Communication,* Laske (1986) described it as "prolegomena," or preliminary remarks, "to a nonexisting study of musical cognition." Although he did not refer to any of the specific ideas contained in the book, one might gather from this review that he regarded environmental sound experience as a kind of foundation on which more specific competencies in speech and music are erected. Soundscape experience predates these competencies in a child's development, particularly if we include both listening and sound-making activities. However, as music progresses in our culture, its definition seems to be embracing all sound material as potentially musical as long as it is organized in some way. John Cage challenged our notion of the role of the composer in dictating such organization by suggesting, as does Laske, that it is the listener who ultimately "organizes" the sound, even random environmental sounds, by the way in which they are perceived and understood. Perhaps we need to reclassify the composer as a "sonic designer" in order to express the breadth of activity, if not materials and context, that may be involved in musical creativity, now and in the future (Truax 1992a).

However, it probably comes down to whether one regards music as the highest form of aural abstraction in cognitive terms, when one regards environmental sound as its foundation. In the future, we may very well come to realize that musical competence based on abstract relationships in sound is merely a specialized version of environmental sound competence. This may come about, first, if we begin to study this latter competence in more detail—in which case I predict that, similar to the acoustical complexity of environmental sounds, we will discover a semantic complexity in our ability to orient ourselves to a dynamically shifting environment through sound. The second reason for the shift away from abstraction may involve a reconsideration of the continued viability of abstract music and its definition of complexity based on internal parameter relationships. I have argued elsewhere (Truax 1994) that social and economic constraints alone may limit the viability of such a definition of music, as currently decreasingly supported by the public sector, in the face of the corporate domination of culture. The best outcome of the dilemma, in my opinion, would be if the inner complexity of music would reflect the outer complexity of the real world, and thereby become reintegrated with it.

In 1974, Laske published a short article, one of his first to appear in North America, entitled "Musical Acoustics (Sonology): A Questionable Science Reconsidered." In it, he outlined sonology as a design science and proposed an information processing, that is, symbol manipulating, approach in its models. He further acknowledged Schafer's work by stating, "The space in which a science of sonic design has to operate is the sonic environment at large, particularly those parts of it in which people live." If the study of acoustic ecology reveals a complex system of human-environment relationships that are made possible through sound, and if music begins to reflect that complexity such that it can only be created and understood in terms of it, then we may well be compelled to revisit Laske's concept of sonology as it will have become indispensable.

NOTE

1. Editor's comment: Laske 1975 is a reprint of Laske 1973.

REFERENCES

Attali, J. (1985). *Noise: The Political Economy of Music*. Minneapolis-St. Paul, MN: The University of Minnesota Press.

Cardinell, R. (1948). "Music in Industry." In D. Schullian and M. Schoen, eds. *Music and Medicine*. New York: Schuman.

Chowning, J. (1973). "The Synthesis of Complex Audio Spectra by Means of Frequency Modulation." *Journal of the Audio Engineering Society* 21(7):526–534. Reprinted in C. Roads and J. Strawn, eds. (1985). *Foundations of Computer Music*. Cambridge, MA: MIT Press, pp. 6–29.

De Poli, G., A. Piccialli, and C. Roads, eds. (1991). *Representations of Musical Signals.* Cambridge, MA: MIT Press.

Koenig, G. (1970). "PROJECT 2: A Programme for Musical Composition." *Electronic Music Reports 3.* Utrecht, The Netherlands: Institute of Sonology.

Koenig, G. M. (1980). "Composition Processes." In M. Battier and B. Truax, eds. *Computer Music.* Canadian Commission for Unesco.

Laske, O. (1973). *Introduction to a Generative Theory of Music.* Utrecht, The Netherlands: Institute of Sonology.

Laske, O. (1974). "Musical Acoustics (Sonology): A Questionable Science Reconsidered." *Numus West* 6:35–40.

Laske, O. (1975). "Introduction to a Generative Theory of Music." *Sonological Reports 1b.* Utrecht, The Netherlands: Institute of Sonology. (Reprinted from Laske 1973.)

Laske, O. (1976). "Toward a Theory of Musical Instruction." *Interface* 5(3):125–148.

Laske, O. (1977). *Music, Memory and Thought: Explorations in Cognitive Musicology.* Ann Arbor, MI: University Microfilms International.

Laske, O. (1981). "Composition Theory in Koenig's PROJECT 1 and PROJECT 2." *Computer Music Journal* 5(4):54–65.

Laske, O. (1986). Review of *Acoustic Communication. Computer Music Journal* 10(2):75.

Laske, O. (1990). "The Computer as the Artist's Alter Ego." *Leonardo* 23(1):53–56.

Laske, O. (1992). "The Humanities as Sciences of the Artificial." *Interface* 21(3–4):239–255.

Mendelsohn, H. (1964). "Listening to Radio." In L. Dexter and D. White, eds. *People, Society and Mass Communication.* London: Macmillan.

Schafer, R. (1969). *The New Soundscape.* Vienna: Universal Edition.

Schafer, R. (1977). *The Tuning of the World.* New York: Knopf.

Simon, H. (1969). *The Sciences of the Artificial.* Cambridge, MA: MIT Press.

Torigoe, K. (1982). *A Study of the World Soundscape Project.* Master's thesis, York University.

Truax, B. (1973). "The Computer Composition Sound Synthesis Programs POD4, POD5 and POD6." *Sonological Reports 2.* Utrecht, The Netherlands: Institute of Sonology.

Truax, B. (1974). "Soundscape Studies, an Introduction to the World Soundscape Project." *Numus West* 5:36–39.

Truax, B. (1976). "A Communicational Approach to Computer Sound Programming." *Journal of Music Theory* 20(2):227–300.

Truax, B. (1977). "The POD System of Interactive Compositional Programs." *Computer Music Journal* 1(3):30–39.

Truax, B., ed. (1978). *Handbook for Acoustic Ecology.* Vancouver: A.R.C. Publications.

Truax, B. (1980). "The Inverse Relation Between Generality and Strength." *Interface* 9(1):49–57.

Truax, B. (1984). *Acoustic Communication.* Norwood, NJ: Ablex Publishing.

Truax, B. (1985). "The POD System: Interactive Compositional Software for the DMX-1000." *Computer Music Journal* 9(1):29–38.

Truax, B. (1986). "Computer Music Language Design and the Composing Process." In S. Emmerson, ed. *The Language of Electroacoustic Music.* London: Macmillan.

Truax, B. (1991). "Capturing Musical Knowledge in Software Systems." *Interface* 20(3–4):217–234.

Truax, B. (1992a). "Musical Creativity and Complexity at the Threshold of the 21st Century." *Interface* 21(1):29–42.

Truax, B. (1992b). "Electroacoustic Music and the Soundscape: The Inner and Outer World." In J. Paynter, T. Howell, R. Orton and P. Seymour, eds. *Companion to Contemporary Musical Thought.* London: Routledge.

Truax, B. (1994). "The Inner and Outer Complexity of Music." *Perspectives of New Music* 32(1):176–193.

Truax, B. (1996). "Soundscape, Acoustic Communication and Environmental Sound Composition." *Contemporary Music Review* 15(1):47–63.

Westerkamp, H. (1988). *Listening and Sound-making: A Study of Music-as-Environment.* Master's thesis, Simon Fraser University, Vancouver, B.C., Canada.

Westerkamp, H. (1990). "Listening and Sound-making: A Study of Music-as-Environment." In D. Lander and M. Lexier, eds. *Sound by Artists.* Banff, Alberta: Art Metropole and Walter Phillips Gallery.

2

Structure as Performance: Cognitive Musicology and the Objectification of Compositional Procedure

Michael Hamman

INTRODUCTION

In his essay "The Humanities as Sciences of the Artificial," Otto Laske points out that though the humanities "form a huge and, historically speaking, heterogeneous domain of research," there nevertheless exists among the humanities a common bond: all of them focus on a reality that is "artificial in comparison with the reality sought by the natural sciences" (Laske 1992:239).[1] This "artificial reality is a result of design, whether one deals with a work or a social institution" (ibid.). Pursuant to this overall view, the objective of Otto Laske's research has been to study musical works in order to determine "the intentions, designs, images, goals, and strategies of the generative processes that yielded them" (ibid.). Laske's project in cognitive musicology considers not only the work of art but the cognitive processes by which it is realized (both for a listener and a composer). As such, Laske recognizes the failure of the standard theoretical paradigm by which objects (scores, sounds, etc.) are considered in isolation from the cognitive processes that give rise to them. According to the standard notion of music theory and analysis, an investigator extracts, from the object under scrutiny, structured models. These models take on meaning within the context of particular *cultural codes*. Thus, for example, a Schenkerian analysis of a score is understood in the context of hierarchical structural codes (hierarchical structures being a child of the Copernican/Newtonian model of the universe) as they are applied to similarly invented notions of counterpoint and harmonic progression. In like fashion, acoustical analysis of sounds yields coded messages in the form of signal representations (McAdams 1987:20, Kopec 1992) that reflect the premise that sound is a phenomenon that can be isolated from its context (Laske 1974:35).

By contrast, cognitive musicology investigates the relationships between musical artifacts and the cognitive processes within which both individual and cultural codes are generated and integrated within a specific task domain. Cognitive musicology is not, therefore, an inquiry into the purely behaviorist aspects of musical performance. It is concerned rather with "the lawful, systematic link that connects behavior with the structural results it produces" (Laske 1977:3).

In this chapter, I wish to examine some aspects of Laske's theoretical work, particularly as they address issues related to the use of computers in music composition and sound synthesis. In the ensuing discussion, I take what Laske terms a "procedural" view of music composition inasmuch as I am concerned with the "how" rather than the "what" of activities operating within musical problem domains. I therefore consider a musical artifact—be it an entire composition or a single sound—from the point of view of the design processes that yield it. A study of design processes requires the specification of the environment in which such processes are engaged. As such, it is necessary to objectify the artifact within the context of its design processes in order to foreground the notion that such an artifact functions within a particular environment and according to the goals for which it is fitted. In this context, an artifact traces a process in which the "inner" becomes the "outer." Computers contribute enormously to this process since they effectively objectify the processes that are otherwise internal. Computers become not merely tools for the making of artistic works (artifacts); they become instruments for the objectification of the very processes by which such works might be made. This view of human/computer interaction, particularly as it occurs in the context of artistic creation, forms a basic theme in Laske's theories and research in cognitive science and in his formulation of composition theory. The contours of this argument are, therefore, presented as they are developed in Laske's own writings on cognitive musicology and composition. During the course of the discussion, I follow Laske's information-processing model of cognition in order to formulate some of the more unorthodox aspects of that model.

TOWARD A PROCEDURAL VIEW OF MUSIC

To begin with, we want to determine what is meant by procedural. In order to offer some insight, I first consider Laske's notion of design. According to Laske (and to cognitive science in general), a design model renders ill-structured problems into particularized task domains in which competence and performance aspects of cognitive activity are combined in order to both define and solve those problems. In the following discussion, a model of memory is proposed that differentiates its competence and performance components within a larger cognitive framework. Such a model reveals knowledge as a process in which performances activate particular modes of competence.

The Artifact as an Object of Human Design

Herbert Simon has proposed a descriptive framework with which one might regard any type of human-made work, or "artifact" (Simon 1969). He distinguishes an artifact as a phenomenon that derives from a system that has been "molded, by goals or purposes, to the environment in which it lives" (op. cit.:ix). In contradistinction to natural objects, artificial objects (artifacts) arise from systems that are synthesized by human beings. While artifacts may be bound to certain laws as defined by the natural sciences, they differ from natural objects precisely because they function in relation to a particular goal, which is defined according to a humanly synthesized design (op. cit.:5). Adaptation of an artifact to a particular goal is dependent upon "the purpose of the goal, the character of the artifact, and the environment in which the artifact performs" (op. cit.:6). Thus, for example, a clock functions as a thing by which we can tell time; its characteristic constructive principles may feature arrangements of gears and springs as acted upon by gravity or a circular grid with a thin spike at its center as acted upon by sunlight: the exact construction is in large part a function of its environment.

How an artifact performs (with respect to the function for which it is designed) depends on the fit between its construction and the environment in which it functions. As such, Simon speaks of the artifact as an "'interface' between an 'inner' environment, the substance and organization of the artifact itself, and an 'outer' environment, the surroundings in which it operates" (op. cit.:7). This allows an explanation of an artifact to be referenced to the purpose or function for which it is designed: "Thus the first advantage of dividing outer from inner environment in studying an adaptive or artificial system is that we can often predict behavior from knowledge of the system's goals and its outer environment, with only minimal assumptions about the inner environment" (op. cit.:8). Such a descriptive framework allows us to begin to talk about artifacts in terms of the functions for which they are designed. Central to this descriptive framework "are the goals that link the inner to the outer system" (op. cit.:11).

The Ill-structured Problem

In order to study such systems, we begin by considering the nature of the specific problems those systems address. Well-structured problems are problems whose specifications meet certain criteria. Such criteria include the requirement that the entire solution space (including initial problem state, goal state, and all intervening states) be definable. Problems that meet such criteria—well-structured problems—are relatively easy to represent with a General Problem Solver (GPS) and are thus regarded as "computable." In contrast, ill-structured problems are characterized, negatively, by their inability to meet such criteria.

Designing a house is an example of an ill-structured problem. For one thing, "there is initially no definite criterion to test a proposed solution"—the problem space is initially undefined (Simon 1973:187). The knowledge base representing possible solutions would have to include all possible materials, techniques, and design processes—a database of obviously prohibitive magnitude. Simon postulates that a design proceeds by transformation of ill-structured problems to much smaller well-structured ones. Such a process might be composed from a combination of a GPS (which at any given moment works on some well-structured subproblem) with a retrieval system, which continually modifies the problem space by evoking from long-term memory new constraints, new subgoals, and new generators for design alternatives.

Laske characterizes the structure of a problem according to the size of the knowledge base required for its solution (Laske 1978:40). As Laske notes, however, the size of the knowledge base is itself not the governing factor. Rather, the ill- or well-structuredness of a problem is determined by two entailments of a large knowledge base. First, a large knowledge base tends to yield a large number of different "representations of knowledge, any number of which might be simultaneously available to the performances of a problem-solver." Second, "a problem-solver operating upon a large knowledge base is able to, or [is] forced to, redefine the problem space during the performance of a task" (ibid.). How such a problem comes to be defined is shaped by the tasks of the problem solver. As a result, "problem definition and problem solution may come along together" (ibid.).

Structural and Procedural Components in Memory

Problem-posing and problem-solving activities make use of memory. Cognitive research defines human mental activity in terms of data components on the one hand and programs on the other. Laske calls these dual realms "structural" and "procedural." The structural component is comprised, roughly, of a database "where the stuff memory contains is stored." The procedural component consists of the "*interpretive* processes that use the information stored in the data base" (Laske 1977:5).

When speaking of structure, the assumption is that the performing system is, for the moment, suspended, at which point one may observe the data that has been processed so far. When speaking of process, on the other hand, focus is on the actions of the performing system upon and within that data (op. cit.:6). In terms of music, this "acting upon" is a matter of linking the perception of sound objects to more elaborate processing functions. According to an information-processing view of cognition, this occurs in two steps. First, sound is pre-processed and stored in various buffers until some representation of it is stored in longer-term memory. Second, that data is acted upon in some manner by a Central Processing Unit (CPU).

While it is unlikely that this separation of structural and procedural components actually characterizes the organization of human memory, it facilitates the investigation of certain issues regarding a cognitive musicology, the principle one of which asks: how are structure and process related in musical memory (ibid.)?

Musical Knowledge

The above question impinges on questions of musical knowledge. In order to frame a discussion of the structure of musical knowledge, Laske begins by conceptualizing knowledge, in general, as constituting two distinguishable components: *competence* on the one hand, and *performance* on the other. Competence refers to "knowledge concerning the structure of the medium within which" particular activities are carried out, while performance refers to "knowledge concerning the ways in which this competence is utilized in the act of" carrying out particular activities (Laske 1973).[2] Operationally, competence constitutes "a set of concatenations of units forming a *musical structure*" while performance constitutes "a set of concatenations of such operations as form a *musical activity*" (op. cit.:2–3). In a general sense, competence refers to the "grammatical" while performance refers to the "strategical" aspects of the musical faculty.

A theory of musical knowledge accounts for both the grammatical and strategical aspects of musical activity, with the following stipulations: first, that "musical competence informs all musical activities irrespective of their strategical differences"; second, that "activities such as the production and/or recognition of sound structures are musical to the extent that they are demonstrably the actualization of musical competence" (op. cit.:9).

Competence/Performance as Framed by the Particularity of Tasks

Designing a computer-based task environment for music composition is tantamount to specifying a theory of performance. In a general sense, a performance model of music takes into account the task specificity of the processes according to which musical competence is evoked in the solution of particular problems. As such, we should understand competence and performance, not as different types of knowledge, but rather as "dimensions of one and the same knowledge being brought to bear on a task" (Laske 1988:3).

Consider, for example, Laske's model of a musician (Figure 2.1).[3] The musician is depicted as a system (M-System) which comprises three subsystems and which is itself embedded in a learning system (L-System). The three subsystems that constitute the M-System are:

1. a knowledge system (K-System),
2. a performance system (P-System),
3. an "understand" system (U-System).

The knowledge system is regarded as a storage facility which is constituted by a declarative component on the one hand, and a procedural component on the other. As described above, the declarative (i.e., structural) component represents assertional knowledge about music, while the procedural component concerns the actual use of such knowledge in the performance of music-related tasks.

Figure 2.1
Model of a musician

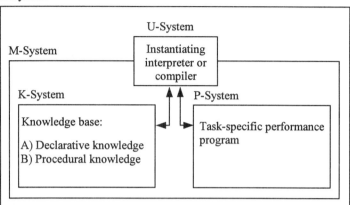

The performance system (P-System) specifies particular tasks. In this case, a task orients a sequence of actions taken toward the accomplishment of a specific goal. Once a task has been submitted at performance time, the understand system (U-System) derives task-specific information (specific, that is, to the task at hand) from the knowledge system (K-System). This task-specific information takes the form of a program. The submission of a task-oriented program to the U-System implies that the U-System is actually either an interpreter or a compiler. As such, the U-System instantiates a General Purpose Program (not shown in the diagram, but running "in the background") along with the data structures associated with general music competence. In other words, the U-System converts generalized data structures into those that are needed by the P-System for the performance of a particular task.

These principles can be demonstrated with an example taken from Laske (1988). Here musical competence is represented as a set of PROLOG assertions, several of which represent an assumption of motivic competence. Under this assumption the musician understands a "motive-x" as comprising three tones, c#–d#–e):

```
element (c#, 1, motive-x).
element (d#, 2, motive-x).
element (e, 3, motive-x).
length (motive-x, 3).
```

Given this small knowledge base, the musician can ask any number of procedural questions, such as

```
-?element(X,1,motive-x).    ;which tone is 1st?
-?element(d#,X,motive-x).   ;which position is d#?
-?element(e,3,X).           ;in which motive is 'e' the 3rd tone?
```

While any of such questions might be appropriate for the given knowledge base, it is significant that those questions actually considered "would depend on the problems the musician is solving, the musician's plans and goals, and the actual task environment (historical situation) in which the musician is working" (Laske 1988:46). These particulars generate the conditions that, in turn, orient the tasks that engage the performance system of a musician. This is another way of saying that the particular problems, plans, goals, and histories that constitute the particular tasks defined within a performance system comprise the exact constraints with respect to which components of the knowledge base (both declarative and procedural) are instantiated (Figure 2.2).

Knowledge as Performance

In this context, the performance of a designer (i.e., a composer) itself becomes a kind of artifact that functions as an interface between an inner environment, as represented by the knowledge system comprising his/her internal state, and an outer environment, as represented by the goals in relation to which the performance system is oriented and the tasks by which it is defined. In this regard, performance is as much a factor in the determination of knowledge as knowledge, per se, is a determinant in the nature of performance.

Such a notion evokes Humberto Maturana's description of the nervous system as a

closed network of interacting neurons such that any change in the state of relative activity of a collection of neurons leads to a change in the state of relative activity of other or the same collection of neurons. From this standpoint, the nervous system does not have 'inputs' and 'outputs.' It can be *perturbed* by structural changes in the network itself. (Winograd and Flores 1987:42)

A *perturbation* is a point of intersection between a system that is defined as an environment and a system that is defined as the organism.

Figure 2.2
Constraints on K-System based on P-System

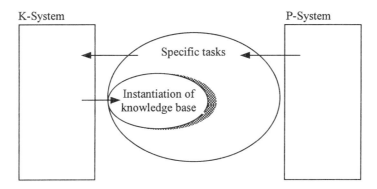

Similarly, knowledge processes can be viewed as consisting of perturbations generated by specific actions within a task domain; a view that sees actions as constitutive agents in the activation of knowledge. From the standpoint of the human performer, however, knowledge and performance constitute a unity in which strategy and know-how are coupled. Each action engages both strategy and knowledge in a feedback loop in which, to some extent or another, each forms an input to the other. The precise nature of this feedback loop is determined by the task environment in which actions are generated.

Such a view of knowledge processes is at variance with the more common one that sees the knowledge system, per se, as generative of the task-specific knowledge used in the formulation and execution of actions. This classical view of knowledge processes is most prominently promulgated within the sciences of human/computer interactivity. It is this subject of interactive computing to which we now turn.

THE OBJECTIFICATION OF DESIGN PROCEDURE

As has already been mentioned, designing a computer-based task environment for music composition is tantamount to specifying a theory of performance. While a computer system, which assists in creative activity, activates an environment for formulating and executing tasks associated with the realization of particular goals, it also frames the intentions, designs, and strategies with which those goals are conceived and, finally, realized. As such, the computer is a tool that enables the composer to specify, in a more or less precise fashion, the processes and objects by which goals are imagined, formulated, and realized. To the extent to which a composer makes use of this potential, a computer system becomes a tool, not only for specifying particular artifacts (scores, sounds, etc.) but for objectifying the very processes by which such artifacts might be modeled. In this regard, the computer is potentially a tool for delineating epistemological frameworks in terms of which one might imagine and realize ideas.

Musical Memory

In order to begin fleshing out this hypothesis, which is of paramount importance in understanding Laske's conception of cognitive musicology, basic issues regarding human memory (as these are explicated in Laske's own writings) are first considered. In his research in human/computer interaction, Laske established criteria that were based on models of human memory.[4] Toward this end he established a model of human memory which defines three domains:

1. temporal constraints,
2. musical pasts,
3. structure of human memory.

The first domain defines three levels of temporal constraints with respect to which musical events might be experienced. These are audio time, conscious time, and interpretive time. Audio time refers to events that occur over time periods of a few milliseconds. Conscious time refers to events that last between a fraction of a second and several seconds. At this level, significant features of an event can be registered in memory such that they can be remembered. Such events can be identified and tagged according to a large number of distinguishing parameters. These include frequency, timbre (characterized by a perception of the overall effect of events occurring at the audio-time level), duration, etc. Interpretive time operates at "the highest level at which sonic events occur" and is "simultaneously the most complex level of all" (Laske 1978:40). The term interpretive refers to the illusion of lasting time, which occurs at this level of temporal structure, and the fact that this illusion is "created by memory through interpretations of events on a high level of abstraction" (ibid.). The term interpretive highlights the fact that structures perceived at this level result from internal interpretive processes that map themselves against a projected passage of time.

The second domain of Laske's model of memory distinguishes "two musical pasts" (op. cit.:41). First, there is the *"cultural past* to which a music and its associated conceptual and compositional software belongs" (ibid.). Second, "there is the *immediate past* into which sounds perceived as music are projected by memory during listening" (ibid.). This later is often called musical context, which can be described as a "semantic model of the current auditory world of a listener" (ibid.).

The third domain of Laske's conceptualization of memory specifies a model of human memory itself. This model relates to the three levels described above (audio, conscious, and interpretive time). Figure 2.3 depicts this model, which consists of a chain of submemories. Each successive submemory along the chain enables more processing time. So, for instance, echoic memory (EM) is a buffer that stores sonic events occurring in audio time and is preperceptual—that is, its contents become perceptible only after they have been stored in perceptual memory.

Perceptual memory (PM) defines events experienced in conscious time as events that last up to several seconds. Perceptual memory stores acoustic information in terms of a totality of its features—that is, it stores it in analog form. By contrast, short-term memory (STM) stores such events as "tokens" that may be used in contextual memory for the purpose of syntactic grouping.

Working memory (WM) is the focal point of moment-by-moment processing: all processing decisions "are made on the basis of the transitory contents residing" here (ibid.). Such contents may be perceptual or contextual in nature, depending on the current problem to be solved. Such contents "define the musical present of which a musician can be conscious" (ibid.). Working memory accesses the central processor (CPU) through short-term memory.

Contextual memory (CM) constitutes "the active portion of long-term memory" (op. cit.:42). Contextual memory "stores the context in terms of which individual events are conceptualized and understood" (ibid.). For this reason, contextual memory "can thus be thought of as holding a model of the current musical world of a composer or listener" (ibid.).

Long-term memory (LTM) contains information that defines a musician's musical past.

Figure 2.3
Information-processing model of human memory[5]

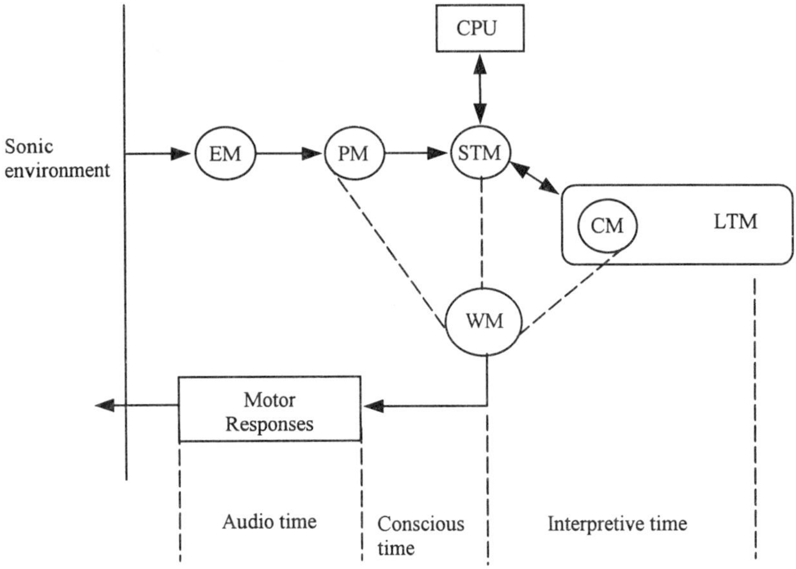

Modified from Laske 1978.

Motor responses direct perceptual mechanisms in an effort to optimize the receipt of input information relevant to that which will help the cognitive system resolve conceptual conflicts and to establish bodily responses according to the semantic concepts gleaned from the input data.

Syntactic and Semantic Considerations of Musical Memory

When considering human memory and its determination in human performance, Laske distinguishes those aspects of cognition that are syntactic from those that are semantic. Syntactic concepts are those which define the various structural levels of a musical object or process. Semantic concepts, by contrast, define interpretations of those structural levels. Semantic concepts are constitutive of the temporal aspects of musical structure as well as the interpretive frameworks according to which relationships within and among such structures are defined. Such interpretive frameworks are dependent on structures according to which perceptual information is stored.

Music-semantic networks evolve through an accretion of moment-by-moment interpretations. At first, an initial input arouses an initial interpretation, which may be largely arbitrary. This interpretation becomes the basis on which further inputs are conceptualized. An interpretive frame—or set of laws—is constructed.

Inputs that violate the integrity of this frame oblige the human agent to reconstruct some principle manifested within that frame, a cognitive action frequently requiring a retroactive resynthesis of previously experienced input material (Laske 1978:42).

Action and Interaction

The manner in which constitutive inputs are rendered within the cognitive system is dependent in large part upon the way in which the organism "navigates," motorily, as a correlate to those inputs. Motor response systems help a human agent to correlate his/her internal state with the input information it receives and to formulate bodily responses with which the environment inferred thereof might be effected. A set of such responses is provided through what is called a *response function* (Newell 1990:43). These are functions (in the mathematical sense) through which a human agent (or any other organism) takes actions within the environment in which it currently exists (ibid.). As some aspect of the environment changes, so too do the outputs of the response function fitted to that particular aspect. When an organism changes its actions, the hypotheses—according to which the cognitive system conceptualizes inputs—themselves are changed. This change results from an alteration of the interpretive frame with which those hypotheses are semantically bound. This alteration of the interpretive frame, in turn, causes an alteration in the response function that orients subsequent actions, and so on (op. cit.:44).

The resulting feedback structure constitutes an interactive system (depicted in Figure 2.4). Each interaction given by the system is "embedded in a sequence such that each becomes part of the context within which further actions follow" (Figure 2.5) (ibid.). As such, a single interaction is of itself meaningless in terms of its capacity for projecting functional information regarding the current environment or of the organism, since such a functionality is defined by a history of interactions (op. cit.:43).

Figure 2.4
Cognitive feedback structure

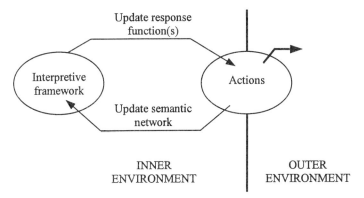

Figure 2.5
Cognitive feedback structure including interactive system

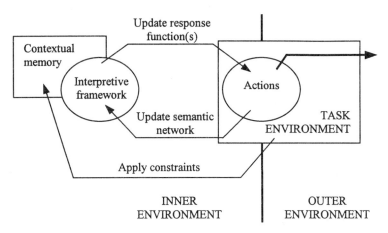

Two things effect this process:

1. the particular goal(s) specified,
2. the task environment in which tasks associated with the realization of those goals are performed.

The goal explicitly differentiates desired states from current states. A task environment encapsulates two pasts—the cultural past and the immediate past—plus a set of tools and materials, along with the knowledge conventions relating their use to the accomplishment of particular tasks. A task environment links two domains: the physical environment in which task performances are carried out and an internal representation of that physical environment in the form of a problem space (Laske 1977:307). The physical task environment delineates a set of tools that are formulated along the lines of goals for which the task environment is fitted. A problem space defines a domain in which particular elements of a given problem (or task) are cognitively linked to their solutions by means of the tools given by the physical task environment. It is within this domain that tools are fitted to those tasks required to realize a goal. Both the response functions and the actions that arise from them are framed not only by the goals at hand but by the constraints generated by the task environment. The feedback loop comprising the resulting interactive system has the qualities shown in Figure 2.5. The task environment forms an input to contextual memory that in turn conditions the ways in which a cognitive system processes input information. The interpretive frame determines the set of laws according to which particular actions are formulated and carried out. The outcomes that emanate from the execution of actions, in turn, orient the framework according to which both elements within the task environment, and the goals and plans of a project, are interpreted.

Composition with Computers as Objectifying Compositional Process

Within such a system, the internal processes by which a human performs actions relevant to specified design criteria become fused with the procedural constraints defined by the task environment. All actions constitute an interpenetration of the representations according to which design goals and design tools are conceived. The internal models formed by the human agent are as much determined by pertinent elements within the task environment as they are by the goals and plans directing the generation of artifacts. Such a system of interaction emphasizes the hegemony of particular historical methodologies while at the same time masking their presence through various forms of acculturation.

However, when a human is somehow enabled to construct elements of the task environment according to criteria that he/she explicitly specifies (as opposed to criteria dictated by historicity and methodology), he/she is in a sense "composing" the very means by which particular goals and plans are framed. In this case, design criteria that are particular to a project become linked with the design criteria according to which the task environment is fashioned. Tasks obtain their particularity, not from some implicitly motivated historical method, but from explicitly motivated criteria that are specific to the problem domain and design goals under consideration. The environment acts as an extension both of that domain and of those goals—an extension that enacts an externalization of internal processes.

Computers are a powerful medium for investigating the means by which plans and goals become realized as artifacts. As a tool, they enable definitions of design criteria according to which compositional activity might be carried out. For this reason, they are valuable tools for composers. To the extent to which composition is "a form of self-reference" (ibid.), as Laske proposes, composition with computers is an attempt "at extending self-reference into the allo-referential domain" (Laske 1980:427). The programmability of the computer gives it the potential for becoming an "intermediate between allo-referential and self-referential" domains (op. cit.:428). To extend compositional activity (which is a self-referential activity) into allo-referential domains (such as computers and theories) is to make "self-reference a topic of the compositional problem," a kind of "meta-composition" (ibid.).

In this context, composition consists in enabling a composer to compose the very means (i.e., elements within the task environment) by which compositional activity might be carried out. The operations and operands that define the task environment themselves become explicit by virtue of their being rendered as formalized elements within a symbolic system such as a computer. Such elements include programs and data structures as well as visual and interactive components. In such an environment, compositional hypotheses are determinative of both the artifacts being designed and the explicitly formulated processes by which those artifacts are designed. Constituted artifacts and their explicitly formulated design processes together project the internal processes of whoever composes them. In a more abstract sense, then, what is self-referential is projected into an allo-referential domain. Through such projection, the otherwise internalized processes of a human agent are externalized as though those processes were given by the task environment itself.

This projective potential of computer systems is their chief contribution to composition theory. It (a computer system) "imagines" us, by externalizing constraints that are otherwise merely implicit. In doing so, it objectifies—or distinguishes—aspects of ourselves that otherwise cannot be distinguished, and therefore are effectively invisible to us. This occurs by virtue of the fact that, in this capacity, computer systems force us to objectify ourselves by making us explicitly encode the processes by which goals and designs are to be imagined and realized. This calls us to understand that which we know "in such a way as to integrate it into a computer program" (Laske 1992:242) or some other representational schema that the computer can understand. By this means the objectifying tendency of allo-referential domains forces us to "scrutinize the types of knowledge that underlie the object of our research" (ibid.) in such a way that "we are modeling in an objectivist manner that part of our knowledge about the object that we intend to explicate (ibid.). Significantly, it "is not the object that has [as a result] changed; it is us. *We have transformed ourselves into a partner of communication between two species of knowledge, one that is alive in us, and another that embodies us in the form of an external 'knowledge base'"* (ibid.).[6]

CONCLUSION

A computer system that itself engenders particular hypotheses of musical knowledge and performance problematicizes the interactions it engages. It does this by turning its focus away from already formulated (but not yet realized) musical objects to those whose formulation (and realization) is contingent upon the actions and decisions engaged within the interaction itself. Many classical computer music composition systems (such as Koenig's PROJECT 1 and 2, (Koenig 1970a, 1970b) Xenakis's stochastic music program (Xenakis 1971), Koenig's SSP (Berg et al. 1980), Brün's SAWDUST (Grossman 1987, Blum 1979), and Berg's PILE (Berg 1979), as well as some that are more recent (such as Kirk Corey's IVORY TOWER [Corey 1990], Eckel's FOO [Eckel and Gonzalez-Arroyo 1994], Choi's MANIFOLD INTERFACE [Choi et al. 1995], and Hamman's RESNET [Hamman 1994] to mention only a few) are designed along these lines. Such systems acknowledge the fact that computer systems are encapsulated theories. They are understood as means for hypothesizing musical knowledge and performance in ways that challenge traditional notions of what music is and how a composer must proceed in order to make it.

In regard to such systems, Otto Laske's research has contributed and continues to contribute significant insight since it explicates a cognitive and epistemological context for evaluating such systems and the models of human activity that they project.

NOTES

1. It should be noted that various engineering fields frequently focus on similarly artificial realities as well.

2. Chomsky makes a similar distinction with regard to language, relating competence to "the speaker-hearer's knowledge of his language" and performance to "the actual use of language in concrete situations" (Chomsky 1965:4).

3. The following description is based on that given in Laske 1977:39–40.

4. The following description is taken from Laske 1978:41–43.

5. Editor's comment: Although by contemporary neuropsychological standards this model of memory is too linear in nature, its visualization here serves to conceptualize research issues (rather than being a documentation of research results). It is a useful conceptual model.

6. Editor's comment: Italics are used by the author for emphasis.

REFERENCES

Berg, P. (1979). "PILE—A Language for Sound Synthesis." *Computer Music Journal* 3(1):30–41.

Berg, P., R. Rowe, and D. Theriault. (1980). "SSP and Sound Description." *Computer Music Journal* 4(3):25–35.

Blum, T. (1979). "Herbert Brün: Project Sawdust." *Computer Music Journal* 3(1):6–7.

Choi, I., R. Bargar, and C. Goudeseune (1995). "A Manifold Interface for a High Dimensional Control Space." *Proceedings of the 1995 International Computer Music Conference*. San Francisco, CA: ICMA, pp. 385–392.

Chomsky, N. (1965). *Aspects of the Theory of Syntax*. Cambridge: MIT Press.

Corey, K. (1990). Unpublished manuscript.

Eckel, G., and R. Gonzalez-Arroyo (1994). "Musically Salient Control Abstractions for Sound Synthesis." *Proceedings of the 1994 International Computer Music Conference*. San Francisco, CA: ICMA, pp. 256–259.

Grossman, G. (1987). "Instruments, Cybernetics, and Computer Music." *Proceedings of the 1987 International Computer Music Conference*. San Francisco, CA: ICMA, pp. 212–219.

Hamman, M. (1994). "Dynamically Configurable Feedback/Delay Networks: A Virtual Instrument Composition Model." *Proceedings of the 1994 International Computer Music Conference*. San Francisco, CA: ICMA, pp. 394–397.

Koenig, G. (1970a). "PROJECT 1." *Electronic Music Reports 2*. Utrecht, The Netherlands: Institute of Sonology.

Koenig, G. (1970b). "PROJECT 2: A Programme for Musical Composition." *Electronic Music Reports 3*. Utrecht, The Netherlands: Institute of Sonology.

Kopec, G. (1992). "Signal Representations for Numerical Processing." In A. Oppenheim and S. Nawab, eds. *Symbolic and Knowledge-Based Signal Processing*. Englewood Cliffs, NJ: Prentice Hall.

Laske, O. (1973). "On Problems of a Performance Model of Music." In *Introduction to a Generative Theory of Music*. Utrecht, The Netherlands: Institute of Sonology.

Laske, O. (1974). "Musical Acoustics (Sonology): A Questionable Science Reconsidered." *Numus West* 6:35–41.

Laske, O. (1977). *Music, Memory, and Thought: Explorations in Cognitive Musicology*. Ann Arbor, MI: University Microfilms International.

Laske, O. (1978). "Considering Human Memory in Designing User Interfaces for Computer Music." *Computer Music Journal* 2(4):39–45.

Laske, O. (1980). "On Composition Theory as a Theory of Self-Reference." In K. Gaburo, ed. *Allos*. La Jolla, CA: Lingua Press, pp. 419–431.

Laske O. (1988). "Introduction to Cognitive Musicology." *Computer Music Journal* 12(1):43–57.

Laske, O. (1989). "Composition Theory: An Enrichment of Music Theory." *Interface* 18(1–2):45–59.

Laske, O. (1991). "Toward an Epistemology of Composition." *Interface* 20(3–4):235–269.

Laske, O. (1992). "The Humanities as Sciences of the Artificial." *Interface* 21(3–4):239–255.

McAdams, S. (1987). "Music: A Science of the Mind?" *Contemporary Music Review* 2(1):1–61.

Newell, A. (1990). *Unified Theories of Cognition*. Cambridge, MA: Harvard University Press.

Simon, H. (1969). *The Sciences of the Artificial*. Cambridge, MA: MIT Press.

Simon, H. (1973). "The Structure of Ill-structured Problems." *Artificial Intelligence* 4:181–201.

Winograd, T. and F. Flores (1987). *Understanding Computers and Cognition*. Reading, MA: Addison-Wesley Publishing.

Xenakis, I. (1971). *Formalized Music*. Bloomington: Indiana University Press.

3

PROJECT 1 Revisited:
On the Analysis and Interpretation
of PR1 Tables
Gottfried Michael Koenig

My first designs for PROJECT 1 (PR1) date from the time when I was taking a course in programming offered by Bonn University and wanted to utilize my newly acquired knowledge for something that had been on my mind for a long time. In the electronic music studio at West (then Northwest) German radio in Cologne I had learned how to work with machines in order to realize compositions and observed in myself a tendency to employ these machines in as rational a way as possible, that is, not to do anything by hand that could be done by a machine. Using sinewaves for sound production held out promises of being able to generate the entire sonic realm synthetically—an illusion, as it turned out. Instead, the constraints of the studio apparatus made themselves felt: they remained instruments, deployed in approximately the same place as orchestral instruments: at the tone (or sound). Despite all hopes, they could not reveal the "atomic structure" of the sounds. A more likely aid seemed to be the computer, with which every detail of a sound's waveform could be mathematically defined. During the programming course, however, I discovered that generating sounds with a computer was a distant prospect. In those days (1963–1964) the machines at Bonn had insufficient memory, there were no D/A converters, and in any case the university's computer department was not equipped for such tasks. I therefore decided to continue my studies in the domain of instrumental music and to write a program whose results could be represented on a line printer.

This program, to which I gave the working title PROJECT 1, developed, by way of various intermediate stages, from a progenitor (Koenig 1970) with scarcely any input data into the current software, which runs on a PC and in the WINDOWS version also outputs the resulting data as a standard MIDI file.[1] This current software also "opens" up all the parameters to the users in the form of input data. I was urged to take this measure by students who came up against the program's limitations while working with it during their studies in Sonology at the University of Utrecht. I myself had to conquer considerable doubts about this opening, for what, as a program, looked like a general description of musical structure with which every composer would be able to speak his own language, turned out to be a composition by the composer Koenig—a composition, though, in the form of countless variants. It was indeed a composition, for before I could start designing PR1 I had envisaged the first piece I wanted to compose with it. However, every detail of that piece needed to be generalized to a considerable extent in order to give the program the necessary scope for experiment. What benefited the program as formalization weakened the composition, which could not be both an original and its generalization at the same time. Reduced to a simple formula, after writing the program and obtaining the first result, I had to search for the original piece, which was hiding behind its own formalization, as it were. The aforementioned opening has accentuated this aspect, because in addition the program now has to bear the responsibility for possible compositions which for good reasons were barred from the original conception.

This is the situation Otto Laske encountered when he made the acquaintance of the program at the Institute of Sonology. I do not remember talking to him about my aforesaid doubts as to the expansion of the input possibilities, but I cannot rule out any such discussion either. By no means would (or did) my doubts deter him from incorporating the program in his research into compositional theory—nor, in a way, from basing that research on the program. There was no need for him to be tormented by the pangs of conscience suffered by Koenig the composer and author of the program; thus unencumbered, he could focus his keen eye on the structures of the program and its results. As he said:

In my understanding, [PROJECT 1 and PROJECT 2] represent a first step towards an artificial intelligence view of composition; they embody an analysis of the data base and the procedures required for performing compositional tasks. My high esteem for these programs has to do with the fact that they are not only design tools for composition, but also provide the composer with an *alter ego* enabling him to unlearn his habitual ways. Programs for music composition by definition provide fresh intelligence that is not available to the composer working manually. It is apt to consider them objectivications of the mental and intuitive faculties of a composer interacting with himself from an outside vantage point. (Laske 1981)

In my original design of the program, the time axis was first plotted. This involved a list of durations, expressed as divisions of a metric unit: 1/1, 1/2, 1/3, 2/3, 1/4, 3/4, etc. Every time point resulting from an accumulation of the time values was to be occupied by a tone or chord (for the sake of simplicity I speak of "chord sizes" that can assume values from 1 to 6). Each single tone was assigned a register number indicating its octave register or a register typical for the selected instrument. Furthermore, the chords were assigned an instrument number and a dynamic value. The instrument number could be interpreted freely, that is, it could indicate a single instrument or a group of instruments. The program prints these data in the form of a "score table" (which Laske calls an "event list").

Laske had this to say about the event list:

The event list has two alternative basic units, the EVENT and the COLUMN (which is a "vertical" string). The EVENT is a microscopic, the COLUMN a macrocosmic unit.

Also, the EVENT is multi-dimensional, the COLUMN one-dimensional. . . . The EVENT is most easily pictured as a *point in space* (such as a pitch-time space) which could be any conceivable space. . . . The COLUMN would be most easily conceivable in the form of a *shape* such as a curve or graph. . . . COLUMNS are linked to each other by mappings. . . . COLUMNS are *hors-temps* (as Xenakis would say), i.e., outside of time, like any deep structure. . . . EVENTS per se (as templates) are not in any time either. Nevertheless, events, when fully interpreted, are elements of surface structure, i.e., actually sounding elements. When COLUMNS are segmented, event groups are formed. (Laske 1988)

Later he wrote:

An *event list* is a two-dimensional matrix in which musical events occur. Reading the rows of this matrix, one learns something about the parametrical properties of successive events, while reading the columns provides information about the development in time of parametrical properties. Without an analysis—manually or program aided—of the matrix, no information about the grouping of events or other properties essential to the design is available. (Laske 1989a, footnote 41)

In the first version of the program, the data printout already identified the row structure in the parameter columns. However, concrete circumstances suggested the use of this row structure for the segmentation of the score table for purposes of analysis. Composing with PR1, I constantly encountered a phenomenon that had long been familiar to me from theory and experience: that single musical elements (e.g., tones) form small cells; that such cells are complementary and form larger units. A single cell is "hungry" for completion or at least for continuation. The cell thus acquires potential for the further development of the form. Such cells are to be found in every parameter, and just as the parameter rows are layered to form ever changing constellations, so are the cells. At the time I called a cell the "smallest musical quantity" and told my students to search the event list produced by PR1 for these smallest musical quantities, crystallization nuclei, so to speak, to which more material—which has to be in the immediate vicinity, though—can attach itself. The nucleus then illuminates the environment, or, in musical terms, the environment of a smallest musical quantity must be analyzed (and interpreted) in terms of its definition. Since this aspect not only seemed important to me for the evaluation of an event list, but apparently also accompanied Otto Laske in his exploration of computer-aided composition, I quote a diary entry of January 31, 1975:

Let us carry out the following experiment in our minds: a single note is written down, then a second, a third and so on; after each note we ask whether the respective constellation is a "musical quantity." By a musical quantity we mean a configuration of elements which contains the germ-cells of a musical *development*, and also indicates the *direction* in which the development should proceed. *The term "development" should not be misunderstood. I merely use it to indicate that the existing context contains "jumping-off" points which can be continued; in the simplest case it merely describes a stationary state or a tendency.*
    Instead of writing down notes in succession, we can use a computer-composed sequence of tones, each individual tone being covered up at first and gradually revealed. At

first we get a single tone, then a pair of tones, then short sequences of tones with the character of a signal etc., until we discover a configuration which I call the *smallest musical quantity*. For present purposes I suggest the term "nucleus." This nucleus can be described quantitatively, for instance according to the following viewpoints (only pitch and duration being taken into account):

a. number of events,
b. number of different pitches,
c. number of different durations,
d. "continuity" of pitches (whether the space between the highest and lowest tones is uniformly occupied),
e. "continuity" of durations (whether the space between the shortest and longest duration is uniformly occupied),
f. concentrations in the pitch and duration range (constant alternation of elements or groupings as extremes).

It would also be possible to have a qualitative description if one were able to imagine all (or at least as many as possible) permutations in terms of the above viewpoints and delete all redundant formations. To illustrate this, imagine a lot of dots giving the impression of a circular surface. Remove all the superfluous dots until there are only enough left over to arouse the compelling association of "circle" and "surface." Applied to the musical example this would mean: there is a minimum number of permutations which completely represent what is inherent in each individual one. I call this description of the nucleus its *potential*.

We use the term nucleus to describe the quantitative configuration of a (small) number of notes. Observation of variant-formation in terms of the form potential involves qualitative determination—the answer to the question as to what is to be done with the nucleus. The nucleus represents a starting position in which the various elements (pitches, durations) are "introduced"; we take a familiar term from form-theory and now call the nucleus an *exposition*.

Whereas the nucleus represents a complete entity—the nucleus is clearly distinguishable from the variants derived from it—its expositional character remains open. If (in a second imaginary experiment) we add a further tone to the nucleus, does it still belong to the exposition, or to a form-section which is plainly separated from the exposition? (Both cases are possible.) If, however, we go on like this, nucleus and variants will separate. We have already agreed that the variant is obtained from the nucleus by means of permutation; the relationship of the two now becomes apparent. We can see how the term "exposition" is becoming extended; nucleus plus variant now "expose" one of the possible relationships between the nucleus and its variants, and in general, between variants. With each additional variant the exposition of these relationships becomes more complete. When the redundancy threshold is reached (i.e., when a further variant adds nothing more to the exposition), the exposition is completed. With regard to the variant there is also something like a smallest musical quantity, "quantity" being on a higher plane here.

I might add that the "nucleus" loses its function of reference when the exposition is completed; it merely represents one of the variants. The exposition meets with the same fate: it is followed by complexes which behave towards the exposition as the variants do towards the nucleus, until this form-level is completed too and the whole exposition disappears. The entire train of thought merely serves to arrange hierarchically a sequence of elements which at a first glance appears to be disorganized.

These are the aspects on which PROJECT 1, and consequently the class at the Institute, are based. The idea was to analyze the computer output, to discover "nuclei" in it and configurations which might be interpreted as variants of a nucleus. We shall see that, considered under this aspect, the definitions we use change as the length of the structure increases. However, strict attention should be paid to verifying definitions quantitatively; indications of interpretative means (including instrumentation and directions for performance) need not be excluded if they can help to make the structural description apparent in the score.[2]

Otto Laske, on the Institute's scientific staff at the time, attended my classes on programmed music. The above passage from my diary was not read out verbatim in class, but the gist of it was discussed during subsequent meetings on February 4, 11, 18, and 25, 1975. There was admittedly a high degree of abstraction in the requirement to discover "smallest musical quantities" in a PR1 output and use them to analyze the entire text, and it surely overtaxed my students at the time. The search for analytical footholds remained a matter of urgency, though, and continued to engross Laske (and me) in the ensuing period. Using PR1, I wrote a series of pieces with the collective title *Segmente*. Between 1987 and 1991 Laske (in collaboration with D. Cantor) developed his PRECOMP program, designed to analyze PR1 scores and help the user in design decisions.[3] Before I discuss a few examples connected with the analysis (and interpretation) of PR1 score tables, here is a brief summary of Laske's outline of PRECOMP.

PRECOMP [is] an interactive working environment, the purpose of which is to simulate the execution of a compositional task on the basis of insights into the sequence of actions of human experts. . . . PRECOMP currently consists of four components:

(A) a generator model derived from G. M. Koenig's PROJECT ONE, which produces score texts (called event lists)
(B) an analysis module showing the deep structure of event lists in a graphic representation[4]
(C) a module which computes structural breakpoints in the event list on the basis of criteria provided by the composer[5]
(D) a module enabling the composer to convert, in accordance with rules selected by himself, event lists into the note lists necessary for scoring with Csound (Laske 1990a)

As Laske informed me in a letter while I was preparing this chapter, A and B have been used by him for compositions such as *Immersion*, for Saxophone. Module C (also written by D. Cantor) cannot, for copyright reasons, be used at present, while Module D, although designed, has not been implemented. According to Laske, in working with PR1 and PRECOMP, it is

the composer's task to understand the structure of the event list and assess its consequences for the design of a musical form. This task is supported by PRECOMP's module B, which shows the composer graphic representations of analysis results, for example how tone density develops in comparison with loudness. . . . After studying several of these representations, the composer is interested to find out what events can act as starting-points of sections of the score he intends to write. (Laske 1990a)

An exhaustive description of Laske's method is given in his essay, "The Computer as the Artist's Alter Ego" (Laske 1990b). [6]

From all his remarks it is obvious that Laske wants to formalize the analysis phase during which the composer is endeavoring to find what I call the "substance" of a PR1-produced score table, so that the analysis can be performed with the aid of the computer. Of course, the analysis can only refer to data not already in the input set and hence known to the composer not only as such but also as intended.[7] Herein lies a typical problem since the composer, when formulating the input data (unless he/she is just playing with the program in order to test its power), already has a result in mind; without this expectation he/she would not have possessed a tool for formulating the input data. Apparently this expectation is only partly fulfilled. While the program is only meant to carry out the composer's orders, that is, produce the intended score, it adds something that is analytically separate from the intention and must itself be investigated. This addition is the direct consequence of formalization, without which the composer—launching a frontal attack, so to speak—would simply write down what he/she envisages with pen and ink. Formalization makes for spaces, which the computer program, lacking imagination, fills with random numbers.

Laske actually referred to this aspect as antagonistic: "In the world of compositional tools, I would place Project One on the side of friendly antagonists more than compositional assistants" (Laske 1988). The occasionally unexpected course of the program results, compared with the composer's intentions or expectations (which he/she believed were in the safe keeping of the input data), can indeed be alarming. For better or for worse he/she must try either to see the unexpected output as (hidden) confirmation or a paraphrase of his/her expectations or, on the basis of the complexity of the results, a way to acquire a new understanding—no longer of his/her plans, but of the surprises they triggered. Composing—I used the metaphor of a frontal attack previously—assumes the guise of a strategy of circumvention. The intention (if there actually is one, for often a composer does not execute a plan but *composes*, i.e., engages in an activity which is fairly likely to produce a composition)—or rather the sum of everything that might result from the intention—is encircled and attacked on all sides at once.[8]

No matter how poetically PR1 score tables are described, the fact remains that they can rarely be transcribed literally, that is, converted straight into a form of musical notation. To illustrate the problems Laske faced in formulating module B in PRECOMP, I shall present a few examples in an attempt to show what footholds are offered by the score table (in my own view).

The examples—treated in isolation to demonstrate possible compositional procedures—were generated by default input data and are taken from the first 108 lines of the first section (Figure 3.1).[9] Almost all the lines of the score are used, only six being omitted (49–54). Several lines occur in more than one example. The columns describe the behavior of parameters I (instrument), E (entry delay), H (harmony), R (register) and D (dynamics). Entry delay is the distance between two neighboring entry points; each entry point is occupied by a tone or a chord. PR1 does not take a tone's or a chord's duration into account. (The word "rhythm" is usually given instead of "entry delay" in the explanations of the examples). The only reason for selecting this specific score table was that, statistically, it contains sufficient material for analysis. Its compositional usability was not assessed, nor does it figure in the discussion of the examples. This simulates a frequent experience of the PR1 user, that is, that only after careful scrutiny of all the details does it become apparent whether a score table is usable or not.

Figure 3.1
PROJECT 1 score table using default settings

```
C:\PR1\IO-PR1\NURSO.OP1        Date: 28.05.1997    15:04:47
--------------------------------------------------------------------------------
SECTION 1                         IN    ED    PI    RE    DY
                                  4     4     4     4     4
--------------------------------------------------------------------------------
#    Instr  Tem  Entry  Delay Pitch                  Register        Dynamics
--------------------------------------------------------------------------------
1    *  8   90   *  1/8  0.125 *  F                  *  5            *  mf
2       8           1/8  0.125    D                     4               fff
3    *  1           1/8  0.125    C#                     6               ff
4       9           1/8  0.125    B   G#                 3  4            ppp
5       3           1/8  0.125    G                   *  6               p
6    *  6           1/8  0.125    F   D                  5  5            f
7       6           1/8  0.125    C#                     3            *  pp
8       6           1/8  0.125    B                      3               pp
9    *  4           1/8  0.125    G# G               *  6  6            pp
10      5        *  0/0  0.0      F                      4               pp
11      7           4/5  0.81     D   C# B               5  5  5         pp
12   *  2   60   *  3/4  0.75     G# G  F D C#            4  4  4  4  4   pp
13      5        *  5/8  0.625    B   G# G            *  3  6  5      *  mp
14   *  3           1/4  0.25     F                      3               fff
15      4           1/3  0.333    D   C#                 6  5            ppp
16      2           1/8  0.125    B   G#                 4  5         *  p
17   *  6           0/0  0.0      G                   *  4               p
18      6           1/2  0.5      F   D                  3  3            p
19      6           0/0  0.0      C#                     6            *  f
20   *  7           3/5  0.6      B   G# G            *  5  4  3         pp
21      7        *  1/8  0.125 *  E   F                  6  4         *  mp
22      7        *  1/1  1.0      G# A  C  C#            5  6  3  6      mp
23   *  9           1/1  1.0      F# G  *               5  5         *  ff
24      1   68   *  2/3  0.666    A#                     4               ff
25      8           1/4  0.25     B   D  D#              3  3  3         ff
26   *  2           2/5  0.4   *  C# D  F  F#            3  3  3  3   *  mf
27      3           3/8  0.375    A                      4               pp
28      6           1/5  0.2      A# G# B                6  6  6         p
29   *  6           2/5  0.4      C   D#                 5  5         *  fff
30   *  4           3/8  0.375 *  F# G  A# G#         *  6  4  3  5      ppp
31      4           1/5  0.2      A                      3               mp
32      4           1/4  0.25     C   C#                 6  4            f
33   *  7        *  1/8  0.125    E                      5               ff
34      7           1/8  0.125    F                      5            *  mf
35      7           1/8  0.125    B   D                  3  4            mf
36   *  5           1/8  0.125    D#                     6               mf
37   *  1           1/8  0.125 *  G#                  *  4               mf
38      9           1/8  0.125    F                      5               mf
39      9           1/8  0.125    E   C#                 6  6         *  f
40      6           1/8  0.125    C                      3               ppp
41      1  120   *  1/2  0.5      A   D                  6  6         *  fff
42      4           1/2  0.5      B   A# G  F#           4  4  4  4      fff
43   *  2           1/2  0.5   *  C   A  G#              3  3  3      *  mf
44      8           1/2  0.5      B   A#*               5  4            mf
45      5           1/2  0.5      G   F  E               3  6  5         mf
46      7           1/2  0.5      C# F#                  4  5            mf
47      3           1/2  0.5      D#                     6               mf
48   *  9           1/2  0.5      D                      3               mf
49      7           1/2  0.5   *  D# E                   5  6            mf
50      6           1/2  0.5      G# D# E                4  3  6      *  mf
51   *  8           1/2  0.5      C#                   *  4               pp
52      8           1/2  0.5      D# E  G#              5  5  5         ff
53      8           1/2  0.5      D# E  G#              3  3  3         p
54   *  2           1/2  0.5      D# E  G# D#         *  6  3  4  5      p
55      1        *  1/3  0.333    E                      4               f
56      5           1/5  0.2      G#                     6               pp
```

(Figure 3.1 continued)

#	Instr	Tem	Entry	Delay	Pitch	Register	Dynamics
57	* 4		0/0	0.0	D#	* 3	* ff
58	4		3/8	0.375	E	5	ff
59	4		3/8	0.375	G#	3	ff
60	4		0/0	0.0	D#	6	ff
61	4		1/5	0.2	E	5	ff
62	4		2/5	0.4	G# D# E	4 4 4	* mf
63	* 3		2/3	0.666	G# D# E G# D#	6 6 6 6 6	ppp
64	3		0/0	0.0	E	3	mp
65	3		2/5	0.4	G# D# E G#	* 5 4 3 4	fff
66	3		* 0/0	0.0	* B	5	mp
67	3		0/0	0.0	B	6	* mf
68	* 3		0/0	0.0	B	5	ff
69	3		0/0	0.0	B	6	p
70	3		0/0	0.0	B	4	ppp
71	* 2		0/0	0.0	B	3	f
72	* 9		0/0	0.0	B	4	fff
73	1		0/0	0.0	B	* 6	pp
74	6		0/0	0.0	B	5	* p
75	7		0/0	0.0	B	3	p
76	5		0/0	0.0	B	3	p
77	4		0/0	0.0	B	* 4	p
78	* 8		0/0	0.0	B	5	p
79	1		0/0	0.0	B	6	p
80	* 6		* 1/1	1.0	B G#	3 3	p
81	9		1/8	0.125	B	* 6	* f
82	7		1/8	0.125	B C	5 4	pp
83	* 5		1/2	0.5	B C E	5 4 6	mf
84	3		1/8	0.125	* A	* 3	ff
85	2		1/4	0.25	F# F D	6 6 6	ppp
86	4		0/0	0.0	C#	4	fff
87	8		1/8	0.125	A# G#*	3 5	* mp
88	1		3/5	0.6	* A# G F# E C# C	4 6 3 5 6 4	mp
89	* 4		1/2	0.5	D#	5	mp
90	4		5/8	0.625	D B A G#	3 4 6 5	mp
91	4		1/4	0.253	* G D#	3 6	mp
92	4	104	* 3/4	0.75	D A# F# F C# A	5 4 3 4 3 6	mp
93	4		3/4	0.75	G# E C B	* 5 5 5 5	* p
94	* 6		3/4	0.75	* D D# F# E	3 3 3 3	ff
95	6		3/4	0.75	F G#	6 6	fff
96	6		3/4	0.75	D D# F# E	5 5 5 5	mp
97	* 5		3/4	0.75	F G# D D# F#	4 4 4 4 4	f
98	5		3/4	0.75	* B C E G# A C#	6 6 6 6 6 6	mf
99	* 7		3/4	0.75	F F# A# D D# G	4 4 4 4 4 4	ppp
100	7		3/4	0.75	* G D# D A# F# F	3 3 3 3 3 3	* pp
101	7		3/4	0.75	E C B C# A G#	* 5 5 3 4 6 6	pp
102	7		3/4	0.75	* F#	5	pp
103	7		3/4	0.75	G B	* 4 3	pp
104	7	79	* 4/5	0.8	D# E G# C	* 5 5 5 5	pp
105	* 8		1/5	0.2	C#	* 6	pp
106	8		1.3	0.333	F A	4 3	pp
107	8		1/3	0.333	A#	5	* ppp
108	8		1/5	0.23	* A# G	6 3	ppp

In order to understand why these examples were chosen (and the analysis "problem" in general), it is useful to know that the parametric data occur in cycles. A cycle contains either similar (regular=r) or different (irregular=i) data in the relevant parameter. "Irregular" means that they come from different places in their list; when data are repeated in a list, there can also be repetitions in the i-cycle. In harmony, for example, "i" consists of (sometimes truncated) twelve-tone rows, each note coming from a different place in the list. However, "r" is defined as a repetition of three- or six-tone groups, or as sequences of chords that begin with the same pitch. The cycles, being of different lengths, rarely begin simultaneously in the various parameters and just as rarely end together. The more often parameter cycles begin or end simultaneously, and the greater the number of parameter cycles that do so, the easier segmentation becomes. Definition of the cycle raises another question. In some cases regular and irregular cycles alternate: r i r i r . . . Each r or i marks a regular or an irregular cycle. However, if the alternation is interpreted as tending towards a balance, the form of the cycle is ri or ir. The same applies to a repeated r or i: rrriii, iiirrr, etc. The following examples favor such alternations of r and i, thus highlighting the analysis problem. If one wants to simplify or modify the problem so that only cycles of form r or i occur in certain parameters, the input data must be altered correspondingly.

THE EXAMPLES

Laske writes: "Most succinctly, the user's task in Project One (as I see it) is that of 'making sense of the event list' (inherited from Schoenberg/Webern). This is a vast field, with *very few* sign posts set by the Project One itself. But it is exactly this near *tabula rasa* of raw materials that accounts for the creativity potential of Project One" (Laske 1988). Laske does not explain why he finds only "*very few* sign posts" or what he means by a "near *tabula rasa* of raw materials." My own findings follow here, and I leave it to the reader to judge them.

Example 3.1 shows the first twenty lines of the score table, here (as in all the following examples) distributed over four octaves as prescribed by the default data and omitting specific instrumentation. Two parameters, both regular, are to be compared: entry delay (E) and harmony (H). In the first bar the rhythmic regularity is easily recognizable; irregular cycles follow. Harmony is based on the repetition of two three-tone groups (f, d, c♯) and (b, g♯, g) until the end of the example. When the congruence of the regular cycles is to be used to articulate the form, there is a slight caesura after the first chord in bar 2.[10] The caesura's importance diminishes as less importance is attached to continuous regularity in the harmony.

For the sake of completeness, regularity in instrumentation is indicated by the brackets labeled I (only three small groups). The dynamics (D) change too: i r i r. Their possible function in the formal articulation is ignored here, but con-

Example 3.1
Score table lines 1–20

*Parameters of primary interest

siderably complicates the picture.

Example 3.2 (lines 66–83) also shows a passage in which parameters E and H are regular for a while. Harmony has a b at every entry point, joined towards the end by g♯, c and c with e. Strictly speaking, the rhythm is only regular in the group of grace notes, not afterwards. The apparent regularity of the second sep-tuplet is caused by the metrical rounding off; the entry delays are actually 1/1, 1/8, 1/8,—all divisions of the metric unit—the 1/8 value already occurring re-peatedly in the list. This is a typical borderline case in which, for the sake of absolute irregularity, the repetition of list values should be avoided or the evaluation should be based on the notation, which is again very regular in the rhythm here.

A group of events played by similar instruments only occurs at the begin-ning; only in the middle of the example is there a regular group of dynamics. How to execute a rapid succession of grace notes on different instruments and with great dynamic variation is not considered here. On this complex Laske writes: "The decisions made by the user are in no way particularly arcane; they usually have very pragmatic reasons (like what are my instruments?, how much time do I have to work on this composition?, should I try something new?), and since such reasons are numerous, depending on the user's task environment, they cannot easily be predicted" (Laske 1988). To this I might add that the pa-rametrical allocation of the columns in the score table is unimpeded (only the pitch data cannot be transferred to another parameter; the dynamic values—eight different ones—and the instrument or register numbers could be redefined by the composer).

In the next two examples the congruence of irregular E and H complexes is sought. Example 3.3 (lines 21–29) fits the bill from bar 3 on; in the first two bars the rhythm of the second and third chords still belongs to a small regular group (both involving entry delays of four eighth notes). Harmony presents itself as a twelve- and ten-tone row and is irregular throughout because of a lack of pitch repetition. The dynamics are regular at first (*mp* twice, *ff* three times), then ir-regular. These cycles thus overlap. Instrumentation is dissimilar, apart from the first two chords.

Example 3.2
Score table lines 66–83

*Parameters of primary interest

It is hard to draw any conclusions from this kind of examination. If we had concentrated on instruments, registers, or dynamic values instead of on rhythm and pitches, we might have arrived at different results in our interpretation of the data. In the case of registers, there is a noticeable difference between the use of narrow and wide ranges. The first two chords are widely spread, the remaining notes staying within a single octave range. An examination of the register pa-rameter in the first two examples provides us with another argument for or against any segmentation we may have in mind, again emphasizing the impor-tance of the composer's interpretation of the output data.

Example 3.4 (lines 66–93) starts in the same place as Example 3.2, but goes further. Congruent irregular cycles are confined to bars 3, 4, and 5, where har-mony, despite truncated twelve-tone rows (seven and eleven, but then twelve tones), is irregular due to a lack of pitch repetition, whereas the entry delays in the first two bars (only regular in the grace notes and subsequently irregular—cf. the commentary to Example 3.2) fall on regular tone sequences. Although con-gruence is confined to bars 3, 4, and part of 5, the environment is shown so that

Example 3.3
Score table lines 21–29

*Parameters of primary interest

Example 3.4
Score table lines 66–93

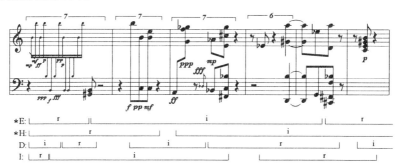

*Parameters of primary interest

we can follow the course of the cycles in context before they enter the congruence zone and after they leave it. Here the instrumentation would only have one regular group, while the regular cycles in the dynamics coincide with the E-H congruence.

I would like to take this opportunity to emphasize the point of this exercise. What we see in these examples are sections from a score table, represented on piano staves, without any indications as to instrumentation. Tones beginning simultaneously are shown as chords, although it would be possible to play them successively (to "horizontalize" them), which would result in a different rhythmic picture and provide ample polyphonic material. But even this "bald" text shows an abundance of layers, a given tone or chord displaying other links in each of its parameters. The door to interpretation is wide open. The question arises of how far such links, which are caused by PR1's composition algorithm in combination with the composer's input data, should be respected. The algorithm, within limits partly determined by that algorithm and partly prescribed by the input data, makes use of random decisions. By that I mean that a cycle could have begun or ended one or two notes sooner or later without rocking the basic principle. I see the real problems of analysis or interpretation in having to weigh the options of faithfulness to the text and tolerance regarding the limits inherent in the text, a choice that virtually encroaches on the text and the conditions of its genesis to the point of total dissolution. Of course the composer who, of his/her own free will and aware of the algorithm, uses PR1 to compose can make his/her decision in complete autonomy. The situation becomes problematic only when the PR1 user wants to find out what the program can do on its own and is therefore forced to take the score data literally.

In the next group of examples we shall examine other parameter pairs more extensively for congruences of regular or irregular cycles: first harmony versus register, and then instrument versus dynamics. Now referring to coupling of parameters rather than to patterns of cycles as discussed earlier, rr, ii, ri, and ir are random comparisons, chosen merely as examples. In rhythm and harmony, which are readily perceived as main parameters, the rr congruence (Examples 3.1–3.2) is particularly effective because it is distinctly group forming. The other extreme, ii congruence (Examples 3.3–3.4), presupposes other compositional intentions (and is meant in the totally opposite sense). We refrain from making an assessment here because the mechanism of group or cycle formation is in the foreground of our discussion. It is this mechanism that, for Laske, provokes the question as to whether there are rule-based procedures for mechanizing assessment, or at least an aid for it.

Example 3.5 (lines 65–83) is practically identical with Example 3.2. It shows one possibility of making regular harmony and irregular register congruent. (It was hard to find another example in the 108-line score.) Congruence is interrupted only in bar 2 by the three single grace notes and the g♯-b chord (the grace notes at the beginning of the second bar obviously form an i-group in the register parameter). Except for the *p* (*piano*) group the dynamics are irregular, as are the instruments.

In Example 3.6 (lines 21–48) the situation is reversed: regular register and irregular harmony are congruent in bars 2 through the middle of 5 and again in bars 7 through the middle of 8. Small notes indicate where the register parameter is not regular. Five irregular harmonic cycles fill the example (twelve, ten, twelve, eleven, and twelve tones per "row").

The final group of examples demonstrates four congruences of instrumentation and dynamics: rr, ii, ri, and ir.

In Example 3.7 (lines 87–108) instrumentation is regular throughout, with the exception of the first two chords: each group is played by the same instrument (or group of instruments). They are marked "a" through "e" to indicate that there are five different instrument numbers in the score table. The dynamics are regular in the groups marked *mp*, *pp*, and *ppp*. Bars 4–8 contain an irregular group.

Rhythm is regular from the last chord in bar 3 to the last chord in bar 11. Harmony is slightly irregular except for bars 5–7, where it consists of a repeated six-tone group (d, d♯, f♯, e, f, g♯).

In Example 3.8 (lines 66–88, cf. Examples 3.2, 3.4, 3.5) the instrumentation and dynamics are, for the most part, irregular. This irregularity is not reinforced by rhythm until after the grace-note group, and by harmony only in the last bar. (The apparent regularity—multiples of eighth notes—is caused by the circumstance that the list elements are multiples of a basic unit.)

At a first glance, instrumentation and dynamics do not appear to be the most important parameters for formal segmentation to comply with. The use of certain instruments is only noticed when effective, whereas dynamics are the expressive parameter par excellence. After all, an unusual combination of instruments and an effective use of dynamics might inspire a composer to subordinate the other parameters and to employ them more in the manner of a commentary or a reinforcement. Here, then, are two more examples that contrast the examined parameters.

In Example 3.9 (lines 57–73) instrumentation is regular except for the last three grace notes (which require two different instruments) and dynamics are irregular except for the *ff* group at the beginning. Congruence is therefore largely confined to the "b" group of the instrument parameter. Rhythm is divided: first irregular, then (in the last bar) regular. Harmony is regular

Example 3.5
Score table lines 65–83

*Parameters of primary interest

Example 3.6
Score table lines 21–48

*Parameters of primary interest

throughout: first a three-tone group (d♯, e, g♯), then (from the grace-note group on) a constant single tone (b).

In Example 3.10, finally, (lines 34–50) instrumentation is irregular throughout; dynamics are regular except for two chords in the second bar (*f, ppp*). This demonstrates almost complete congruence in the ir relationship. Apart from the last two chords (a three-tone group: d♯, e, g♯), harmony, too, is irregular. Regularity in rhythm adds nothing to the structural articulation.

We have seen that in an "average" PR1 score table, because of overlapping parameter cycles, countless groupings are possible, caused by the congruence of constant characteristics (such as regularity and irregularity). The more congruent cycles there are, the more distinctly such a passage stands out from its context. At the same time, this diversity poses a problem: in the first place because the constellation of congruences is constantly changing; and in the second because the borders of different congruences are often close together. This blurs the demarcations. This effect is enhanced by constellations that are difficult to interpret in any situation, such as rapidly changing dynamics or rapidly changing instruments in groups of grace notes (or other very short time values). True, the score table used for the examples is the more or less arbitrary result of using the default input data. The more goal oriented the input data, the easier it is to interpret the table, because it is oriented towards interpretability. The examples have

Example 3.7
Score table lines 87–108

*Parameters of primary interest

also shown, though, that some passages lend themselves to different interpretations, as in lines 66–93 (Examples 3.2, 3.4, 3.5, 3.8). The rhythm and harmony parameters were congruent in terms of both regularity (Example 3.2) and irregularity (Example 3.4). If the regular version of harmony is preferred, it is congruent with an irregular register (Example 3.5); instrument and dynamics are also irregular (Example 3.8). One could, by regarding this as a key passage, try to see the possible groupings in the other lines as variants of this prime passage and interpret them correspondingly in the transcription of the score.

Our discussion of the examples has also shown that PR1—a far cry from a composing machine—does not supply any solutions for compositional tasks. In Laske's words: "Project One does not deliver solutions, it is a *problem-posing tool* of the first order, and a framework for compositional thinking" (Laske 1988). This property would have emerged more clearly if we had compared several score tables, possibly with different sets of input data. We would then have seen that, given suitable input data, it is possible to grope one's way toward a score that embodies the optimal conditions for its interpretation. With PRECOMP Laske pursued a path that by no means rules out correction of the input data but adds a second tool that simplifies the final interpretation by preparing it. Like the first tool (PR1), this second tool derives from rule-based

Example 3.8
Score table lines 66–88

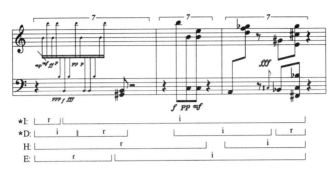

*Parameters of primary interest

thinking. Laske would like "to introduce the computer generally as a means to rule-based musical thinking. Musical thinking is a *process*, and processes can be represented in computer programs by procedures. That is why the computer may also be seen as a possible means of research into, and the articulation of, musical processes, those mental processes whose result is sociologically defined as music" (Laske 1989b).

The composer as a maker of music has a music-theoretical interest in finding out how he proceeds, or how he *could* proceed, when composing. He is interested, then, in possibilities of composing, in possible—not existing—music. Since his formulation of the [compositional] question anticipates procedural methods, the musical theory he favors is a "procedural" one, oriented towards the structure of musical activities. It is thus closely related to research into artificial musical intelligence, which likewise poses the question of "how." The questions that preoccupy him are focused on such problems as: how do I proceed when composing, how is my decision-making structured, how do musical effects

Example 3.9
Score table lines 57–73

*Parameters of primary interest

Example 3.10
Score table lines 34–50

*Parameters of primary interest

relate to musical procedures, what procedures can be developed in order to reach goal X? The answers to these questions are theories which are set down in programs. These theories are then empirically verified by being acted on accordingly. (Laske 1981–1982)

NOTES

1. For the Windows version and MIDI facility I am indebted to Rainer Wehinger, director of the computer music studio at the Musikhochschule, Stuttgart.

2. Quoted in Koenig 1979. The passages in italics are subsequently added commentaries for publication of *Protocol* (Koenig 1979).

3. Laske 1990a. See also Cantor 1989.

4. For example, see Laske 1990b:58–60.

5. See Laske 1992.

6. Editor's comment: It should be noted that as a result of PRECOMP's capabilities, there is a difference in Koenig's and Laske's analytic approach to the score table. The former composer, as demonstrated in this chapter, places emphasis on congruences of regular and irregular parametric cycles as a way of determining potential formal demarcations. Laske, on the other hand, emphasizes aggregates of parameters (i.e., sections of the score table) observed as belonging together when viewed in PRECOMP's graphic representation of the event list. Laske does not take parametric regularity and irregularity into account explicitly, though the graph clearly shows such relationships. Thus, while Koenig's approach is tied to the way PROJECT 1 actually generates a score table and is *hors temps* (outside time), Laske's is based in real time.

7. Not that the actual sequence of events in the result could be seen from the input data. We can however assume that a composer capable of envisaging contexts in connection with rules and thus of establishing rules for desired contexts harbors expectations fraught with experience when setting rules, or recognizes in the result the rules and hence his expectations. (By rules I mean the input data, the algorithm and their interaction.)

8. Elsewhere I employed the metaphor of a landscape in which many paths are possible but not yet defined. (Cf. Koenig 1993.)

9. In this connection it is neither possible to specify the format of the input data nor to explain the rules according to which the program uses the input data. I must therefore ask the reader to take the following examples as given facts. References to PR1, its algo-

rithms and data spaces are to be found in almost all of Laske's writings pertaining to PR1. Cf. also *Protocol* (Koenig 1979 and Koenig 1980).

10. Editor's comment: In a letter further explaining this, Koenig says, "After the first chord in the second measure, the congruence of E and H ceases [thus the term caesura] and it is up to the composer, who analyzes the context before writing the score, to mark this fact in some form or other."

REFERENCES

Cantor, D. (1989). *A Knowledge Acquisition System for Segmentation in Music*. Ph.D. diss., Department of Computer Science, Boston University Graduate School.

Koenig, G. (1970). "PROJECT 1." *Electronic Music Reports 2*. Utrecht, The Netherlands: Institute of Sonology (now Royal Conservatory, The Hague).

Koenig, G. (1979). "Protocol: A Report of the 1974/75 Class in Programmed Music at the Institute of Sonology." *Sonological Reports 4*. Utrecht, The Netherlands: Institute of Sonology (now Royal Conservatory, The Hague). [A German version of this text appears in *Ästhetische Praxis. Texte zur Musik*, vol. 4, PFAU-Verlag, Saarbrücken (BRD), 1998.]

Koenig, G. (1980). "PR1XM" (Manual). Utrecht, The Netherlands: Institute of Sonology (now Royal Conservatory, The Hague).

Koenig, G. (1993). *Ästhetische Praxis. Texte zur Musik*, vol. 3. Saarbrücken, Germany: PFAU-Verlag.

Laske, O. (1981). "Composition Theory: A New Discipline for Artificial Intelligence and Computer Music." In *Music and Mind*, vol. 2 [of collected papers published 1971–1981]. San Francisco, CA: International Computer Music Association, pp. 157–196.

Laske, O. (1981–1982). "Computermusik und Musikalische Informatik." *Neuland* 2:209–213. [H. Henck, ed., Cologne, Germany.]

Laske, O. (1988). "Observations about PROJECT 1." Unpublished manuscript.

Laske, O. (1989a). "Kompositionstheorie: Ein neues Konzept musikalischer Theorie." Unpublished manuscript.

Laske, O. (1989b). "Die Integration neuer Technologien in die Denkweisen der Musiker." Unpublished manuscript.

Laske, O. (1990a). "Zwei Ansätze zur musikalischen Wissensakquisition." Unpublished manuscript.

Laske, O. (1990b). "The Computer as the Artist's Alter Ego." *Leonardo* 23(1):53–66.

Laske, O. (1992). "AI and Music: A Cornerstone of Cognitive Musicology." In M. Balaban, K. Ebcioglu, and O. Laske, eds. *Understanding Music with AI*. Menlo Park, CA: AAAI Press, pp. 272–276.

Part II

Cognitive Musicology

4

A Brief Overview of
Otto Laske's Work
Joel Chadabe

For more than twenty-five years Otto Laske's articles have been puzzling many of his colleagues around the world. Musicians, after all, know about music; but Laske's concerns have been interdisciplinary, touching upon not only music but also computer science, artificial intelligence, philosophy, and psychology. The questions that have so often occurred to me, as his old friend and colleague, are probably the same questions that have occurred to numerous others: What exactly is he getting at? What is the relevance of these articles? What, exactly, *is* Laske? Musician? Psychologist? Philosopher?

Laske, indeed, has always been a prolific writer, but it has not always worked to his advantage. His many papers and articles have functioned as tools for himself to formulate his ideas as much as they have been communications of those ideas; and in the aggregate—partly because each article contains such a wealth of allusions and short detours, and partly because each article represents a thought in progress that will eventually be transformed into another article—they challenge our basic understanding of what his theoretical work is about.

This brief sketch of his ideas is based on conversations between Laske and myself in 1988, 1994, and 1996. In writing this chapter, I have two goals in mind. First, I want to provide a map that traces the main routes of his research so that others might better explore its details. Second, I want to outline what I see as the historical significance of his work: Laske is the first person to seek to understand musical compositions as the results of explicable mental processes.

THE FIRST IDEAS

Laske began as a thoughtful composer. It is from his own music that his theoretical ideas have grown, and throughout most of his career, he has thought of composing as the center of his activity. As he put it, "Composing was always my major interest. I was always interested in a theory of composition . . . the process." Indeed, all of his theoretical work grew out of his early composing in Utrecht. He had gone to the Institute of Sonology in 1970 at the invitation of

Gottfried Michael Koenig, and as he began to work in the electronic music studio—in fact, it was the first time he had worked in such a studio—certain questions coalesced in his mind. He asked himself, for example, whether or not there were rules that governed the way sounds came together. As he said:

I started being interested in generative grammars for music. Pierre Schaeffer had investigated how sound was structured by and in itself and suggested a taxonomy of *objets sonores*. He also thought that what really was needed was a treatise on how musical objects are linked to one another. That's what I wanted to do. I wanted to investigate linkages between sounds by investigation into the musical process, because that's where the linkage occurred.

Laske's goal became the formulation of "a theory of *making* music," as against a theory of music as every other composer might have thought of it. He put the phrase in active terms—"making music"—because, in his words,

The way to understanding music is by doing it, whether composing, listening, analyzing, performing, theorizing . . . all the tasks that require an active involvement in music. My personal involvement is in composing, because composing is so comprehensive. It involves listening, analyzing, and performing. . . . I disagree with traditional views that composing is separate from analysis and listening.

Many composers don't think about the process by which they compose, but do it intuitively, making it all the more difficult to explain. Drawing upon musicologist Charles Seeger's concepts of music knowledge versus speech knowledge, Laske pointed out that music knowledge is intuitive and reticular. Speech knowledge, on the other hand, is logical and linear and is the means by which we articulate our analyses of musical processes. Laske thought in both ways. He said, "As human beings, we don't live in one world alone. We continually negotiate between different worlds of knowledge." So Laske, as a thoughtful composer, began by asking about this relationship as it relates to composition.

As a first step toward discussing Laske's first answers, however, we might ask other questions: Why did it seem important to understand the process of making music? Why would the question have come to his mind in the first place?

On one level, Laske's answers were universal. They were the answers of a man of all ages: "To understand ourselves better. To know what to do! Having choices. If we do, we'll do music better. Or to do it differently, to find new ways of doing it. Musical activity is a self-discovery activity. We don't want to repeat what we did yesterday." He was espousing well-known wisdom in saying that knowledge leads to resources, choices, and informed decisions.

On another level, he was a man specifically of his own time. By 1970, our concept of musical instruments, in the sense of devices used to produce sounds, had expanded to include electronics; and electronic instruments were capable of producing a wide range of sounds, including those that had previously been thought of as noise. The ubiquitous influence of John Cage, as well as the approaches to electronic music represented by *musique concrète* and *elektronische Musik*, had put new ideas in the air. By 1970, any sound had become permissible in music, and traditional music theory—which dealt mostly with harmonic tension and release and the closed musical forms of tonality—was woefully inadequate for illuminating such a music. To be sure, individual composers had documented their own musical ideas: Cage, for example, had explained his chance procedures; Pierre Schaeffer had speculated on issues of connecting sounds; and Karlheinz Stockhausen had developed forms based on serialism and statistics. But there was no general theory of this new music. It was natural that Laske would see the need for a new "theory of linkages," or a "generative grammar," as he put it. In the vacuum, he asked himself: What are the general issues of coherence and communication in a new type of music that can use any sound? And he proceeded to look into the issues in an unusual way. Rather than deal with relationships between sound objects, as Pierre Schaeffer had proposed, Laske saw the problem as one of understanding the process by which music was made, that is, composed, analyzed, and listened to. Why did composers, Laske asked, combine sounds in certain ways?

The predominant structural paradigm in the sciences of the 1960s, whether or not articulated in just these terms, was General System Theory. A system was viewed as a functioning whole, a dynamic process, that functioned in a certain way because of the way its parts were organized. Further, a system could be understood in terms of its functioning, its organization, and its history. Making music was, in Laske's view, a dynamic process that functioned as it did according to the way its component parts interacted; and the component parts, as he analyzed them, were the composer's personality, background, and tools (i.e., instruments) at hand. A finished composition, in his view, was not the point. A finished composition was but a fixed souvenir of a productive moment in a continuing process of making music.

Laske's task, then, was to discover a way in which the dynamic process of doing music could be described. What language could be used? Clearly, because there was no specialized musical terminology in which a dynamic process could be described, it was an interdisciplinary issue. Laske perceived that music could not be separated from the rest of the world and that an understanding of a dynamic musical process had to draw upon general knowledge dealing with dynamic processes. He needed a metaphor to draw together observations and to construct concepts that belonged to what he called "a universe of discourse." What was the best metaphor?

Although the basic principles of General System Theory—dynamic process, interactive components, and development through time—provided an underpinning for virtually every idea that Laske has formulated since the 1960s, he quickly abandoned it as a specific model for composing. In 1970, he instead adopted as a model the idea of a composer's changing sense of musical grammar. He focused on the formulation of a generalized syntactic model; in that pursuit, he was particularly influenced by Koenig's composition program called PROJECT 1, which involved an approach Laske later said he took on faith. PROJECT 1 defined techniques for creating musical structures apart from any particular sounds. By using this program Laske could isolate grammar as a subject of experimentation. And it is worth mentioning that this line of thinking— defining the nature of a process without defining any material in which the process is manifest—is also characteristic of system-theory thinking. Growth, for example, can be discussed without discussing anything particular that grows.

Laske sought to verify his ideas in his own composing. Following the structural procedures of PROJECT 1, he began by creating *events*, which were groupings of unassigned parametric values that represented the structure of something to be determined later. He then used the events to form *objects*, which were groupings of events that made musical sense. Higher-level objects could contain lower-level objects, such as a *phrase object*, for example, that might cause tones to be grouped in a particular sequence. Laske then represented the objects in common practice notation so that he could hear them. But each particular score represented only one possible interpretation of the grammatical structure.

Laske was also influenced by Noam Chomsky's writings—in particular Chomsky's distinction between analytical and generative grammars. An analytical grammar was a set of rules derived from an analysis. A generative grammar, on the other hand, was a set of principles for synthesis. Laske found the concept of a generative grammar liberating. Laske realized he had always been talking about generative grammar when referring to composition. And like Chomsky, Laske pondered the relationship between meaning and grammar. Laske proposed the following formula: semantic (meaning) = syntax (grammar) + sound.

By 1972, however, Laske had concluded that a study of grammar itself was too narrow to yield the insights he sought. Grammar, as he saw it, assumed static rule-based relationships between objects; and although grammar types might have changed through history (from tonality to serialism, for example), the changes had been from one static model to another. Further, following a grammar seemed to him, at the time, constraining, as if grammar represented chains one had to cast off to achieve the freedom of creativity. Laske later said, looking back, "I saw creativity as anti-grammar."

In 1973, influenced by Herbert Simon's discussions of computer-simulated problem solving in *Sciences of the Artificial* (Simon 1969), Laske began to focus on problem solving rather than grammar as the metaphor most useful for understanding the music-making process. In terms of the problem-solving metaphor, making music was goal-oriented behavior based on planning. This process, consequently, was a succession of tasks performed, sometimes at different levels, each task leading to the next. Describing it in system-theory terms, Laske formulated the interactive components of the process as: (1) a composer's basic musical knowledge and understanding of the rules of music, (2) a composer's way of using knowledge in the process of making music, and (3) the particular tools used by a composer in making music. Laske explained it this way:

For me, then, there were three notions that took on equal relevance: *competence, performance*, and *task environment*. Competence is knowledge of musical grammar, a knowledge of sound linkages. Performance is *doing*; it's observable activity—the expression of competence. The task environment is the environment in which performance is done. It structures our thinking, our doing. We are interacting with it so we cannot help but be inspired by it, constrained by it. In electronic music, it is something that can be designed to a composer's liking. When I choose a program to work with, I'm designing my task environment. The electronic music studio's relevance is not in its physical configuration but in the fact that it is an environment that one [can] redesign and choose and be aware of as a set of constraints that inform[s] one's work.

Having defined the components of the process, Laske then concentrated on understanding the dynamics of the process, and he quickly saw that the key was in understanding what he called performance. He formulated two questions. First, how is a composer's performance influenced by that composer's understanding of grammar and by the environment in which that composer is working? And second, how can I find an answer to the first question?

It was at that time (1973) that Laske made his first major foray into empirical research. He launched a two-year project to analyze and document the steps taken by a group of children—sons and daughters of people he knew through the Institute of Sonology—while they were working with electronic sounds at the institute's PDP-15 computer. Barry Truax was also at the Institute at the time. His musical ideas were consonant with Laske's approach and he wrote the software that Laske used in the experiment. This software, called OBSERVER, allowed Laske to record what the children did as they solved musical problems. Laske explains, "That's how I saw computers: as a new data source. We would place the children in front of the teletype and whatever they typed was stored and later analyzed so that we could say, 'This is what children do when they compose melodies.'" When Laske left Utrecht in 1975, he had not yet finished the OBSERVER project. As a postdoctoral fellow at Carnegie-Mellon University from 1975 to 1977, he attempted to simulate OBSERVER's action protocols in an artificial intelligence language. But it was, in fact, a project only a team could have completed. Unfortunately, OBSERVER remains unfinished.

TRANSITION TO A NEW APPROACH

During the period immediately following his years in Utrecht, Laske continued to develop his earlier ideas. His scope of inquiry was enlarged to include listening as a creative act. He sought to answer questions through experimentation and empirical research. In 1978, as visiting faculty at the University of Illinois at Urbana, he asked graduate students to listen to Debussy's *Syrinx* and analyze it in terms of harmony, melody, rhythm, and timbre while talking aloud about what they were doing—for example, "Now I'm looking at the second phrase and linking it."[1] In 1983 at the Conference on Music, Emotion and Reason (Ghent University, Belgium), he delivered a paper called "Toward a Computational Theory of Listening."[2] The paper applied the metaphor of problem solving to analysis and listening. It portrayed the latter as a stepwise progression from hearing sound to formulating understandings of longer-term structures. Laske points out, "People listen to music on different levels at the same time, developing ideas of the overall structure at the same time that they're hearing the sounds."

During the 1980s, Laske lived in the Boston area. He worked at first as a designer of expert systems and then as a consultant in artificial intelligence for

Arthur D. Little. The 1980s, for Laske, were also years of extraordinary artistic involvement and activity. For example, in 1981 he and Curtis Roads organized Newcomp, a concert organization based in Cambridge. As Newcomp's artistic director for ten years, Laske organized sixty-five multimedia concerts featuring works by more than three hundred composers, filmmakers, choreographers, poets, video artists, and performance artists with concerts in Munich, Bonn, and Warsaw in addition to the series in Cambridge. He also administrated the annual Newcomp composition competition with an international board of jurors. Perhaps Laske's most important work from the '80s is seen in his compositions, poetry, and theories concerning the compositional process (which he referred to as composition theory). As a realization of his thoughts on composition theory in the late 1980s, Laske collaborated with a doctoral student at Boston University to implement PROJECT 1 on a Macintosh computer. In contrast to Koenig's original program, however, PRECOMP, as Laske called this new software, contained four modules: PROJECT 1 itself; an analysis module; a form-design module that, similar to OBSERVER, captured the composer's actions while working; and an unfinished module that Laske designed to convert PROJECT 1 output into a CSOUND score.

In 1991, Laske decided to study developmental psychology at Harvard University. By that time, he had concluded that grammar and creativity are not at odds with one another, that they are not separate but are interactive components of a process, and that creative people expand and transform grammar rather than rebel against it. He had also realized, as he later said, "that the meaning we make of our lives is a way of understanding our approach to composition." He developed a notion of what he called *biography*—by which he meant a composer's total history and evolving sense of self—to convey the idea that meaning, grammar, and sound are not separate dimensions of a musical process but, rather, are integrated within one evolving personality. In a 1994 lecture called "Creating Music as an Articulation of Prelinguistic Senses of Self" (published for the first time in this volume), he speculated, "It is my hunch that the composition of art works, and the composition of self in infancy before the emergence of the verbal self, have many things in common." Laske had re-oriented his research designs toward creativity in general. His own self-image had also changed. In that same paper, he refers to himself as "a composer and poet who is also a developmental psychologist."

THE SIGNIFICANCE OF LASKE'S WORK

Whereas in the nonmusical world a theory conveys the excitement of a new speculation that may or may not eventually be verified, the musical world often sees theory as the analysis of old compositions and the reaffirmation that those compositions follow certain rules. It is obvious that Laske uses the word in the nonmusical, speculative sense when he describes himself as a "theoretician of the musical mind who develops theoretical ideas on the basis of empirical research as well as compositional experience." He thus imbues the word "theory" with new musical meaning. Further, because Laske's approach has been to analyze the processes that produce compositions rather than the compositions themselves, his work represents a major reorientation of music theory.

In my view, the primary importance of Laske's work is in its relevance to new interactive compositional approaches that will soon emerge in the musical mainstream. His work is relevant because it relates the nature of musical activity to human personality and development rather than to a set of rules; and consequently, it enables composers to better understand what constitutes a satisfying musical activity for a performer or listener and to create interactive compositions accordingly. Laske's ideas, in short, help us understand how to achieve and cause others to achieve higher levels of musical creativity and reward.

NOTES

1. Editor's comment: See Laske 1984.
2. Editor's comment: See Laske 1986.

REFERENCES

Laske, O. (1984). "Keith: A Rule System for Making Music-Analytical Discoveries." In M. Baroni and L. Callegari, eds. *Proceedings of the 1982 International Conference on Musical Grammars and Computer Analysis*. Florence, Italy: Leo S. Olschki, pp. 165–200.

Laske, O. (1986). "Toward a Computational Theory of Musical Listening." In F. Vandamme, J. Broeck, and H. Sabbe, eds. *Proceedings of the 1983 International Conference on Music, Reason, and Emotion*. In *Communication and Cognition* 18(4):363–392.

Simon, H. (1969). *The Sciences of the Artificial*. Cambridge, MA: MIT Press.

5

Portrait of an Extraterrestrian
Bernard Bel

C'est un extra-terrestre!

This was my wife's exclamation the first day she saw Otto Laske. After years of communication through the Internet, our short encounter in 1990 had turned to a kind of recognition exercise—gathering reminiscences of a common world. Ours was indeed the virtual one of global culture, but we soon discovered a shared suspicion towards ethnocentrism, cultural prejudice, and illusory speech knowledge.

Otto Laske was born in Olesnica (Silesia) and graduated in philosophy under Theodore Adorno in Frankfurt-am-Main (Germany). In the late 1960s he went to Boston to complete his training as a composer. Later he studied and worked in the United States, Canada, the Netherlands, Finland, and other countries. He speaks fluent French and writes poetry in English and German.

The man from another planet was bound to become the target of controversial debates often arising from single-sided views on his work. I find it very difficult to introduce such a multifaceted intellectual *démarche*, ranging from philosophy, psychology, sociology, computer science, let alone the practice of poetry and music. A conventional academic survey of Laske's writings—focusing on products to the detriment of processes—might betray his commitment to action science. This chapter is therefore an attempt to trace the premises of his theoretical work in computational musicology. Being a subjective account, it may be taken as a reconstruction of Laske's favorite themes in the light of experience in the related field of music software engineering.

COMPETENCE VERSUS PERFORMANCE

Early writings of Otto Laske should be reviewed in the context of the early 1970s, when uncompromising ideas about competence and performance were dominating the field of linguistics (Chomsky and Halle 1968). Unlike musicologists applying generative models to music, Laske did not attempt to formulate a model of musical competence ("an intrinsic, tacit knowledge distillable into a grammar," [Laske 1993:210]) opposed to performance:

Performance, giving rise to individual compositions, and thus requiring, as its theoretical analog, a musical poetics, deals with musical activities as deviations from grammaticalness which result from mental and psychological factors external to the grammar, such as finiteness of memory, aesthetic intention, and pursuit of personal strategies. (op. cit.:214)

The musical notion of performance, in Laske's view, did not coincide with the Chomskyan concept recalled here. In a musicological sense, it was that part of the musician's knowledge that pertains to his use of competence and of local knowledge under real-world conditions (Laske 1992a:10).

Competence itself needed to be reviewed in the light of an action theory. And with regard to musical competence, providing a logical explanation of musical activity (i.e., amenable to performance prediction, [ibid.]) was confronted with several open questions: "In music, then, who was the native speaker? The composer, listener, instrumentalist, conductor, music analyst—who? What did the tasks these different experts were pursuing have to do with each other, if anything" (Laske 1993:217)?

Laske anticipated an important conceptual change that was later enacted by (ethno)linguists gaining insights into the historical dimensions of languages. Studies on pidgin languages, notably, suggest that linguistic competence (here meaning *domain-specific knowledge*) may be constructed from performance—constructed, indeed, and altogether maintained, since human languages are subject to growth, decline, and even death (Hagège 1996:35). This is also the case with aurally transmitted musical forms that do not rely on permanent knowledge substrates. If so, envisaging musical competence as a cumulative process, rather than a rigid assemblage of universal and local axioms, may provide a new explanatory framework accounting for change in the so-called immovable traditions.

Besides Chomsky's generative linguistic model, Laske was influenced by the work of Michael Kassler (1963). However, he found limitations in Kassler's attempt to derive a theory of music systems from individual pieces of written music. At first, the theory seemed to deny the importance of problem solving: "the procedural basis of any theory of music as something humans do, rather than just understand" (Laske 1993:211). In addition, Kassler's analytic approach was based on example-based composition, a theory of "existing musics" bypassing the problem of musicality, the domain of "possible musics."

In retrospect, [Kassler's] work is limited by the same assumptions that underlie contemporary work in expert systems. Frequently, the resulting knowledge bases embody only those elements of an expert's knowledge that are pure competence, and public knowledge at that, leaving out the expert's performance in real time, and his idiosyncratic local knowledge of how his performance fits into a particular task environment. (ibid.)

AN EXPERIMENTAL STUDY OF PERFORMANCE

Unexpectedly, the issue of musicality raised by Laske is of great relevance outside the western musical world from which it originated. When dealing with improvisatory techniques in aurally transmitted musical systems, ethnomusicologists tend to minimize, if not refute, compositional (i.e., problem-solving) processes. In the West, the status of a composer may only be granted to musicians claiming musical competence (assessed by experts and certified by academic records). In the broad view of social-cultural anthropology, this idea may be challenged as laden with Eurocentric prejudice (Blacking 1989). It is also interesting to deal with musical creativity from a cognitive perspective, with the hypothesis that music improvisation might be tractable as real-time composition.

During the early 1980s, Jim Kippen and I conducted field work in India, aiming at the development of a formal-language representation for tabla music and its implementation in a computer system named BOL PROCESSOR (Kippen and Bel 1989a). The methodological approach was one in which the computer could be incorporated into the process of data collection, representation, and analysis in order to "facilitate an 'apprentice-like' interaction between informants and analysts where priority may be given to the modeling of informants' and not analysts' views" (ibid.). The BOL PROCESSOR was a sort of expert system in which a preliminary set of syntactic pattern rules (an extension of Chomskyan grammars) was proposed by the analyst on the basis of hypotheses about compositional strategies. In a related experiment (Kippen and Bel 1989b), the initial model could be inferred automatically from ordered sets of examples. The machine was then requested to derive sentences (strings of terminal symbols), which were played or recited by the analyst so allowing expert musicians to assess their quality and accuracy. In addition, to prove that the current model was representative of the full scope of the compositional scheme under investigation, it was necessary to invoke a proof procedure (membership test) for any sentence proposed by the informant as a correct variation. Thus, grammars were not aimed at describing a particular musical item, nor a finite set of musical items (a corpus), but a composition scheme (named *qaida* in Hindi/Urdu) yielding a virtually infinite set of acceptable compositions.

The interaction between the expert, the machine, and the analyst in BOL PROCESSOR experiments may be summarized in Figure 5.1 which Laske (1992b:285) later extended to the western context. Informants' analytical observations were thus incorporated into the model in order to correct the machine's inadequacies and to help in the formulation of increasingly valid hypotheses of musical structure.

Our work came in support of the view that this type of improvisation qualifies as (indeed, real-time) rule-based composition. This may apply to other improvisational practices where grammaticality (consistent decisions about well-formedness) is relevant, exemplifying cultural knowledge that is quantified (through encoding), non-hierarchical, reasonably coherent, consistent, and above all bounded (Kippen and Bel 1989a).

Figure 5.1
Interaction between the expert, machine and analyst in BOL PROCESSOR experiments

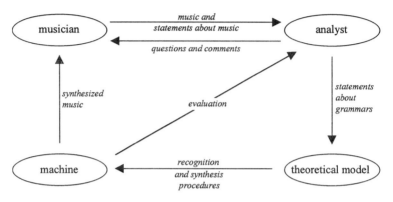

Source: Kippen, J. and Bel, B. (1989a), "Can the Computer Help Resolve the Problem of Ethnographic Description?" *Anthropological Quarterly* 62(3):133. © CUA Press. Used with permission.

Inaccurate investigations of real-time cognitive processes mislead musicologists who reduce improvisation to a virtuoso combination of precomposed fragments. This amounts to a conceptualization of the underlying process as example based rather than rule based. Precomposed fragments and "precompiled" strategic knowledge certainly play a role in tabla improvisation. But an exclusive example-based approach presupposes the existence of models (examples) and calls for a methodology in which these may be derived from existing musical pieces: analytical grammars illustrating (instead of explicating) music competence. As put by Laske (1992c:211), "This is analogous to trying to derive a French grammar from individual poems by Stéphane Mallarmé."

PROCEDURAL AND DECLARATIVE KNOWLEDGE

The BOL PROCESSOR experimental setup for improvisational knowledge acquisition may be compared with Laske's (1973b, 1992b) and Truax's OBSERVER programs in which musicians (notably children between ages five and twelve) were given simple compositional tasks for which traces of their mental processes could be analyzed. The comparison raises the issue of procedural (action-oriented) versus declarative (description-oriented) knowledge, which has been the topic of passionate debates in the artificial intelligence community.

A pattern grammar in the BOL PROCESSOR resembles a Chomskyan grammar in its attempt to describe a (virtually infinite) set of sentences (a formal language) acceptable by an idealized expert. In a formal grammar, rules are applied in an arbitrary order. Thus, the specification of the problem, "Generate a sentence," is clearly separated from the method of solution. This is the typical declarative approach on which logic programming languages like PROLOG have been based (Kowalski 1985:82).

Contrasting to this, action protocols traced by OBSERVER are stepwise procedural descriptions of the compositional process. There was also procedural knowledge in the early BOL PROCESSOR grammars, as rules were partially ordered, thanks to the intuitive layering of grammars (Kippen and Bel 1992). Besides, new features in the "BP2" version (used as a composition assistant[1]) include "flags" denoting states, global numeric variables, conditional jumps, and real-time interaction with the MIDI environment (Kippen and Bel 1994). This amounts to using programmed grammars (Laske 1993:224), that is, introducing strategical or performance constraints monitoring derivations in the context of a specific real-time problem-solving task. Unlike abstract generative grammars, programmed grammars qualify as "an integral component of a musical agent or robot functioning in a specific task environment" (ibid.).

Current developments of knowledge models, notably object-oriented systems, point at a comprehensive encapsulation of combined declarative and procedural representations. Modeling human activity presupposes a trade between generality, relevance and accuracy. OBSERVER protocols are extremely relevant and accurate, but they do not easily lend themselves to generalization (inductive inference). On the other hand, formal grammars are accurate and easy to manipulate inductively (see Kippen and Bel 1989b), but their relevance to musical activities such as composition and listening may be questioned.

VERBAL KNOWLEDGE, ACTION KNOWLEDGE

It may be clear from the above discussion that computational modeling attempts to elude pseudoproblems caused by natural-language aesthetic discourse, thereby challenging illusions fabricated by verbal knowledge. Uncritical reliance on speech definitions of artistic creativity, notably, undermines debates on modernity and tradition, which are biased by culture-specific perceptions of change (Lath 1988, Zarrilli 1987). Does artificial intelligence yield practical insights into such an interdisciplinary problem?

If you take a practitioner of some domain, your theory of knowledge in the domain, and attempt to embody a part of that knowledge in a computer program destined for interactive use by the practitioner, you have already decided that creativity is discipline-based. This may do you a lot of good in research regarding scientific creativity, but it does not bode well for studies, say, in poetic or musical creativity, where creativity may be unique or idiosyncratic before it becomes discipline-based (if it ever totally does), not to mention the fact that the competence in question may be largely "action knowledge," and thus essentially non-verbal . . . as in music or dance. In the described set-up, you have made the further determination that what interests you is how extant problems get solved, rather than how new products are forged and new problems get defined. . . . You are simply following a cultural script that tells you what is creative, and all you want to do is to find out how, in detail, processes deemed creative are being carried out in a step-by-step fashion. (In other words, you are exemplifying, but not explaining, creativity). . . . The goal of defining a retrospective theory of creativity is perhaps a one-sided undertaking; . . . what may equally matter is an action science approach to creativity, where the primary problem is not "Where is creativity," but "How can we transport creativity from here to there?" Of course, these two pursuits are not divergent, but ultimately convergent, issues. (Laske 1992d)

This leads to a clarification of the distinction between mainstream science and an action science:

A mainstream science gives retrospective accounts of creativity as documented or observed on the basis of traces of past processes deemed creative in light of cultural valuation. . . . By contrast, an action science "seeks to enact communities of inquiry in communities of social practice" (Argyris [et al.] 1985:12). It is dealing with living practitioners, and consequently is based on concurrent reports and on negotiations, unable to detach its practice from that of living practitioners. An action scientist is a "creativity consultant." (Laske 1992d)

Focusing on musical activity (instead of theories of musical artifacts) provided a reinterpretation of the paradigm of "computation" underlying cognitive musicology, "where [paradoxically] one attempts to formulate a theory or machine (thus an alloreferential construct) explicating a self-referential activity" (Laske 1992a:13). "However, it took some time to realize that the Cartesian notion of knowledge (viz., the separation of knowledge from action and being-in-the-world) that underlies most artificial intelligence research . . . is largely inapplicable to music research" (op. cit.:5).

SONOLOGY AS A SCIENCE OF THE ARTIFICIAL

Otto Laske told me that his work had been considerably enriched by Simon's book, *The Sciences of the Artificial* (1969), which he read nonstop the day he acquired it. To start with, Simon gave him a substantial theoretical base for a distinction between sonic and sonological concepts, which may be paralleled with the "etic" and "emic" components of speech.

In music, sonic entities are the elementary sound units isolated by acoustic analysis, while sonological components are equivalence classes constructed on these units by the cognitive-perceptive auditory system. In his introduction to a generative theory of music, Laske identified sonetics as a *science of the real* versus sonology as a *science of the artificial* (1975:35–52), the specific agenda of the latter being "the design of sound artifacts . . . leading to the formulation of performance models of music: (1) Sound Engineering and Sonic Representation, (2) Pattern Recognition and Sonological Representation, (3) Musical Representation and Definition of Intelligent Musical Systems" (Laske 1973a:354–355).

Sonology, "both a grammatical and a strategical, that is, problem-solving theory of music listening" (Laske 1993:217), may be checked against Pierre Schaeffer's (1966) phenomenological analysis of listening. Making the *intention d'entendre* the basis of listening, Schaeffer "concentrated on the patterns and qualities of listened-to sound as a phenomenon in and by itself, unrelated to the musical grammar and sources of production" (Laske 1993:218).

According to Laske, Schaeffer's recognition procedure in which the listener makes a transition from a repertory of input sound objects (*objets sonores*) to a configuration of output musical objects (*objets musicaux*) seems to imply two different, though interrelated, recognition strategies: listening (associated with sonority) and understanding (associated with musicality) (op. cit.:219). In the domain of listening, Laske draws a parallel between these two strategies and the concepts of performance and competence, claiming that Schaeffer "makes sonority, thus listening, a topic of a discipline in its own right, called sonology, while . . . accounting for musicality is a matter of formulating a musical syntax and semantics, in contrast to sonology" (op. cit.:220). If so, Schaeffer's theory fails to account for the recognition of sound objects qua musical objects, that is, how sound and sense come to be related in music.

In sum, a science of musical problem solving requires an intimate understanding of relations between the sonological component and the higher levels of sound organization termed as syntax and semantics (Laske 1972:29). "Where sonology goes beyond both the grammatical and performance domain, it is a theory of auditory imagination forming part of epistemology and aesthetics" (Laske 1993:217).

The coupling of syntax-semantical and sonological components in musical grammars is difficult to implement in computer composition programs. Many software environments exhibit advanced sound synthesis techniques with little scope for structural design. Conversely, compositional software often relies on the popular electronic instrumentation available in the MIDI studio, in which conventional macro events and the twelve-tone system are taken for granted.

When faced with the problem of developing a composition environment (e.g., BOL PROCESSOR BP2) expanding the boundaries of what is musically possible in both the Indian and Western contexts (Kippen and Bel 1994), we opted for a twofold definition of *time objects* (or sound objects): (1) a sequence of elementary actions performed on a music instrument, for example, a stroke on a drum or a stream of input/output MIDI messages; (2) a set of metric and topological properties relating to proximity constraints. These properties (e.g., "this object may be dilated up to 200% of its basic duration," or "this object shall never be overlapped by the preceding one.") embody time objects with "pertinent traits" that make them "well-formed in various musical contexts" (this pertains to sonority, Laske 1993:219). As to elementary actions, dealing with both output and input objects extended the time-object concept to programmed interactions with the outer environment (e.g., synchronization).

The instantiation of time objects (which turns them to musical objects) is the result of two processes: first, an arrangement of terminal symbols (a kind of score) produced by the grammar; then, a constraint satisfaction (time-setting) algorithm invoked to shape and locate all time objects mapped to the terminal symbols found in the score (Bel 1992). These processes combine several complementary aspects of computation: top-down (rule-driven) and bottom-up (data-driven); declarative and procedural; symbolic and numeric; stipulative and interactive; etc. Music software engineering nowadays has become more pragmatic and less innovative in some respects. However, after discovering the KYMA music system three years ago, Otto Laske told me that his whole theorization of composition would have been different if he had imagined the environment offered by new technology.

Asserting that artificial intelligence (based on symbol manipulation, i.e., reasoning) may play an essential role in constructing music-understanding systems, Laske questioned the connectionist approach (based on networks of formal neurons) in the light of Schaeffer's paradigm:

Neither acoustics or psychoacoustics, sciences of the real, can explain the intention d'entendre of which Schaeffer, the phenomenologist, had rightly spoken, but for which he could not fully account. It remains to be seen whether connectionism, which construes the intention d'entendre as rooted in human biology, will fare better than Schaeffer in this regard. (Laske 1993:220)

TASK ENVIRONMENT

Historical anthropology of music investigates relations between musical works and the societies in which they were commissioned, produced, performed, and appreciated. Its conclusions may often collide with the relatively romantic idea of individual artistic genius determining cultural processes. Laske's contemporary perspective reconciles both views by stating the importance of the task environment in which individual artists are operating. As put by Bernard Vecchione (1992:295):

Music has become something to produce in agreement with a certain number of protocols, programs, know-hows, questionings, problematics, instilled by designers into the devices they construct (hardware, tools and software). Thus, the task environment implies a certain type of questioning and the formalization of compositional or musicological problems, sometimes leading to a dialogue between human and machine . . . , the music-producing musician and the music being produced, or the machine and the musicologist envisaged as partners.

Further, Laske (1990a:55) states,

The task environment of a computer-assisted composer is more than a set of tools and materials. It is rather a habitat in which the composer lives, and its elements are partners in an ongoing conversation. Much of this environment consists of programs that act as external memories holding musical knowledge; the programs represent objectified thought, without which the composer cannot function. The task environment provides the point of origin of the composer's problem-solving.

As a consequence, a more accurate (and therefore) more abstract representation of music imposed itself. Beyond music as an emotional experience, the idea of music as a form of knowledge, or a "form of thought" (Vecchione 1992:295), has progressively emerged:

The computer has changed the potential of music theory, since, for the first time, it has given composers a tool for capturing their processes, and for articulating a theory of music based on their knowledge of compositional planning and problem-solving. This is even the case for composers who never program themselves, but rather use existing computer programs, or no programs at all. (Laske 1989:46)

The structured musical task environments now in existence already form a repertory for musicological research. These systems are the embodiment of musical intelligence in many forms, and while the knowledge bases they incorporate are in most cases not very novel, the way in which they represent and distribute musical knowledge is revolutionary. (Laske 1992a:21)

THE ARTIST'S ALTER EGO

Laske's motivation for seeing the "computer as the artist's alter ego" (Laske 1990a, 1991) is rooted in the foundations of a cognitive anthropology expanding its scope beyond the behavioral study of mental mechanisms.

The program on which computers depend is an artifact that serves our goals; it is written in a language of our invention, and becomes embodied in a physical machine of our design. In an anthropological perspective, such a program is not different from a work of art. . . .

In an epistemological perspective, of a science of the artificial, what we do thereby is to model ourselves, our knowledge, with the aid of an artifact conceived by us, called a "logic machine" or "computer." Writing a program for a computer thus is a metaphorical expression for "programming ourselves," or a part of ourselves, and of our understandings. (Laske 1992c:241)

To the despair of reductionists, Laske addressed the question of mental processes taking psychological and sociological dimensions into account:

In a cognitive perspective, human artifacts are always grounded in an individual way of knowing that is simultaneously a social way. It is the task of the humanities to reconstruct that knowing, either in order to convince of the value of its products, or to better understand them, or both. . . . What engages us are the intentions, designs, images, goals, and strategies of the generative processes that yielded them, which have no natural or factual a priori necessity. (Laske 1992c:240–241)

It is, in fact, the relationship between the (individual and social) processes, on the one hand, and the artifacts, on the other, which is in question in the humanities, and not only the structure of the artifacts (as is believed in aesthetic disciplines), nor only the structure of the mental processes underlying artifacts (as is believed in artificial intelligence). Well understood and utilized, and supported by a reflected epistemological culture, the computing machine, or "computer," can be used as a research tool for validating that relationship which is of such capital importance to the humanities. (op.cit.:244–245)

A FINAL NOTE

This picture is not complete. The reader should listen to Laske's music and appreciate his poetry. His essay on Charles Olson's projective verse (Laske 1990b) reveals a connection between these two sides of his creative genius.

Our common planet has also been occupied by dancers engaged in choreo-graphic research. In a modern world dominated by the craze for "connectivity," it is increasingly compelling to care for innovative explorations of space and time.

NOTE

1. BOL PROCESSOR (BP2) is available from //ftp.ircam.fr/pub/music/programs/mac/BP2 and Info-Mac mirror sites (see ftp://ftp.hawaii.edu/mirrors/info-mac/help/).

REFERENCES

Argyris, C., Putnam, R. and D. Smith. (1985). *Action Science.* San Francisco: Jossey-Bass.

Bel, B. (1992). "Symbolic and Sonic Representations of Time-Object Structures." In M. Balaban, K. Ebcioglu, and O. Laske, eds. *Understanding Music With AI.* Menlo Park, CA: AAAI Press, pp. 64–109.

Blacking, J. (1989). "Challenging the Myth of 'Ethnic' Music: First Performances of a New Song in an African Oral Tradition, 1961." *Yearbook for Traditional Music* 21. New York: International Council for Traditional Music, pp. 17–24.

Chomsky, N., and M. Halle (1968). *Principles of Generative Phonology.* New York: Harper and Row.

Hagège, C. (1996). "Introductory Speech." *Le Journal du CNRS*, January:35.

Kassler, M. (1963). "Sketch of the Use of Formalized Languages for the Assertion of Music." *Perspectives of New Music* 1(2).

Kippen, J., and B. Bel (1989a). "Can the Computer Help Resolve the Problem of Ethnographic Description?" *Anthropological Quarterly* 62(3):131–140.

Kippen, J., and B. Bel (1989b). "The Identification and Modeling of a Percussion 'Language,' and the Emergence of Musical Concepts in a Machine-Learning Experimental Set-Up." *Computers & Humanities* 23(3):199–214.

Kippen, J., and B. Bel (1992). "Modeling Music with Grammars: Formal Language Representation in the BOL PROCESSOR." In A. Marsden and A. Pople, eds. *Computer Representations and Models in Music.* London: Academic Press, pp. 207–238.

Kippen, J., and B. Bel (1994). "Computers, Composition, and the Challenge of 'New Music' in Modern India." *Leonardo* 4:79–84.

Kowalski, R. (1985). "Logic as a Computer Language in Education." In L. Steels and J. Campbell, eds. *Progress in Artificial Intelligence.* Chichester, West Sussex: Ellis Horwood, pp. 71–92.

Laske, O. (1972). *On Problems of a Performance Model for Music.* Utrecht, The Netherlands: Institute of Sonology.

Laske, O. (1973a). "In Search of a Generative Grammar for Music." *Perspectives of New Music* Fall/Winter 1973 and Spring/Summer 1974 (Double issue):351–378.

Laske, O. (1973b). "Toward a Musical Intelligence System: OBSERVER." *Numus West* 4:11–16.

Laske, O. (1975). "Introduction to a Generative Theory of Music." *Sonological Reports 1b.* Utrecht, The Netherlands: Institute of Sonology.

Laske, O. (1989). "Composition Theory: An Enrichment of Music Theory." *Interface* 18(1–2):45–59.

Laske, O. (1990a). "The Computer as the Artist's Alter Ego." *Leonardo* 23(1):53–66.

Laske, O. (1990b). "On the Projective Purpose of the Act of Verse: Composition by Field." ISTAR seminar on artistic creativity, Marseille, France.

Laske, O., guest ed. (1991). Composition Theory. *Interface* 20(3–4). [Issue devoted to composition theory.]

Laske, O. (1992a). "Artificial Intelligence and Music: A Cornerstone of Cognitive Musicology." In M. Balaban, K. Ebcioglu, and O. Laske, eds. *Understanding Music with AI*. Menlo Park, CA: The AAAI Press, pp. 3–28.

Laske, O. (1992b). "The OBSERVER Tradition of Knowledge Acquisition." In M. Balaban et al., eds. *Understanding Music With AI*. Menlo Park, CA: The AAAI Press, pp. 258–289.

Laske, O. (1992c). "The Humanities as Sciences of the Artificial." *Interface* 21(3–4):239–255.

Laske, O. (1992d). "Creativity—Where Should We Look for It?" Abstract submitted to the AAAI Spring Symposium on Artificial Intelligence and Creativity. [See "Creativity: Where Do We Look For It?" Invited paper, National Conference on AI, Workshop on Creativity, Stanford University, Palo Alto, CA. In T. Dartnall, ed. *Creativity, Cognition, and Computation*. The AAAI/MIT Press, 1996.]

Laske, O. (1993). "A Search of a Theory of Musicality." *Languages of Design* 1(3):209–228.

Lath, M. (1988). "The 'Modern,' the 'Traditional,' and Criticism in the Indian Classical Tradition." *Sangeet Natak* 89–90:5–15.

Schaeffer, P. (1966). *Traité des objets musicaux*. Paris: Éditions du Seuil.

Simon, H. (1969). *The Sciences of the Artificial*. Cambridge, MA: MIT Press.

Vecchione, B. (1992). "La recherche musicologique aujourd'hui—Questionnements, Intersciences, Métamusicologie" (Followed by commented abstract by O. Laske). *Interface* 21(3–4):281–322.

Zarrilli, P. (1987). "Re-membering Performance." *UCLA Journal of Dance Ethnology* 11:4–21.

6

Adequacy Criteria for Models of Musical Cognition

Marc Leman

INTRODUCTION

In his monograph, *Music, Memory, and Thought* (Laske 1977), Otto Laske develops a memory theory of music cognition based on an attribute theory of musical representation. The attribute theory assumes that aspects of musical representation can be cast in terms of predicate assignments. For example, the properties of duration, height, and articulation can be attributed to a note; other predicates, such as crescendo or articulation-structure can be attributed to a configuration of notes, etc. However, a paradigm shift in cognitive science—which took place in the mid-1980s—has profoundly changed the way in which we now think about musical representation and memory control. In particular, attributes are no longer considered to be valid entities for representations of musical perception. Instead, musical representations are conceived of in terms of images. Control structures based on production systems have been exchanged for dynamical systems in terms of neural networks. Moreover, the whole concept of what constitutes a valid model of music cognition seems to have been put into question.

In retrospect of twenty-five years of cognitive musicology, the focus of research seems to have evolved away from a Cartesian towards a naturalistically oriented approach. In the Cartesian approach, it is assumed that music cognition has an autonomous status that can be studied independently from the physical structure of the acoustical environment. In the naturalistic approach, it is assumed that music cognition is highly dependent on the nature of the musical sound environment. At least in Europe, it seems that naturalism currently has a profound impact on the transformation of the old systematic musicology. The new approach is cognitively oriented, with an emphasis on empirical data, computer simulation, and the musical sound environment (Leman 1997b). Empirical data come from psychoacoustics, experimental psychology, and brain science. Computer simulation in particular seems to become accepted by an increasing number of musicologists as a basic research tool for testing theories of musical perception and cognition. The musical sound environment is thereby considered to be a starting point for any serious scientific approach to music theory.

In this context, and as a result of the increasing interest in computer modeling, it is important to look at how computer models are currently evaluated and justified. A central concern is indeed whether a model is somehow *adequate*. Criteria of adequacy play a central role in scientific justification. The aim of this chapter is to go deeper into the problem of adequacy and its interpretation within the above mentioned Cartesian and naturalistic approaches.

WHAT IS AN ADEQUACY CRITERION?

Adequacy criteria pertain to often tacitly assumed reasons why a model of (musical) perception and cognition should be accepted as valid or true. In accord with the correspondence theory of truth, a criterion for adequacy is therefore often a method to find out whether a model has some correspondence with reality. Hence, notions such as falsification and corroboration may be involved. However, studies in the history of science have pointed out that the criteria for testing the validity of theories are also bound to a prevailing paradigm (e.g., Kuhn 1962). A change of paradigm may imply a change of adequacy criteria. Owing to the fact that a paradigm shift took place in the short period of twenty-five years of cognitive musicology, it is clear that much of what is to be said about adequacy criteria of models should be included within a more comprehensive discussion about the two paradigmata.

In what follows, it is argued that the assumed adequacy criteria of the Cartesian modeling approach are no longer accepted (in the sense of being sufficient) within a naturalistic epistemology of music. The main problem is not whether these models are true or false within their paradigm, but whether researchers are, in 1998, still prepared to accept the nature of the proposed models.

ARTIFICIAL INTELLIGENCE MODELS AS EPISTEMOLOGICAL MODELS

It is known that O. Laske's view on music cognition has been profoundly influenced by research in artificial intelligence (AI) (Laske 1988) and the related branch of information processing psychology. At that time, AI research was attractive because it provided a paradigm of how to think about human cognition in terms of mental processes. For centuries, theories of human cognition had been cast in terms of descriptive metaphors (either speculative or justified by empirical data). With AI, a new method was introduced by which theories of mental processing could be described in formal terms as quantitative metaphors called formal models. The main feature of a formal model is that it is operational and testable. Testing refers to a procedure by which a model can give answers to particular questions. Operationalization is conceived of in terms of information processing procedures, in particular, manipulations of symbols that show how a certain task is solved within a defined set of constraints. AI claimed to be able to say something about the internal mechanisms of the human mind by means of symbol-manipulation. This post-neopositivist interest in cognition came as a reaction to behaviorism, in which the study of mental processes was thought to be of no value for psychology.

In AI, however, adequacy has often been conceived of in terms of practical relevance, that is, the ability to solve a task in an intelligent way. The main concern, then, is not whether the model tells something about human cognition; rather, the idea is to use strategies of human perception and cognition in order to build machines that mimic human intelligence. Such machines can be helpful tools in industry, medicine, education, or any other application domain, such as music. Several AI researchers have indeed noticed that music provides a rich and ill-defined domain that is therefore suitable to demonstrate the practical relevance of particular AI techniques (Balaban et al. 1992, Camurri 1993). K. Ebcioglu's program for the harmonization of Bach chorales (Ebcioglu 1987) is a well-known example. The program is based on a set of rules, compiled by the author on the basis of a musicological analysis of Bach's style in harmonizing chorales. The program takes as input a choral melody, and it produces acceptable four-part harmonizations as output.

What is of interest here is the relationship between AI and psychology. This relationship has always been particularly intricate, and questions could be raised whether AI relied on psychology for making tools that exhibit intelligent behavior or whether psychology relied on AI to justify its theories. This mutual ambiguity had a profound impact on the assumed adequacy criteria for models.

FROM PRACTICAL TO EPISTEMOLOGICAL RELEVANCE

In the case of Ebcioglu's model, we take for granted that the author's motivation was to show that machines are capable—to some degree—of composing music in the style of J. S. Bach. Basically, the author wanted to show the usefulness of a particular search-heuristics in a rule-based expert system. In other cases, such as of D. Cope's EMI-project (Cope 1989), practical usefulness may pertain to the ability of the program to produce novel music in a predefined style. Here the adequacy of the model is interpreted in terms of artistic relevance, rather than a practical scientific or industrial one.

But what is most curious is the ease with which AI allows one to shift from practical relevance (either industrial or artistically oriented) to epistemological relevance, from solving practical problems to the belief that the model may tell us something about the perceptive and cognitive functions of humans. For example, one may argue that Ebcioglu's model uses musical knowledge to solve harmonization tasks. Hence, the set of rules that implement that knowledge may be seen as a formal description of a cognitive activity, and consequently, the conclusion is that the model tells something about the way in which humans accomplish the Bach harmonization task. Ebcioglu gives a hint in this direction when he says, "We were instead viewing this research as a venture out in the frontiers of the capabilities of expert systems, and as a tool for a more precise understanding of the Bach chorale style and Schenkerian analysis as applied to the microcosmos of the chorales" (Ebcioglu 1987:9).

IDEALIZED MODELING AND PROTOCOL ANALYSIS

The ease with which a shift from practical relevance to epistemological relevance could be achieved in the early days of AI research was inspired by the way in which modeling itself was realized. In order to model intelligence, one starts from a general model called a cognitive architecture. Hence, given a system that is able to solve particular tasks in an "intelligent" way, it is straightforward to claim that what the model does is because it is an adequate model of human cognition.

The shift from machine to human mind is thus somehow imbedded in the bare concept of modeling intelligent behavior. N. Stillings et al. (1995) draw on D. Marr's distinctions between knowledge level, functional level, and physical level. These distinctions are at the core of the modeling paradigm in AI and cognitive science. The analysis of intelligence at the knowledge level describes what is done to solve a certain task. The analysis at the functional level describes how a certain task is carried out in terms of a functional description and representation. Finally, the analysis at the physical level describes how the functions are actually physically implemented.

In Laske's *Music, Memory, and Thought* (MMT), the models are called process models rather than functional computer models. At the knowledge level it is described what kind of memory tasks are involved in music processing. At the functional level, it is described how symbol-manipulation is done. However, to have a real functional level, the process model should be implemented on a machine, which in this case was actually not accomplished. Rather, the model is described in terms of a general cognitive architecture and the logic of production systems. What is of interest here is the way in which attributes (as symbols) can be manipulated and processed by different memory blocks (Figure 6.1).

One may criticize this approach by saying that it is purely speculative. The question is thus if such an idealized model can ever be tested. First of all, one may argue that the process model is in accordance with the existing theories about echoic memory, short-term memory, and long-term memory. Secondly, it can be argued that the model relates to the real world by means of a metaphorical transfer. Human cognition is thereby interpreted as a device that works with constrained operations on symbols and structures of symbols, similar to the computer model. Adequacy, in that sense here relies on (a) the integration of existing knowledge about an abstract architecture of cognition, and (b) the a metaphorical transfer of the process model onto the mental processing mechanisms of the human mind.

The focus on explicit though highly idealized process models was considered to be a final stage of the theory construction process and a first step toward straightforward concretization in terms of a computer implementation. In addition protocol analysis was at the time conceived to be an acceptable postbehavioristic, introspective methodology. In MMT, and especially in "Keith: A Rule-System for Making Music-Analytical Discoveries" (Laske 1984), Laske has

Figure 6.1
Laske's memory model

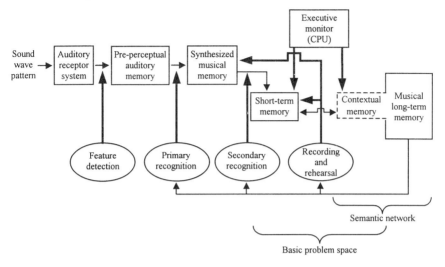

made use of verbal reports, which are then explained by making correspondences between observations of the performance and predictions of the process model.[1] As such, the model is believed to be adequate insofar as the behavioral analysis fits with the assumed processes of the information processing model.

PSYCHOLOGICAL MODELS AND TESTING

In the short history of cognitive musicology, the highly idealized approach of MMT was followed by an attempt that aimed at a more concrete implementation and testing. Explicit psychological models of musical cognition processes were then designed in such a way that quantitative predictions about data would be possible.

The semiformal and rule-based *Generative Theory of Tonal Music* (GTTM) by F. Lerdahl and R. Jackendoff (1983) is an example of a theory with clearly psychological aspirations, and it is of interest here to have a look at it because it is often praised as a most adequate model of music cognition. As with MMT, however, the model is still described at a high level of idealization. Interestingly, the model is said to be adequate because it is supposed to shed light on general psychological issues of musical information processing. The authors claim "Linguistic theory is not simply concerned with the analysis of a set of sentences; rather it considers itself a branch of psychology, concerned with making empirically verifiable claims about one complex aspect of human life: language. Similarly, our ultimate goal is an understanding of musical cognition, a psychological phenomenon" (op. cit.:6) The model is argued to be adequate because it provides a solution to the task of perception-based analysis and the assumption that this can be shaped in terms of some rule-based grammar. The success of GTTM, in contrast to MMT, has been that it was possible to straightforwardly implement the model and test it either by psychological experimentation or by computer modeling (e.g., Deliège 1987, Heeffer and Leman 1986, Jones et al. 1988). Implementation of the so-called preference rules was easily done because the model was rather concrete about the assumed grammar for segmentation of notated melodies. In addition, the basics of this grammar could seemingly be tested. The connection to the real world was based on a set of segmentation rules that operate on the attributes of notes: duration, articulation, instrument (called: timbre), height, and so on.

CONCRETIZATION AND ECOLOGICAL VALIDITY

It may be argued that both action-protocol analysis and hypothesis testing, the two methods for testing the adequacy of formal models described thus far, suffer from a lack of ecological validity. The assumed correspondence with the data of the real world depends (too) much on the goodwill of the researcher (or reader) to actually see this correspondence. It is indeed far from evident how a set of symbols (notes on a score) can be called a relevant representation for the acoustical representation of music. Testing the preference rules of GTTM on subjects may turn out to work fine, but do we therefore have to accept the set of formal rules as an adequate model of music perception? What, then, about auditory processes and peripheral signal processing? What about virtual pitch processing and segregation at the lower perceptual levels? What about the fine aspects of perception, those that relate to tuning, expressing, accentuation, etc.?

All these aspects seem to be idealized. Yet, humans live in a world of sounds, and musical thoughts depend on it. How can a model that is completely deprived of this world then simulate processes that are fundamentally based on the physical structures of the world? How does one think about a model of perception that is not connected to the musical sound environment when this sound environment is reduced to bare symbols on a score? The authors argue that only cognitive issues are at stake here, irrespective of their implementation. But are there any cognitive issues that are independent of their environment? Does such a Cartesian model tell us anything at all about the world from which it is itself deprived? Is the assumed autonomy of mental processing itself a valid assumption in music cognition research?

In this context, it is perhaps instructive to recall that the idealized assumptions are not limited to classical rule-based symbolic approaches. Neural networks and connectionist models may suffer from much the same ailments. For example, in J. Bharucha's neural network for a study of chord facilitation (Bharucha 1987), the concepts of pitch, chord, and keys are attributed to the nodes of the network and the relationships between the nodes are then handwired in order to reflect the constraints between the concepts of tone, chord, and key in tonal music. Yet, the model is assumed to be adequate because the output of machine chord facilitation seems to fit with psychological data. But note that the rather loose criterion of adequacy-as-hypothesis testing is here replaced by a stronger criterion of adequacy-as-correspondence-between-computer-output-and-psychological data. This is an improvement because it implies a much more concrete notion of model—less metaphorical or idealized, so to speak. But the model still suffers from the same Cartesian approach as it is deprived from any contact with the constraints of a musical sound environment. Can we accept such a model to be adequate for music perception?

Laske, Lerdahl and Jackendoff, and Bharucha argue that their system explains properties of music perception and that the burden of adequacy depends on the way in which the model is interpreted as a task-specific hypothesis testing device. Laske's theory of perception has been indirectly tested using composition tasks and action-protocol analysis. Lerdahl's and Jackendoff's model, as well as Bharucha's, has been tested in perception tasks. In all cases, however, the model is isolated from the musical environment and the programmer/reader has to assume possible links with the outer environment at a metaphorical level. The operational theory, process model or computer model is therefore only adequate as long as one accepts the metaphor.

ADEQUACY, IDEALIZATION, METAPHOR, AND PARADIGM

The function of idealization and gradual concretization (called: *factualization*)[2] has been dealt with by W. Krajewski in the context of a discussion about scientific theories (Krajewski 1977). What is interesting here is his definition of an idealized model. An idealized model is defined as an ideal limit of a sequence of real objects with diminishing value of some characteristic parameters. For example in GTTM, the parameters related to auditory perception are set to zero, although we know that in reality, these parameters are not zero. According to Krajewski, idealization is an important phase in the construction of theories. However, in testing the adequacy of rival theories, factualization is considered to be a necessary step. But the problem with the Cartesian approach is that no factualization is possible. Rather, factualization is exchanged for metaphorical transfer. Otherwise stated, in the Cartesian paradigm, factualization (which is always necessary in order to test a model) is subsumed under the more general notion of metaphorical transfer.

Factualization and adequacy are thus related to metaphorization. A transfer of thoughts from one domain to another is a common strategy of human thinking (Johnson and Lakoff 1980), and it works well provided that one agrees about the domain of application onto which the model is projected. Metaphors, however, may lose their appeal as the research paradigm changes. In particular, problems arise when we no longer accept an idealized model of a cognitive architecture as a paradigm for modeling or when we no longer accept scores to be a corresponding input for acoustical stimuli. Adequacy criteria, therefore, seem to be highly dependent on research paradigms.

Paradigms refer to a pool of pragmatic constraints that typically mark scientific communities (Batens 1991). Such a pool is not a fixed set of statements about scientific work. Rather it is a collection of thoughts of how to deal with data, theories, methods, and epistemological justification. As such, the set of criteria for adequacy should be seen as part of a larger scientific framework that allows scientists to decide to what degree something is acceptable or not acceptable. An AI model can therefore be loosely interpreted as an epistemologically relevant model, but its adequacy depends on whether we can accept the metaphorical transfer as a relevant act of factualization.

BEYOND METHODOLOGICAL SOLIPSISM

The symbol-based approach to cognitive science assumes that perception and cognition can be studied by means of models that simulate performance (how it works) by means of formal operations (numerical or string-based) on symbols (Newell 1980). The competence of the model (what it does) is understood by assigning the formal symbols to concepts, that is, by providing a semantic interpretation. Obviously, the interpretation of the computer model is based on the attitude of methodological solipsism (Fodor 1981). It implies that the existence of the physical world is not denied, but it is kept separated from the model. Consequently, the relationship between the model and the physical world can only be justified by the programmer who is standing between the physical world and the model (Figure 6.2).

The formal entities, on which rules or dynamic constraints are operating, impose a distinction between form and content (or signifier and signified)—mental and physical world. Consequently, meaning assignment in the mental system is somehow assumed to be carried out by another device: the self, or the will. In modeling, of course, it is the programmer who plays the role of the model's self and who assigns meaning to the formal entities. The model is thus the result of the modeler's conceptualization of the world.

One may conclude that the attitude of methodological solipsism entails a metaphorically defined concept of epistemological relevance that results from the specific position of the programmer as gateway between computer model and environment. According to W. Clancey (1993), these attitudes are the result of a category mistake in which the description of the outer world in terms of fixed a priori concepts are confused with the ontology of the model. It is certain, how-

Figure 6.2
The Cartesian modeling strategy. The modeler interprets the environment and forms a representation of that environment using concepts and relationships between concepts. The knowledge is formalized in explicit terms, and a model is constructed using a proper formal language.

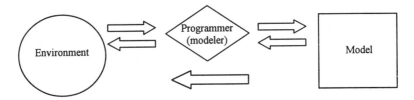

ever, that the position of the model maker, as well as the way in which the programmer is related to the model and the environment, is a central issue in this discussion.

Yet, the implied triadic relationship between programmer, model, and environment is a problematic one that often transcends the discussion about symbolic versus connectionist modeling. Above, it was argued that connectionist methods do not guarantee ecological validity. In counterpoint with that view, Vera and Simon (1993) argue that environment-based intelligent systems are quite compatible with the symbol-systems point of view and the idea of interaction with the external environment. However, a practical solution to the denotative and hence arbitrary character of symbols can only be given when sensory input systems are somehow hooked to symbols. Reasoning with these symbols is then constrained by *situated action*: feedback to actions in a context or by internal constraints among sensory inputs. Whether such an approach is called symbolic, or hybrid (involving nonsymbolic and symbolic techniques) is not really relevant here. Obviously too, anything can be called symbolic as long as it refers to a pattern.

In this context it makes sense to distinguish between different types of patterns such as signals, images, and symbols. Images are typical nonsymbolic patterns in that their meaning or function in the model is not assigned by denotation but by filtering aspects of the acoustical environment. The auditory information processing system can indeed be considered a filtering system. It filters part of the acoustical environment in terms of a limited range of frequency and amplitude and encodes this filtered information in terms of activities of basic, though massively interconnected, information entities (neurons). The properties of neurons can also be described in terms of filters. Encoded physical signals, however, are called images. As such, images are said to reflect properties of signals. Signals are objects in the external environment, and consequently, the definition of images assumes an intrinsic interaction with the environment. This interaction is situated at the level of the model. With symbols, this interaction is situated at the level of the human interpreter of the model. Yet it is perfectly possible to develop systems in which symbols emerge from the interaction with the musical environment (Camurri and Leman 1997).

In models that are deprived of an environment, the test of adequacy seems to rely ultimately on the approval of the programmer and the inclination of the reader to accept the metaphorical implications of hypothesis testing. The attitude of methodological solipsism is in that sense quite ambiguous: expert systems can be argued to be epistemologically relevant, while models with psychological aspirations can be argued to have a purely practical relevance. However, in the context of a newly emerging naturalist paradigm, in which the notion of factualization is implicitly assumed in the methodology, the Cartesian notion of adequacy is no longer accepted to be sufficient. The main argument is that models should be related to a functional analysis of the brain and the environment. Otherwise, the model is not accepted as a valid testable model but only as a general metaphor for musical cognition. A most important requirement now is that the input to both computer models and human subjects should be the same, rather than just having some correspondence. In particular, score representations are therefore no longer accepted to be valid inputs for a psychological model. This requirement, however, implies an ecological approach (see below).

The notion of hypothesis testing as it has been formulated in the information processing psychology of the '70s (Lehnert 1984) is indeed a rather general concept, compared to the requirement that a model should reflect the low-level functions of the brain. But how far can we go? Do we really have to model ion streams in neural cells? If not, one may argue that hypothesis testing can be done at many different levels of human behavior (including the brain level) and that relevant neuronal information processing does not necessarily urge one to implement all the tiny details of the dynamics of single cells. Again, the notion of factualization may play a crucial role in a better understanding of the problems involved.

THE SUBSYMBOLIC APPROACH

In answering the question of what constrains a good model, A. Clark (1995) remarks that the task-specific input-output correspondence between a computer model and human perception/cognition is only of marginal epistemological interest. Additional constraints should largely come from disciplines such as psychology and psycholinguistics (psychomusicology in our case) and neuroscience and brain theory (neuroanatomy, neurochemistry, lesion studies, and research on the single cell, circuit, and systems level). According to Clark, an acceptable model of human information processing must respect the results of such studies. It is argued that the (above mentioned) distinction between knowledge level, functional level, and physical level does not afford a useful conceptualization of the relations between studies of the brain and computational models. The idea of a single knowledge level is clearly an oversimplification, as is the idea of a single level of algorithmic specification. According to Clark, Marr's (Stillings et al. 1995) three-level distinction needs to be multiplied and even that may lead to problems. What is mere detail for one explanatory level may be crucial for another level. He proposes Arbib's schema theory as an alternative to the competence/performance/physical levels. A schema, according to Arbib (1995), is both a store of knowledge and a way of controlling that knowledge: neither aspect can be separated from the other. This notion of schema is in agreement with the one in *Music and Schema Theory* (Leman 1995).

A. and N. Sharkey (Sharkey and Sharkey 1995) distinguish between the following constraints of adequacy for models of cognition: (1) they simulate the actual behavior involved; (2) they provide a good fit to the data from psychology experiments; (3) the model, and its fit to the data, is achieved without explicit programming or hand-wiring; and (4) the models often provide new accounts of the data. What is most different from the previously mentioned Cartesian approach is the requirement that the model is achieved without explicit programming or hand-wiring. Nevertheless, the authors argue that even when one adopts this ecological viewpoint, a number of decisions have to be made by the programmer, such as about the architecture of the net, its initial structure, the learning technique, the learning parameters, the input/output representations, and the training samples. But even this can be argued to happen in connectionist modeling. The problem, however, with most models is what the Sharkeys call the "unrealistic tailoring of the environment." Especially in music research, the problem of realistic tailoring is an acute one. Because of an historically developed language of musical performance, scores have often been taken to represent the musical environment. Yet, the score is a skeleton representation, deprived of inherent forces and constraints that actually reign in music (Leman 1993).

From the above discussion it follows that, first, the distinction between the three independent levels of modeling is no longer valid; second, that a number of additional constraints can be formulated in order to test the adequacy of a model; and third, that any modeling will involve the hand of a programmer who makes decisions about what aspect of the world should be modeled. But the main fundamental distinction with the Cartesian approach then seems to be that the model is no longer considered a system that is isolated from its environment. Factualization should especially be concentrated on the realistic tailoring of the environment. What follows is a deeper look into an analysis of the ecological modeling approach. Afterwards, an overview of adequacy criteria is presented that may be relevant in a naturalistic approach.

ECOLOGICAL MODELING AND THE MODELING ENVIRONMENT

D. Cohen and R. Jeger-Granot (1995) describe a framework for music research that is based on the idea that different kinds of so-called influences operate on different stages of musical activities. These influences are related to psychoacoustics and cognitive constraints but also to the stylistic ideal and aspects of consciousness such as the personality of the composer. It is obvious that music modeling too must take into account a number of levels of description and a general framework within which the modeling operation is carried out. Computer modeling, however, may not be able to handle all these constraints within an ecological setting. Following is a discussion of some basic aspects of an ecological setting.

Modeler, Environment, and Model

Modeling is done within a defined set of constraints called the modeling environment, or the space in which modeling takes place. By the end of the nineteenth century, it was realized that a theory of music had to be formulated within a framework of at least three constraint levels (Leman 1995):

- Sound acoustics,
- Processes of sensorial perception and Gestalt formation, and
- The cultural environment.

In view of computer modeling, it is important to carefully analyze the set of constraints that define these levels. To start with, it is instructive to compare the modeling approach of Figure 6.3 with the Cartesian approach presented in Figure 6.2. The modeler here is no longer the interpreter of the environment and inventor of all aspects of the model, rather, his role is limited to defining the interactions between a bare model and the environment. Categorization within the model now proceeds by extracting information from the physical stimuli of the environment and by self-organization. In principle, the modeler has no direct access to the knowledge represented in the model. The evaluation of the model has to be based on appropriate testing with stimuli. The so-called bare model may account for low-level physiological mechanisms that are responsible for the emergence of global phenomena at higher levels of observation.

The Human Information Processing System

What aspects of the model, then, are predefined, and what aspects are the result of the interaction with the environment? The architecture of the Human Information Processing System relies on proper regularities and principles that are assumed to be common to the members of all cultures. At this level, it makes sense to distinguish between:

- sensory information processing: eyes, ears, and other sense organs are assumed to be the same for the members of all cultures.
- perceptual information processing (apperception): it is assumed that the dynamics that underlie processes such as grouping (including both segmentation [in time] and segregation [of voices]) and fusion are the same for the members of all cultures.
- cognitive information processing: it is assumed that the dynamic principles of learning, categorization, and association are the same for the members of all cultures.

Of course, these assumptions (often called universals) have appeal as general

Figure 6.3
The ecological modeling strategy. The modeler defines the conditions for an interaction between a system and the environment. The dynamics are formalized using a proper formal language. Representations are formed in the model through interaction with the environment. Afterwards, the model needs to be tested in order to make explicit what has actually been learned.

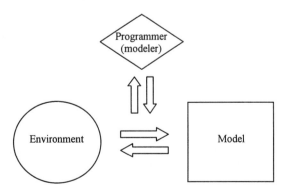

working hypotheses. Much of the research about the Human Information Processing System makes abstraction of small individual differences, deficiencies, and/or possible physiological adaptations to particular properties of the environment.

What is important, however, is that the information processing of a Human Information Processing System is based on a memory representation of the environment or the most relevant parts of it. Unlike the Cartesian approach, in which a memory representation of the environment is a conceptualization of the modeler, we adopt the point of view that auditory representation is reflecting basic filtered physical properties of the environment. What needs to be modeled, then, is the way in which the auditory system processes information at this physiological level of information processing.

Especially in auditory perception, we believe that the physical properties of the sounds may have a large impact on the memory representations. In pitch perception, for example, the effects of virtual pitch perception should be taken into account as this is indeed the basis of tonal center perception and harmony. In addition, segregation will need to be based on physiological properties of the auditory system. Wang (1996) has developed a model of primitive auditory segregation based on a neurocomputational theory that clearly suggests the dependency of perceptual organization on synchronization correlations between different groups of neurons. As in the previous example, the effect depends on the nature of the stimulus. If in the sequence ABABAB, the frequencies of the tones A and B come too close, or the durations become too long, then one does not hear the sequence as two streams (A . A . A .) and (. B . B . B) but as one stream.

One may observe, first of all, that particular features of the sound environment may have a large impact on the perception of the objects. A good example is the effect of pitch shifts, which are caused by a periodicity analysis of the temporal structure envelope of a signal (Langner 1997). Such effects, of course, can only occur when the Human Information Processing System is somehow reflecting the properties of the sound environment. Therefore, simulations of musical perception and cognition must take into account aspects of the way in which the environment is encoded. This involves a particular conception of a metric representation that is different from the one used in the formal-linguistic Cartesian paradigm. In short, we say that representations in the Human Information Processing System do not point to objects in the sound environment; rather, they reflect filtered and metric properties of this environment. The distinction between pointing to and reflecting has much to do with the distinction between symbols and images. The notion of image is therefore an important concept in naturalistic musicology.

A second observation is that the experience of particular perceptions (such as those based on fusion and grouping) may be the result of applying defined constraints on the sound environment. The feedback on sound from the Human Information Processing System is an illustration of the intrinsic ecological basis of music perception. Octave enlargement [systematic stretching in the upper and lower register] is based on sensory feedback but we may extend the idea to different types of feedback including perceptual and cognitive. The use of pseudo-polyphony in the works of J. S. Bach may be conceived of as an example of exploiting perceptual constraints of grouping (segregation), whereas the organization of sounds using particular scales may be related to learned schemata. In general, the feedback of the Human Information Processing System, seen as the set of constraints imposed on the sound environment, is in fact what defines the musical environment.

The usefulness of different levels of description is also evident from the above example. In order to explain a phenomenon such as octave enlargement, it makes little sense to describe the quantum structure of the ions that flow through the neural membrane at the moment of excitation. Of course, this information is necessary to understand how neurons work, but it is not necessary to model neuronal functioning at this level in order to develop a working model of perception. It is good to know that our building is built on solid ground, but once we know that the foundations are stable, we do not need to give a detailed description in order to discuss other aspects of the architecture.

Contrary to the symbolic-functionalist approach, the subsymbolic-functionalist approach aims to describe the functions of the Human Information Processing System in terms of the underlying physical system. As such, functionalism can be in agreement with reductionism provided that functional principles closely match the input/output properties of the physical carrier.

For example, if tone fusion can be modeled in terms of an autocorrelation function (Meddis and Hewitt 1991, VanImmerseel and Martens 1992), then this function should be based on input/output functions of the physical carrier system. Neurophysiological studies (Langner 1983, Schreiner and Langner 1988) indeed show that some type of cross-correlation may be carried out by the brain to do a periodicity analysis of the acoustical signal. In a similar way, higher level functions such as perceptual learning and schema-based recognition should be ultimately based on neurophysiological findings.

The Musical Environment

Because of the particular properties of the sound and the auditory system, musical sounds are perceived as objects rather than acoustical signals. The auditory system thereby does not function as a mere recorder of sound, but it filters the signals and actively disentangles the acoustic wave and constructs the perceived entities by segmentation, segregation, and ultimately categorization. Bregman (1990) has referred to this process as auditory streaming. In the previous paragraph, we have seen that perception may be influenced by properties of the signal as well as the way in which the Human Information Processing System encodes and processes the signal.

In the example of the enlarged octaves, the Human Information Processing System imposes constraints upon the sound environment in order to facilitate fusion. This condition may be called a musical condition—albeit it is one imposed by mechanisms that are operating at the periphery of the Human Information Processing System and have probably nothing to do with learning. In a similar way, pseudopolyphonic settings (as in African xylophone music) obey certain rules related to speed and ambitus of the tones that are used. The particular settings may foster segregation or it may dissolve it; the effect is due to neural mechanisms of perception (Bregman and Ahad 1995). In a similar way, but more related to learning, a schema for tone perception (which resides in the Human Information Processing System) has been conditioned by the musical environment in which tones (having a particular timbre) are combined into particular configurations. The impact of the schemata on the musical environment may be such as to strengthen a desired tone's semantic effect, in combination with timbre fusion, segregation and segmentation.

Generalized, we may define the musical environment as the set of constraints which the Human Information Processing System imposes on the sound environment such as to foster (ap)perception. This rather general definition involves feedback dynamics that should be taken into account while working out a model of music cognition. The feedback can be observed at two different time scales, one which applies to the life cycle of, and one which applies to generations and populations of a Human Information Processing System. The first is related to psychomorphological processes—those processes that determine how form and structure emerge in the Human Information Processing System's interaction with music. The second is related to histomorphological processes—those which determine how form and structure emerge in culture (e.g., as stylistic ideal reflected in cultural objects or systems).

The modeling paradigm discussed in this chapter is restricted in that it applies mainly to the time scale of psychomorphology. It is a modern version of a psychoacoustically-based Gestalt theory whose aim is to explain how global order as a mental phenomenon emerges from the interaction of elementary processes.[3]

On the other hand, a given musical environment is often the result of a histomorphological development by which generations of Human Information Processing Systems have imposed new constraints on the sound environment. Such constraints may eventually lead to the emergence of a stylistic ideal—a set of highly abstracted structures and beliefs that find their sediment in cultural objects as properties of style (such as Baroque, Rococo, Romantic, etc.).

Obviously, the constraints imposed on the sound environment—which are often associated with the perceptual modalities of pitch, rhythm and timbre, and streaming—are related to the different processing stages of the Human Information Processing System (sensorial and perceptual, as well as cognitive). Sensorial and perceptual constraints are typically associated with the psychomorphological level. Cognition on the other hand, also involves the histomorphological level. And when music information processing is involved, then the histomorphological level is always involved.

Different cultures show large differences in the constraints imposed on the sound environment, which suggests that the feedback dynamics are nonlinear. The effects of learning and schema-dependent feedback often mask the fact that the underlying information processing principles are common to all cultures. A description of the musical environment is therefore not a simple task.

The Implementation Environment

The implementation environment comprises the tools that are used to model and run the simulation. From a purely theoretical point of view, the implementation environment is not important. The present generation of computers is based on the Turing machine, and its operations can in principle be carried out with pencil and paper. In practice, of course, the implementation environment is an important factor in cognitive science because the feasibility of a simulation often depends on the availability of powerful computer equipment (Carreras and Leman 1996).

Research in cognitive science is often based on a small-scale artificial world that does not fully integrate the idea of ecological modeling. When theories of music cognition are tested under more realistic conditions, then the amount of data is huge and the computational efficiency of the model (its coming to an end within limited time constraints) becomes a critical factor in research. In simulations that incorporate a realistic physical environment, fast computing is crucial.

Limitations of a Naturalistic Approach

The pursuit for a naturalistic approach to cognitive modeling is often tempered by a number of difficulties and methodological limitations.

- The Constraint of Monomodality: The interaction of a human listener with the environment is basically multimodal, involving different senses in a unified way. Even if we limit the sound environment in an acousmatic setting (the so-called listening-behind-a-curtain condition—which is the case when we listen to the radio or CD player), the basis on which the interaction takes place is not necessarily limited to sounds. The effect of sound on the Human Information Processing System is more than just a response of the auditory system. Movements of the body are particularly connected to the perception of the beat and phrase, and the apperception of emotion and affect is associated with kinesthetic and synesthetic processes (apperception of movement and colors) (Broeckx 1981). At present, however, multimodal perception is far beyond the scope of the current modeling paradigm, owing to a limited knowledge of how different modalities of perception interact.
- The Constraint of Context-Sensitivity: The impact of a context on signs has been discussed at length in the semiotic literature. Signs indeed get their meaning because they are occurring in a context of other signs that, together, contribute to a background against which the meaning of a particular sign is pronounced. This aspect can be captured by modeling. However, the musical environment is also embedded in a functional context in the sense that music often has a role within a larger social (and multimodal) event. This aspect too is neglected when dealing with pure audio modeling. In fact, the point of view adopted is a listener who sits in an armchair and who listens to recorded music without moving or using music for any other function than listening.
- Extramusical Influences: The set of constraints imposed upon the sound environment has been defined in musical terms, such as the use of a particular selection of devices to produce sounds (instruments), a selection of a scale, harmony, polyphonic setting, and so on. From the point of view of composition, several of these constraints can be applied as rules for composition. In recent compositional practice, some rules explicitly take into account auditory properties of the Human Information Processing Sys-

tem, but this is not a necessity. The generation of sounds is often inspired by concepts that are nonmusical and that may originate from pure mathematical models. Although these extramusical influences may have found a sediment in music (as a sort of stylistic ideal for composing, cf. serialism), it may be very difficult, if not impossible, to retract them. The ecological paradigm presented here is therefore mainly restricted to musical behavior in which perceptual learning is involved. It does not take into account sources that go beyond perception.

The musical environment has a rather wide scope, while the modeling paradigm seems to be applied to a small part of it. This is indeed acknowledged, but the paradigm should be evaluated with respect to criteria for scientific research, not with respect to its scope. After all, the scope is wide enough to account for musical phenomena that have been discussed for centuries, such as the previously mentioned effect of timbre and tonal fusion, an explanation of the sense for tone center perception, emergence of the beat, auditory streaming, and so on. Less well understood, but feasible within the constraints of the current paradigm, is the role of the above-mentioned feedback mechanisms that lead to the emergence of styles and stylistic concepts in the long term. The latter is especially intricate because it may include all kinds of constraints that do not have, at first sight, a direct relation to music.

ADEQUACY AND EPISTEMOLOGICAL RELEVANCE—ADDITIONAL CONSTRAINTS

In what follows, several candidate criteria for adequacy are proposed. Most of the criteria fall under the heading of the so-called convergence paradigm (Leman 1997a). In this approach, it is assumed that the adequacy of models should be tested within an interdisciplinary context of experimental psychology and brain research. Convergence implies a pursuit of comparison and correlation at different factualized levels of the model between results obtained by different research methodologies.

Input-Adequacy

By input-adequacy it is understood that the input environment for computer modeling, behavioral research and brain research should be the same or converge toward each other.

Input to Computer Models. Although this constraint may sound trivial, it is a remarkable fact that models of music perception score very poorly with respect to an adequate tailoring of the input environment. One aspect of this is concerned with the nature of the musical input. The input is often cast in terms of a simplified and highly abstract representation of real stimuli: a set of notes (as in a score), a set of musical microfeatures (Gjerdingen 1989), abstract input vectors (Kaipainen 1996), or simplified virtual pitch patterns (Laden and Keefe 1991, Leman 1991). However, in models that claim to provide an account of music perception, one would at least expect that the input to the model is identical to the acoustical stimuli used in the psychological tests.

A second aspect deals with the scope of the musical input. Models that assume that music perception is largely determined by data-driven perceptual learning may limit the input environment to a set of test stimuli. Some timbre studies rely on the idea that the similarity between timbres is somehow reflected in mental maps through perceptual learning. The input is then a limited data set that can also be used in discrimination studies (Toiviainen et al. 1995). In studies related to tone center perception, however, the aim is rather to show that listeners, when exposed to tonal music, develop particular structures that reflect some basic properties of the circle of fifths. The input environment can be limited to particular chords, cadences, or short musical fragments (Leman 1991), yet the burden of the proof is to show that invariant information can indeed be extracted by exposing the model to real music (Leman and Carreras 1997). The pursuit for a realistic tailoring of the acoustical environment is an essential aspect of a naturalistic approach to musicology.

Input for Brain Studies. The methods for noninvasive studies of the brain may provide direct or indirect evidence for representation and memory. Analysis based on positron emission tomography (PET) and functional magnetic resonance imaging (fMRI) allow a direct view on the activated brain areas (Martin et al. 1991). In the near future, the resolution in time as well as in space may become sufficiently fine to uncover details of cognitive processing of music. For the time being, however, electroencephalogram (EEG) signals are perhaps more appropriate because of fine temporal resolution obtained by this technique (da Silva and Pijn 1995). Gevins (1996) argues this could become the primary tool for studying the neurophysiology of cognition in natural contexts. PET and MRI indeed require heavy machinery whereas EEG can be done in natural settings. New methods have recently increased the spatial resolution of the EEG so that source modeling can be applied as well.

A number of musical studies have concentrated on event-related potentials (Cohen and Erez 1991, Cohen and Jeger-Granot 1993, Janata and Petsche 1993, Janata 1995). Event-related potentials (ERP) are EEG signals that depend on the context in which the stimulus is presented, such as whether a stimulus is expected or a surprise. The size of the response in an individual record is small in relation to the amplitude of the fluctuations of the ongoing brain activity so that numerous records must be averaged in order to reveal the characteristic evoked potential (Martin 1991). Consequently, the input environment may need to be submitted to a particular test paradigm with many trials in order to fulfill some conditions of measuring. Typically, the input is designed to isolate and manipulate specific cognitive processes, while eliminating or holding constant other task-related activities. For cognitive studies, typically, twenty-five to one hundred trials are averaged to form a clear response. Other studies, such as (Petsche et al. 1996, Zatorre et al. 1996) have concentrated on a realistic musical input, rather than short melodic or harmonic sequences. But the aim is rather to test general hypothesis about musical imagery.

Input for Behavioral Studies. The input used for behavioral studies is less dependent on technological constraints and allows a greater flexibility.

Output-Convergence

As discussed in previous sections, a straightforward requirement for the adequacy of models is that the output should somehow relate to human behavior or human brain activity. Again, it is possible to distinguish between different kinds of outputs related to computer modeling, psychological studies, or brain studies.

Output of Computer Modeling. Adequacy has sometimes been tested in terms of a qualitative evaluation of the musical output. In this tradition, T. Järvainen (1995) adds a quantitative test in terms of a comparison between a multilevel statistical analyses of the machine improvisation and human improvisation. In the context of the convergence paradigm, the suggestion is that the output of a computer model should somehow be compared with the results from behavioral studies as well as brain studies. Thus far, however, most models have been restricted to behavioral data, or they remain highly idealized models in which behavioral data are compared with brain studies.

In our study of tone center perception the aim has been to make the model as concrete as possible. A memory representation of the musical environment is obtained by exposing the model to a representative musical environment, such as Book I of Bach's *Das Wohltemperierte Klavier*, played by K. Gilbert on a clavichord. After training, the model is handled as an artificial human listener. Acoustical stimuli are presented and responses are recorded that allow for the specification of a tone profile for tone center recognition. The test paradigm is similar to the techniques used by C. Krumhansl in her studies of pitch perception (Krumhansl 1990) and hence, a comparison with behavioral data is straightforward. Figure 6.4 gives an example of a computer output in terms of a tone profile. It is compared with profiles from human subjects (Leman and Carreras 1997).

Output of Psychological Studies. Psychological research is based on a multitude of techniques for data analysis. In the '70s, multidimensional scaling was introduced as a mathematical technique to interpret psychological data in terms of mental representations. This technique has turned out to be of utmost importance for music research because it used behavioral data to construct a space in which the perceived objects are related to each other. Listeners typically have to estimate the similarity between perceived objects. The resulting similarity judgments are then interpreted as metrical distances and the relationships between the objects are represented accordingly. The resulting maps are called mental representations. The paradigm, known as cognitive structuralism (Shepard 1982), has first been explored in studies of tonality perception (Krumhansl and Shepard 1979, Krumhansl 1990), later also in studies of timbre perception (Grey 1977, 1978; Grey and Gordon 1978; Kendall and Carterette 1991; Iverson and Krumhansl 1993). Perhaps more than any other area of perception, the multidimensional scaling technique, despite its limitations, has led to a remarkable set of quantitative data that can be used to test the output-adequacy of computer models.

Figure 6.4
The tone profile of a computer simulation ("simulation" below) is here compared with a tone profile of human subjects ("experts," "intermediate group," "novices"). The same stimuli have been used. They consisted of three chords (establishing a tonal context of C-major) followed by a major triad chord on the different degrees. Human subjects have to rate how well the last chord fits with the context. The profile of the computer simulation is obtained by comparing the network activation of the last chord with the network activation after the context.

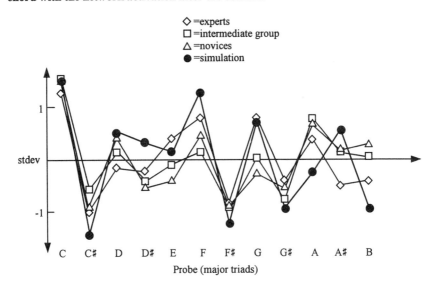

Output of Brain Studies. Brain studies may provide different types of output. They are partly dependent on the nature of the techniques used (Zatorre 1997, Tervaniemi 1997, Janata 1997, Besson 1997). In general, one may distinguish between studies that concentrate on the localization of cognitive functions and studies that concentrate on association and global aspects of brain activity. Näätänen and collaborators (Näätänen 1990, Tervaniemi et al. 1993) have focused on the ERP-component, called the MMN or mismatch negativity, which reflects a mismatch process between sensory input from a deviant stimulus and a short-duration memory trace developed by the standard stimulus. The results show that the MMN amplitude correlates with the pitch-discrimination performance.

Functional-Reductionism and Factualization

Input/output convergence does not yet guarantee an optimal selection between models. Consider a situation in which two models, A and B, are available and they simulate the same cognitive phenomenon, using very different principles of encoding, but they produce the same output (e.g., in terms of a metric). It is clear that in such cases the criterion of input/output convergence may not be sufficient.

Any computer model is a functional model in the sense that processes at the physical level are described by means of functions. Functional reductionism assumes that the global input/output function can somehow be split up into several partial functions, and this at different levels of factualization. Such an idea is in accord with the above suggested requirement of gradual concretization. In that, a model can use components provided that the input/outputs are somehow justified by another model of the mechanisms involved. What is important here is that the causality of the model should be scientifically justified. Functional reductionism thus implies that the model should ultimately be reduced to the levels at which neurons operate. Still lower levels would involve models of chemical reactions and ultimately particle physics. It is clear, however, that the adequacy criterion does not require an actual realization of all these levels. It suffices to show that the functions can be causally linked up with the lower levels.

Interconvergence and Pragmatical Factors

Functional reductionism may fail because of practical problems in that brain science does not always provide straightforward answers to questions concerning cognitive functions. Up to a certain level, the models may rely on neurophysiological data, but very often these data do not provide sufficient information to justify some functions. Interconvergence implies that the adequacy criterion involves an interdisciplinary approach in which convergence is sought by comparing very different methodological approaches such as psychoacoustics/psychology and auditory physiology/brain research. If different and independent methodological approaches lead to the same result, then we may assume that the approaches reinforce each other. Typically, computer models may give deeper insights into the dynamics involved. Interconvergence is thus a criterion that relates to the interdisciplinary context.

In particular, if physiological data are not available, the model can be evaluated within the broader concept of pragmatic justification. This entails that the adequacy of a model should be related to a number of pragmatic factors, that is, methods, beliefs, and the status of the field with respect to other sciences. Obviously, computer models are often discussed with respect to the existing pertinent literature in the field. This is itself an act of knowledge justification that should be carried out for any model. In absence of any functional-reductionist evidence, however, a good analysis of the pragmatic factors may provide an additional help for a demonstration of the adequacy of the model.

ADEQUACY AND CONVERGENCE

In the previous section, adequacy has been linked to convergence within an interdisciplinary context. The issue of convergence is of course not entirely new. It has been considered by neuroscientists and cognitive scientists for a while (e.g., Kandel 1991). The basic idea is that the outputs of totally different research paths are somehow related to each other. For instance, event-related potential component analysis can be associated with perceptive and cognitive functions (Näätänen 1990, Janata and Petsche 1993, Janata 1995). Brain imaging techniques may come up with information about representation, perhaps even brain locations of functions (Martin et al. 1991).

Some recent developments in the computer modeling of music perception (Leman 1994, 1995; Cosi et al. 1994; Toiviainen 1996) are pointing in the direction of a new—although often implicitly assumed—criterion for adequacy based on the notion of convergence. Up to now, however, these applications have been restricted to showing convergence between computer models and psychological data. It is straightforward, however, to relate the results obtained by very different methodologies, including brain research, and to extract from it a general paradigm for music research.

A central aspect of convergence seems to rely on the idea that representations can be cast in terms of a metric that can then be compared with a metric obtained by totally different methods. In cognitive psychology, the use of multidimensional scaling has been important because it allows one to map out mental representations in terms of a spatial metric (McAdams 1993). In a similar way, computer models have been used that map out representations in terms of metric spaces. If it is possible to map out the results of brain imaging techniques or indirect methods based on evoked potentials by means of a metrics, then it is clear that we can compare the results of different methodologies.

CONCLUSION

The advent of computer technology has opened many new opportunities for cognition research. Among these is the possibility to simulate processes of perception and cognition by means of models. In the past, and in many of Otto Laske's works, the adequacy of a model has often been conceived of in terms of abilities to shed light on general psychological issues. It was understood that models should stand hypothesis testing in terms of how well the output confirms or contradicts one or several psychological hypotheses. This chapter aimed to give an analysis of the notion of adequacy within the general context of cognitive musicological research. In particular, it was shown that the notion of adequacy is related to the concepts of idealization and factualization which, in turn, largely depend on the prevailing paradigm. The degree of factualization, however, seems to depend on the paradigm. In the Cartesian approach, the high degree of idealization of the model is justified by a metaphorical transfer to action-protocol analysis or behavioral research. In the naturalistic approach, the aim is to make a model as concrete as possible. As a consequence, more stringent criteria for adequacy are needed for the evaluation of a model. In particular, adequacy criteria have been proposed within an interdisciplinary context of behavioral and brain research in which both the notion of convergence and ecological modeling are important.

POSTSCRIPTUM

In this chapter I have argued that the so-called Cartesian modeling approach and its associated theory of musical memory representation based on attributes no longer provide a paradigmatic model for adequate modeling of musical perception and cognition. What Laske considered to be the task of sonology—namely, providing a link between the perceptual attributes or the musical categories of mental representation on the one hand and the acoustical world on the other—was initially not taken seriously enough and was largely underestimated by researchers.[4] This is probably due to the prevailing AI paradigm that was very much conceptual oriented. Nevertheless, this task has become a main issue in cognitive musicology, and the actual implementation of music perception models soon revolutionized the methodology as well as the entire theory of musical representation. Gradually it became clear that perception is largely based on auditory image representation and gesture representation rather than attribute representations. The task of sonology could therefore only be approached by adopting a radically different research paradigm, one with a main focus on acoustical, psychoacoustical, and low-level perceptual processes. As shown in *Music, Gestalt, and Computing* (Leman 1997b), some progress has already been made in areas such as the perception of pitch, harmony, timbre, texture, and rhythm as well as in the analysis of musical expressivity.

When I reread Laske's work carefully, I get the impression that the modeling approach proposed was much inspired by a desire to account for creative processes in composition, rather than perception. In that field, I must admit, conceptual analysis is *still* a valuable first step.

NOTES

1. Editor's comment: It should be noted that all of Laske's methodologies are built around the need to circumvent verbal reports and explain them by direct, nonverbal interactions between the musician and the computer program. Laske has written that "In cases where human knowledge is mainly action knowledge, as in music, methods of verbalization, as used in different kinds of interview, are insufficient to capture an expert's knowledge. . . . Intuitions and actions must be captured on line . . . by building a programmed environment embodying a model (a) of the expert's task, (b) of the expert's physical environment, and (c) of the cooperation between system and expert" (Laske 1992). (Also, see Laske's writings on OBSERVER and PRECOMP.)

2. Factualization, in short, is the concretization of abstract theories such that they can be implemented in a real-world environment.

3. The term *morphology* is often used in biology to characterize processes that entail forms and structure by means of dynamical processes. A morphology points to forms and structures of organisms or groups of organisms. Thus, in general terms, morphology is the study of structure or form. Forms can be of any kind and the distinction between psychic forms and historical forms is an attempt to distinguish between the emergence of forms within one organism (e.g., seen from a mental or brain functioning point of view), and a group of organisms over time, whose collaborative activity and continued interaction may lead to emergence of features that surpass the individual. The latter is related to the creation of a cultural context or environment.

4. Editor's comment: See chapters 2 and 3 of Laske 1973, entitled respectively, "Some Postulations Concerning a Sonological Theory of Perception," and "Is Sonology a Science of the Artificial?" Laske 1975 is a reprint.

REFERENCES

Arbib, M. (1995). "Schema Theory." In M. Arbib, ed. *The Handbook of Brain Theory and Neural Networks*. Cambridge, MA: MIT Press, pp. 830–833.

Balaban, M., K. Ebcioglu, and O. Laske, eds. (1992). *Understanding Music with AI: Perspectives on Music Cognition*. Cambridge, MA: MIT Press.

Batens, D. (1991). "Do We Need a Hierarchical Model of Science?" In J. Earman, ed. *Inference, Explanation, and Other Frustrations: Essays in the Philosophy of Science*. Oxford: University of California Press, pp. 199–215.

Besson, M. (1997). "The Musical Brain: Neural substrates of Music Perception." In M. Leman, ed. *Foundations of Neuromusicology: Proceedings of the Third Meeting of the FWO Research Society on Foundations of Music Research*. Ghent: IPEM, University of Ghent, pp. 26–41.

Bharucha, J. (1987). "Music Cognition and Perceptual Facilitation: A Connectionist Framework." *Music Perception* 5(1):1–30.

Bregman, A. (1990). *Auditory Scene Analysis: The Perceptual Organization of Sound*. Cambridge, MA: MIT Press.

Bregman, A., and P. Ahad (1995). "Demonstrations of Auditory Scene Analysis" (examples 7–9). Auditory Perception Laboratory, Department of Psychology, McGill University (Audio CD and Booklet).

Broeckx, J. (1981). *Muziek, Ratio en Affect: Over de Wisselwerking van Rationeel Denken en Affectief Beleven bij Voortbrengst en Ontvangst van Muziek*. Antwerpen: Metropolis.

Camurri, A. (1993). "Applications of Artificial Intelligence Methodologies and Tools for Music Description and Processing." In G. Haus, ed. *Music Processing*. Madison, WI: Oxford University Press, A-R Editions, pp. 233–266.

Camurri, A., and M. Leman (1997). "AI-Based Music Signal Applications: A Hybrid Approach." In C. Roads, G. D. Poli, and S. Pope, eds. *Musical Signal Processing*. Lisse, The Netherlands: Swets and Zeitlinger.

Carreras, F., and M. Leman (1996). "Distributed Parallel Architectures for the Simulation of Cognitive Models in a Realistic Environment." In D'Hollander, E., G. Joubert, F. Peters, and D. Trystram eds. *Parallel Computing: State-of-the Art Perspective: Proceedings of the International Conference PARCO 95*. Gent, 19–22 September 1995. Amsterdam: Elsevier.

Clancey, W. (1993). "Situated Action: A Neuropsychological Interpretation, Response to Vera and Simon." *Cognitive Science* 17(1):87–116.

Clark, A. (1995). "Philosophical issues in Brain Theory and Connectionism." In M. Arbib, ed. *The Handbook of Brain Theory and Neural Networks*. Cambridge, MA: MIT Press, pp. 738–740.

Cohen, D., and A. Erez (1991). "Event-Related-Potential Measurements of Cognitive Components in Response to Pitch Patterns." *Music Perception* 8(4):405–430.

Cohen, D., and R. Jeger-Granot (1995). "Constant and Variable Influences on Stages of Musical Activities." *Journal of New Music Research* 24(3):197–229.

Cope, D. (1989). "Experiments in Musical Intelligence (EMI): Non-Linear Linguistic-Based Composition." *Interface* 18(1-2):117–139.

Cosi, P., G. Poli, and G. Lauzzana (1994). "Auditory Modeling and Self-Organizing Neural Networks for Timbre Classification." *Journal of New Music Research* 23(1):71–98.

da Silva, F., and J. Pijn (1995). "EEG Analysis." In M. Arbib, ed. *The Handbook of Brain Theory and Neural Networks*. Cambridge, MA: MIT Press, pp. 348–351.

Deliège, I. (1987). "Grouping Conditions in Listening to Music: An Approach to Lerdahl and Jackendoff's Grouping Preference Rules." *Music Perception* 4(4):325–359.

Ebcioglu, K. (1987). *Report on the Choral Project: An Expert System for Harmonizing Four-Part Chorales*. Technical Report RC 12628, IBM, Thomas J. Watson Research Center, Yorktown Heights.

Fodor, J. (1981). *Representations*. Cambridge, MA: MIT Press.

Gevins, A. (1996). "Electrophysiological Imaging of Brain Function." In A. Toga and J. Mazziotta, eds. *Brain Mapping—The Methods*. London: Academic Press.

Gjerdingen, R. (1989). "Using Connectionist Models to Explore Complex Musical Patterns." *Computer Music Journal* 13(3):67–75.

Grey, J. (1977). "Multidimensional Perceptual Scaling of Musical Timbres." *The Journal of the Acoustical Society of America* 61(5):1270–1277.

Grey, J. (1978). "Timbre Discrimination in Musical Patterns." *The Journal of the Acoustical Society of America* 64:467–472.

Grey, J., and J. Gordon (1978). "Perceptual Effects of Spectral Modifications on Musical Timbres." *The Journal of the Acoustical Society of America* 63(5):1493–1500.

Heeffer, A., and M. Leman (1986). "Chunking as a Method for Concept Acquisition." *Proceedings of the ECAI-86*, vol.2. Brighton, UK.

Iverson, P., and C. Krumhansl (1993). "Isolating the Dynamic Attributes of Musical Timbre." *Journal of the Acoustical Society of America* 94(5):2595–2603.

Janata, P. (1995). "ERP Measures Assay the Degree of Expectancy Violation of Harmonic Contexts in Music." *Journal of Cognitive Neuroscience* 7(2):153–164.

Janata, P. (1997). "Understanding the Activation of Human Cortex by Auditory Images: A Perspective Derived from Recording the Brain Electrical Activity of Musicians Performing Musical Imagery Tasks." In M. Leman, ed. *Foundations of Neuromusicology: Proceedings of the Third Meeting of the FWO Research Society on Foundation of Music Research*. Ghent: IPEM, University of Ghent.

Janata, P., and H. Petsche. (1993). "Spectral Analysis of the EEG as a Tool for Evaluating Expectancy Violations of Musical Contexts." *Music Perception* 10(3):281–304.

Järvainen, T. (1995). "Tonal Hierarchies in Jazz Improvisation." *Music Perception* 12(4):415–437.

Johnson, M., and G. Lakoff (1980). *Metaphors We Live By*. Chicago: University of Chicago Press.

Jones, J., B. Miller, and D. Scarborough (1988). "A Rule-Based Expert System for Music Perception." *Behavior Research Methods, Instruments, and Computers* 20(2):255–262.

Kaipainen, M. (1996). "Representing and Remotivating Musical Processes: Modeling a Recurrent Musical Ecology." *Journal of New Music Research* 25(2):150–178.

Kandel, E. (1991). "Brain and Behavior." In E. Kandel, J. Schwartz, and T. Jessell, eds. *Principles of Neural Science* (Third Edition). Amsterdam: Elsevier.

Kendall, R., and E. Carterette (1991). "Perceptual Scaling of Simultaneous Wind Instrument Timbres." *Music Perception* 8(4):369–404.

Krajewski, W. (1977). *Correspondence Principle and Growth of Science*. Dordrecht, Holland: D. Reidel.

Krumhansl, C. (1990). *Cognitive Foundations of Musical Pitch*. New York: Oxford University Press.

Krumhansl, C., and R. Shepard (1979). "Quantification of the Hierarchy of Tonal Functions within a Diatonic Context." *Journal of Experimental Psychology: Human Perception and Performance* 5:579–594.

Kuhn, T. (1962). *The Structure of Scientific Revolutions*. Chicago: Chicago University Press.

Laden, B., and D. Keefe (1991). "The Representation of Pitch in a Neural Net Model of Chord Classification." In P. Todd and G. Loy, eds. *Music and Connectionism*. Cambridge, MA: MIT Press, pp. 64–83.

Langner, G. (1983). "Neuronal Mechanisms for a Periodicity Analysis in the Time Domain." In R. Klinke and R. Hartmann, eds. *Hearing—Physiological Bases and Psychophysics*. Berlin: Springer-Verlag.

Langner, G. (1997). "Temporal Processing of Pitch in the Auditory System." *Journal of New Music Research* 26(2):116–132.

Laske, O. (1973). *Introduction to a Generative Theory of Music*. Utrecht, The Netherlands: Institute of Sonology.

Laske, O. (1975). "Introduction to a Generative Theory of Music." *Sonological Reports 1b*. Utrecht, The Netherlands: Institute of Sonology. (Reprint of Laske 1973.)

Laske, O. (1977). *Music, Memory and Thought: Explorations in Cognitive Musicology*. Ann Arbor, MI: University Microfilms International.

Laske, O. (1984). "Keith: A Rule-System for Making Music-Analytical Discoveries." In M. Baroni and L. Callegari, eds. *Proceedings of the Musical Grammars and Computer Analysis*. Florence, Italy: Leo S. Olschki, pp. 165–200.

Laske, O. (1988). "Can We Formalize and Program Musical Knowledge? An Inquiry into the Focus and Scope of Cognitive Musicology." In M. Boroda, ed. *Musikometrika I*. Bochum, Germany: Studienverlag N. Brockmeyer, pp. 257–280.

Laske, O. (1992). "The OBSERVER Tradition of Knowledge Acquisition." In M. Balaban, K. Ebcioglu, and O. Laske, eds. *Understanding Music with AI*. Menlo Park, CA: AAAI Press, pp. 259–289.

Lehnert, W. (1984). "Paradigmatic Issues in Cognitive Science." In W. Kintsch, J. Miller, and P. Polson, eds. *Method and Tactics in Cognitive Science*. Hillsdale, NJ: Lawrence Erlbaum Associates.

Leman, M. (1991). "The Ontogenesis of Tonal Semantics: Results of a Computer Study." In P. Todd and G. Loy, eds. *Music and Connectionism*. Cambridge, MA: MIT Press, pp. 100–127.

Leman, M. (1993). "Symbolic and Subsymbolic Description of Music." In G. Haus, ed. *Music Processing*. Madison, WI: Oxford University Press, A-R Editions, pp. 119–164.

Leman, M. (1994). "Schema-Based Tone Center Recognition of Musical Signals." *Journal of New Music Research* 23(2):169–204.

Leman, M. (1995). *Music and Schema Theory—Cognitive Foundations of Systematic Musicology*. Berlin, Heidelberg: Springer-Verlag.

Leman, M. (1997a). "The Convergence Paradigm in Music Research." *Journal of New Music Research* 26(2):133–153.

Leman, M., ed. (1997b). *Music, Gestalt, and Computing: Studies in Cognitive and Systematic Musicology*. Berlin, Heidelberg: Springer-Verlag.

Leman, M., and F. Carreras (1997). "Schema and Gestalt: Testing the Hypothesis of Psychoneural Isomorphism by Computer Simulation." In M. Leman, ed. *Music, Gestalt, and Computing. Studies in Cognitive and Systematic Musicology*. Berlin, Heidelberg: Springer-Verlag, pp. 144–168.

Lerdahl, F., and R. Jackendoff (1983). *A Generative Theory of Tonal Music*. Cambridge, MA: MIT Press.

Martin, J. (1991). "The Collective Electrical Behavior of Cortical Neurons: The Electroencephalogram and the Mechanisms of Epilepsy." In E. Kandel, J. Schwartz, and T. Jessell, eds. *Principles of Neural Science* (Third Edition). Amsterdam: Elsevier.

Martin, J., J. Brust, and S. Hilal (1991). "Imaging the Living Brain." In E. Kandel, J. Schwartz, and T. Jessell, eds. *Principles of Neural Science* (Third Edition). Amsterdam: Elsevier.

McAdams, S. (1993). "Recognition of Sound Sources and Events." In S. McAdams and E. Bigand, eds. *Thinking in the Sound—the Cognitive Psychology of Human Audition*. Oxford: Oxford University Press.

Meddis, R., and M. Hewitt (1991). "Virtual Pitch and Phase Sensitivity of a Computer Model of the Auditory Periphery." *Journal of the Acoustical Society of America*. 89(6):2866, 2894.

Näätänen, R. (1990). "The Role of Attention in Auditory Information Processing as Revealed by Event-Related Potentials and Other Brain Measures of Cognitive Function." *Behavioral and Brain Sciences* 13(2):201–288.

Newell, A. (1980). "Physical Symbol Systems." *Cognitive Science* 4:135–183.

Petsche, H., A. von Stein, and O. Filz (1996). "EEG Aspects of Mentally Playing an Instrument." *Cognitive Brain Research* 3:115–123.

Schreiner, C., and G. Langner (1988). "Coding of Temporal Patterns in the Central Auditory Nervous System." In G. Edelman, W. Gall, and W. Cowan, eds. *Auditory Function: Neurobiological Bases of Hearing*. New York: John Wiley and Sons.

Sharkey, A., and N. Sharkey (1995). "Cognitive Modeling: Psychology and Connectionism." In M. Arbib, ed. *The Handbook of Brain Theory and Neural Networks*. Cambridge, MA: MIT Press, pp. 200–202.

Shepard R. (1982). "Structural Representations of Musical Pitch." In D. Deutsch, ed. *The Psychology of Music*. New York: Academic Press.

Stillings, N., S. Weisler, C. Chase, M. Feinstein, J. Garfield and E. Rissland (1995). *Cognitive Science—An Introduction*. Cambridge, MA: MIT Press.

Tervaniemi, M. (1997). "Pre-Attentive Processing of Musical Information in the Human Brain." In M. Leman, ed. *Foundations of Neuromusicology: Proceedings of the Third Meeting of the FWO Research Society on Foundations of Music Research*. Ghent: IPEM, University of Ghent, pp. 10–17.

Tervaniemi, M., K. Alho, P. Paavilainen, M. Sams and R. Näätänen (1993). "Absolute Pitch and Event-Related Brain Potentials." *Music Perception* 10(3):305–316.

Toiviainen, P. (1996). "Optimizing Auditory Images and Distance Metrics for Self-Organizing Timbre Maps." *Journal of New Music Research* 25(1):1–30.

Toiviainen, P., M. Kaipainen, and J. Louhivuori (1995). "Musical Timbre: Similarity Ratings Correlate with Computational Feature Space Distances." *Journal of New Music Research* 24(3):282–298.

VanImmerseel, L., and J. Martens (1992). "Pitch and Voice/Unvoiced Determination with an Auditory Model." *The Journal of the Acoustical Society of America* 91(6):3511–3526.

Vera, A., and H. Simon (1993). "Situated Action: A Symbolic Interpretation." *Cognitive Science* 17(1):7–48.

Wang, D. (1996). "Primitive Auditory Segregation Based on Oscillatory Correlation." *Cognitive Science* 20:409–456.

Zatorre, R. (1997). "Brain Imaging Studies of Musical Perception and Musical Imagery." In M. Leman, ed. *Foundations of Neuromusicology: Proceedings of the Third Meet-*

ing of the FWO Research Society on Foundations of Music Research. Ghent: IPEM, University of Ghent, pp. 2–9.

Zatorre, R., A. Halpern, D. Perry, E. Meyer, and A. Evans (1996). "Hearing in the Mind's Ear: A PET Investigation of Musical Imagery and Perception." *Journal of Cognitive Neuroscience* 8(1):29–46.

7

Modeling Musical Thinking
Jukka Louhivuori

BACKGROUND, FIELD WORK, AND THE PHENOMENOLOGICAL LEVEL

At the time when I was working on my dissertation, the topic of which was variation in Finnish spiritual folk songs (Louhivuori 1988), I was faced with the fact that I would never be able to understand this phenomenon without understanding the cognitive processes of the human mind. Singers I studied in different villages sang the same songs differently. Sometimes the differences were only marginal. For example, small changes appeared in the rhythm or melody. Sometimes it was only after careful comparison that two melodies might be seen to have the same origin. I very soon realized the relativity of the concepts of similarity and dissimilarity. The boundaries between classes of melodies or melody families are evidently fuzzy. The categories and classificatory systems with which we operate are artificial and do not always follow those of the folk singers. I had become convinced that to understand variation in folk music I had to be familiar with the functioning of the musical mind.

One of the main reasons I wished to study the human mind was that the musical material I was examining was based on oral tradition. The singers did not know music notation; for them the only way to keep their tradition alive was to hold the whole repertoire in their memory. This means that most of the phenomena the researcher is faced with concerning the musical aspects of the tradition could be viewed from the perspective of the musical mind and memory. The facts concerning spiritual folk songs can be summarized as follows:

- Spiritual folk songs are learned orally.
- Many different forms of the "same song" exist at the same time in the tradition.
- Singers hear the songs in many different forms because the songs exist in different forms in the villages where they live and that they visit.
- The songs do not differ only from village to village, but the same person may also sing a song in different ways at different times, or even during the same performance.

- The differences concern most aspects of singing (meter, rhythm, melody, contour, tonality, intonation, structure of the songs, and so on).
- Parts of different songs (whole phrases or smaller details) may be transferred from one song to another.
- General aspects of a certain song or group of songs (tune families) may be borrowed from another song or group of songs (tonality, meter, structure).
- Some of the songs can be found in almost identical form in every part of the area, while others have no fixed form, every singer singing the song differently.

These findings forced me to look at how a musical tradition is transferred from one generation to another and how music is perceived, learned, and stored in memory in oral tradition. There are also questions of how the contents of the memory effect the way we perceive music, how music is processed during the retrieval, how music is processed during the time it is being stored in the memory, how music is re-created during recall. Questions of a more general nature also came to mind. For example, What function do spiritual folk songs have for the singer? What is the role of music in society? In what ways can music be used as a means to dominate other people? Unfortunately I have never had time to go into these more anthropologically motivated research questions, but hopefully that time will come.

THEORETICAL BACKGROUND AND ALTERNATIVES

These research questions were very much the same as those asked by Albert Lord in his studies of Balkan epic songs (Lord 1960). His employment of the concept of formula, borrowed from linguistics, was very useful to me. At the time I was working on my thesis (1985–1988), fuzzy logic (Zadeh 1978) was "up-to-date" as was generative grammar. Lerdahl and Jackendoff's book on the generative theory of music had just been published (Lerdahl and Jackendoff 1983). Johan Sundberg had applied generative methods in his studies of Swedish nursery tunes (Sundberg 1972); later Sundberg and Lindblom tried to understand the question of variation using the same method (Sundberg and Lindblom 1975, 1976).

From these theoretical starting points I began to build up a model, which could explain, or at least help us understand, learning processes and other aspects of oral tradition. The basic idea of the model is described in Figure 7.1. During his lifetime the singer perceives melodies in many different forms (Figure 7.1a). For many different reasons, for example, the acoustical traits of a room (echoes, etc.), and/or because many different forms of the melodies are performed at the same time, the singer does not actually hear melodies "sharply"—some parts of the singing remain unclear (question marks in Figure 7.1b). The singer has in his mind melody formulae that have been heard and learned earlier (Figure 7.1d). By using these formulae the singer fills the gaps that originated when the melodies were perceived (Figure 7.1e). Replacing the concept of formula with the more recent term schemata, the phenomenon can be described as follows: preexisting schemata direct the perception and production of melodies.

Figure 7.1
Relationship of cognitive processes and variation in spiritual folk songs

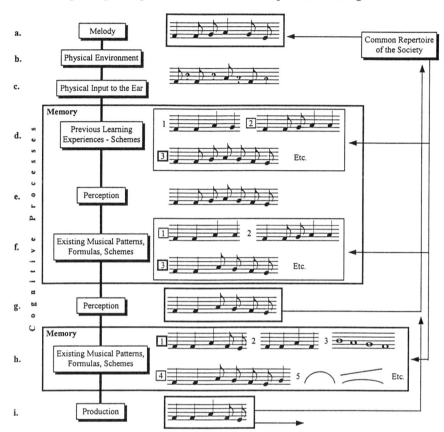

In the process of storing different formulae in his memory, the singer will hear these songs again in many different forms. The consequence will be that some forms of the formulae become stronger while others become weaker (Figure 7.1f). During the process of recreating the melody, the singer uses new forms of the formulae (Figure 7.1g). In oral tradition this process will never end: melody formulae are undergoing change in the singer's memory. The singer combines formulae in different ways during different performances. The following musical examples (Example 7.1a-c) show variations one of the informants used in repeating the first phrase of the song. Every repetition of the "same" phrase was sung differently. The probabilities of different paths are represented by the thickness of the arrows.

The same phenomenon is illustrated in Figure 7.2. The different formulae are represented by the different letters (b1, b2, b3; c1. . . , etc.); probabilities of different paths are represented by the thickness of the arrows.

Example 7.1
Variations of a single phrase in repeated performances

EPISTEMOLOGICAL BACKGROUND AND TESTING MODELS BY SIMULATION

After working with this model I had arrived at a crucial point from an epistemological point of view. I had to take a stand concerning the plausibility of the model. Who knew if the model was correct or not? At this point Otto Laske came into the picture. In his article, "Introduction to Cognitive Musicology," one of the main points he made was that the history of musicology is full of interesting hypotheses that have never been tested (Laske 1988). Was this also the case with my study? Perhaps I had developed an interesting model, but it needed to be tested. The usefulness and plausibility of this model were equal to those of other models musicologists have developed during the history of musicology. Sundberg discussed the same issues in his article "Generative Methods in Language and Music Descriptions" (Sundberg and Lindblom 1976).

The advantages of testing models by simulation are clear. Besides offering the opportunity for getting to know how the model works, this method forces the researcher to consider the reasons why certain aspects of the model do not work. In doing this, new and perhaps important aspects of the musical style being studied will come to light. From the testing of models, new research questions might arise, which musicologists have not before understood. In the case of my investigations into oral tradition, the problem was how the model should be

Figure 7.2
Probable paths of melody variation

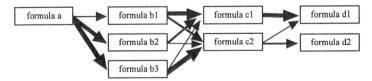

tested. Should methods used in the field of experimental psychology or artificial intelligence be incorporated?

LIMITATIONS OF AI AND THE BEGINNINGS OF THE PROJECT IN COGNITIVE MUSICOLOGY

During this period development in the field of artificial intelligence was very rapid, and a lot of interesting musical applications had emerged (e.g., Ebcioglu 1988). The atmosphere was enthusiastic, and people were optimistic about the potential of AI technology to provide new and interesting methodological tools for musicologists. Artificial intelligence seemed to be one possible answer to my methodological problems.

After I had finished my dissertation I was tired of my research topic and planned to start a new phase of my "scientific career" by concentrating more on such areas as statistical methods (Louhivuori 1990) and later multimedia. I had been working with Finnish folk hymn singing, oral tradition, and the question of variation for fifteen years. Adapting a new paradigm and research topic was much more difficult than I had imagined. Far from feeling my mind refreshed and being motivated to start the study of new aspects of musical life, I felt myself to be homeless. Then I met with Otto Laske at a conference in Marseilles ("Music and Information Technology" organized *by laboratoire musique et informatique de Marseille* in 1990). After we discussed my work, he strongly recommended I continue with the topics started over a decade before. The argument for this was that a researcher with this much experience might have deep insight into the problems of this specialized research field. The value of this knowledge should not be underestimated. Instead of trying to find new research topics, one could try to find new methodological aspects, a new point of view.

At the same time, the Finnish Academy of Science had plans to start a research project on cognitive science. A research group was founded in the Department of Music in the University of Jyväskylä. Only a year before (1989), Laske had visited our department and had given excellent lectures on the relationship of cognition and music. We had an opportunity to discuss different modeling methods with him and especially the present state of AI technology and the future of AI and music. During these discussions Laske warned us of the limitations of AI techniques, especially as applied in music. Many important questions surfaced. How could the learning of music be modeled with rule-based systems? How could we solve the problem of knowledge acquisition? What was the epistemological basis of these models, and were they really models of the human cognitive system? How were we going to represent the temporal aspects of music? How were we going to solve the problem of the representation of melodies? We understood that if we were going to work with rule-based AI models, we would be faced with serious problems. It would not be meaningful to work for many years building up models whose epistemological bases would be weak.

NEURAL MODELING

Otto Laske provided us with an alternative possibility for modeling musical thinking, namely, artificial neural networks. As far as I know he has not worked with these models himself, but he was able to foresee the advantages they offered. In 1988 I attended a conference at Lancaster University called "Computers in Music," where I heard a number of interesting lectures—including Marc Leman's presentation on artificial neural networks. This lecture convinced me of their power and applicability to the study of oral tradition, the learning of music, and other topics I was interested in (see for example Leman 1990, 1991). From that point on I have tried to construct models of human musical cognition and have tested these models by means of simulation with artificial neural networks. The advantages of these networks are their ability to learn, to generalize, to complete incomplete patterns; their high tolerance for incomplete or erroneous information; their epistemological relevance (as brain metaphors); and their ability to handle nonsymbolic information.

Instead of Finnish spiritual folk hymns, I initially constructed models of rune song singing. One of the reasons for this decision was the limited capacity of the computers available to me. In order to keep models to a reasonable size, the small ambitus of rune song melodies would be of advantage. Also, from the rhythmical point of view, rune song singing was reasonably easy to model.

The results were surprising. The artificial neural network model was able to learn the main features of rune song singing, and it was even able to create new variants in the style of the performer we were modeling (Louhivuori 1992). Perhaps the most interesting result was that the model created a variant that it had not been taught, but which I later discovered in another Finnish performer named Anni Tenisova. Still some serious problems remained. The representation we used was not plausible from an epistemological point of view. We represented melodies by using the so-called piano-roll method. In this representation, researchers have to organize the melodies into layers "by hand," and note durations can only be of certain previously fixed lengths. Further, the way the memory was modeled was problematic. First I tried to get around this by using so-called shift registers. This type of memory has at least three disadvantages (Gjerdingen 1989, 1990; Kaipainen 1994; Kaipainen et al. 1995):

1. Although this method defines a mathematically unlimited amount of memory with a very simple formulation, the computational resolution defined by the number of decimal places and the capacity limitations of the network architecture, in practice, set an upper limit to the memory available. It turns out that this limit is not psychologically and biologically plausible.
2. The practice runs the risk of confusing a recent weak signal with an earlier but stronger signal.
3. There is the possibility that such a method will not always distinguish between the effect of recentness and that of repetition. For example, in the case of the schematic sequence ABCBD, there is the possibility that the value for B, increased by repetition, may become higher than that of the most recent event, D.

The consequence was that although the results were very promising, the model itself did not meet our requirements.

PRESENT STATE OF THE MODEL

At about the time we realized these problems (1994), the Academy of Finland started a new project on cognitive science; and again we were fortunate enough to be involved. Together with Petri Toiviainen and Mauri Kaipainen, we began to construct a model that would be more plausible from the epistemological point of view. The aim of our study was to build up a model that would be capable of resolving the ambiguity of sequences that differ only with respect to their temporal contexts. It also would be able to locate the boundaries of structural units in music, to group sequences in a musically acceptable manner, to remain robust and flexible enough to manage different or changing tempi and pitch, and, at the same time, to have credibility as a "mental model" the brain could work with (Kaipainen et al. 1995).

An understanding of the importance of the dynamic and contextual aspects of music was crucial. The need for a new representation of melodies was also obvious. By combining the experience Petri Toiviainen had with his timbre models (Toiviainen 1996, Toiviainen et al. 1995) and the experience he and Mauri Kaipainen had with self-organizing neural networks (Kohonen 1984)—and especially with adding temporal aspects into static networks—we were able to build a new model based on self-organization (Kaipainen et al. 1995). The principle of self-organization seems to be a primary property of the human cognitive system. A very important step was also the fact that we left out graphic notation and started to work with real sound!

With this new model we were able to teach the system the main aspects of Finnish rune song singing using the method of self-organization. The model behaved in a very similar way to human singers in the oral tradition. Its characteristics are the same as Albert Lord described in his famous book on Balkan epic singing. Lord understood the mechanism of remembering in a modern way, that is, he saw it as a dynamic rather than a static system. A singer does not learn epic songs by heart but creates them after previously learned models. The art of these singers is based on mastering traditional musical components. Lord wrote that the singer's

task is to adapt and adjust [the form of the theme] to the particular song that he is recreating. It does not have a single "pure" form either for the individual singer or for the tradition as a whole. Its form is ever changing in the singer's mind, because the theme is in reality protean; in the singer's mind it has many shapes, all the forms in which he has ever sung it, although his latest rendering of it will naturally be freshest in his mind. It is not a static entity, but a living, changing, adaptable artistic creation. (Lord 1960:94)

Although we have been surprised by the properties of self-organizing artificial neural networks, we are well aware of the many problems yet to be solved. For example, we should represent the acoustic input that comes into the cochlea by using ear models instead of autocorrelation—though this will probably cause a lot of trouble in the interpretation of the output of the model. In its present state, the model has no sense of meter. How to solve this problem is at the moment an open question. Another limitation of the model is that it utilizes absolute pitch representation, which means it is not able to recognize transpositions. Further, time and frequency need to be improved. In order to solve these problems we must rectify the problem of limited computing capacity.

IN THE FUTURE

The direction Laske recommended to me during our discussions has been much more fruitful than I could ever have imagined. At present, the end of this particular road is not yet in sight. There are a number of challenging problems waiting to be better understood or even solved.

The artificial neural network model we developed might provide an opportunity to test theories concerning the origin of emotions—for example, Meyer's implication theory (Meyer 1956)—since it has the ability to anticipate future situations. By letting the model generalize, for example with melodies, via the most or least probable memory traces, it is possible to generate melodies that should differ in their emotional content when rated by human listeners. Putting the model in touch with the outside world—that is, by allowing it to generate melodies that will be part of the general musical environment—makes it is possible to study the problem of musical ecology (Kaipainen 1995).

It might be possible to model intentional stages of the mind by studying the organization processes of the model. This idea is based on the supposition that the origin of intentionality is in the tendency of the system (the human mind) to organize the input material into topological order. This is related to the concept of homeostasis introduced first by W. B. Cannon in his book, *The Wisdom of the Body* (1939). The aim of the organism is described as being to achieve a stable state. When the system receives stimuli that are incompatible with it in its present state, it starts to rebuild the topological map. Using the terminology of cognitive psychology, this corresponds to the concept of accommodation. If the system has the ability to move, it is more likely to rebuild the map in a way that helps it—to build up a new scheme. If the system is able to organize the new input on the map without dramatic changes in the topological order, the process corresponds to the concept of adaptation. The new stimuli will be adapted to existing schemes.

In the course of evolution the brain has developed the ability to organize stimuli that come to it through different modes (auditory, visual, tactile, and so on) in an ecologically meaningful manner in order to build up a practical and useful model of the physical environment. The main function of the brain seems to be to self-organize these stimuli. This process gives off a feeling of satisfaction. Such an emotional response is known to anyone who has ever solved a problem. The problem can be very concrete, but solving abstract scientific or aesthetic problems may also produce a strong emotional response.

In my view artistic experience has the same origin. The art object—music for example—should be capable of being mapped in a meaningful way onto topological maps. The task of the composer or artist is to build up auditory structures that are not boring, which means that the mapping process should not be too easy. If the original map and the auditory structure we are perceiving are at an appropriate distance apart, the mapping process takes time, and at the end of the process, when the system is again in a stable condition, we have a feeling of satisfaction. If the auditory stimuli are too complicated compared with the present topological order, the organization process takes too much time, and we have a feeling of not understanding. In this case the system will have difficulties in achieving a stable level, the homeostatic level will not have been reached.

If artistic experience is seen in these terms, the possibility exists to measure the amount of "artistic power" of the stimulus (input). It is clear that artistic experience also includes many other aspects—for example, associations with other human activities. Experiences we have had during our lives are sometimes of great importance (e.g., vital affects such as swinging in mother's arms [see Stern 1985]). Emotions are based on human experiences, and some are difficult or even impossible to model using computers. With the present state of our model we have used only vectors representing auditory information, but there are no obstacles to adding vectors representing visual, tactile, motor, or other types of information.

It is clear—and this is a point that can never be stressed too much—that this kind of modeling can never equal the richness of real human life. The amount of information we receive at every moment is enormous. We should keep in mind that the idea of modeling is not to try to get a full picture of every aspect of human life. But, by concentrating on certain specific research problems, we have the possibility of confirming or disproving particular hypotheses we may have formed concerning certain limited aspects of the human cognitive system.

Still, more serious problems remain. Computer simulations will never tell us how it feels to listen to music. The subjective aspect of listening to music should be studied using different methods. The content of subjective experience is a human property, which can be discussed with other human beings but not with computers.

If it turns out to be true that self-organizing artificial neural networks can be used in the study of the origin of emotions and artistic expression, we will have taken a much larger step in the direction of understanding music than ever suspected. However, it should be kept in mind that in the course of the history of cognitive science a great deal of optimism has given way to realism and pessimism. These crises can be seen as turning points, after which a new and more powerful paradigm has replaced the old one (e.g., the change from rule-based AI to artificial neural network models). We should not quickly reject any method that has demonstrated its power, especially in the study of music. But we should be ready to change the paradigm as soon as its explanatory power is weaker than that of available other methods.

SHARING EXPERIENCES OF LIVING

I have been thinking about the latest turn Otto Laske's scientific interest has taken. Perhaps his interest in clinical work says something essential about music and about human life in general (Laske 1995). One of the most valuable aspects of human life is after all sharing our experience with other human beings. If we want to understand human life in its full richness and unexpectedness, we may have to share our ideas and, what is more important, share our experience of living in order to help other people make sense of their own lives. This means not only mapping certain aspects of human life into topologically meaningful order, but mapping (organizing) the whole of life into order. To the extent that I have learned anything essential about human life, it seems to me that we are destined to spend our existence searching for mental equilibrium, homeostasis.

Otto Laske has, in my view, been one of the most influential people in the field of musicology during the past three decades. I realize that this is saying a great deal. And it is, of course, true that other people too have turned the thinking of musicologists in new directions. Many trends have combined to push musicology in a homogeneous direction, one that has a strong epistemological basis, is able to build up powerful explanations concerning music, has the ability to provide theoretical and methodological models for other disciplines, and is able to provide plausible explanations for the origin of emotion and of artistic experience.

Laske has always been a very sharp and insightful critic. In addition to this, he has been able to offer alternative directions, which have turned out to be very successful. The power to move the whole discipline in a new direction is an achievement worth appreciating. His wide experience in academic, as well as industrial fields, together with his work as a composer, have given him the capacity to look at music and musicology from an exceptionally wide perspective. He has had the ability to clearly see problems that musicologists working in a much narrower field are too far inside to see. An inability to view the whole picture prevented many people from noticing, that the "king is without clothes." The time has come to wear them!

REFERENCES

Cannon, W. (1939). *The Wisdom of the Body*. Special ed. 1989. Birmingham, AL: Classics of Medicine Library.

Ebcioglu, K. (1988). "An Expert System for Harmonizing Four-part Chorales." *Computer Music Journal* 12(3):43–51.

Gjerdingen, R. (1989). "Using Connectionist Models to Explore Complex Musical Patterns." *Computer Music Journal* 13(3):67–75.

Gjerdingen, R. (1990). "Categorization of Musical Patterns by Self-Organizing Neuron-like Networks." *Music Perception* 7(4):339–370.

Kaipainen, M. (1994). *Dynamics of Musical Knowledge Ecology: Knowing-What and Knowing-How in the World of Sounds*. Helsinki: Acta Musicologica Fennica 19.

Kaipainen, M., P. Toiviainen, and J. Louhivuori (1995). "A Self-organizing Map That Generates Melodies." In P. Pylkkänen and P. Pylkkö, eds. *Proceedings of the 1995*

International Symposium on New Directions in Cognitive Science. Saariselkä, Finland. Hakapaino, Helsinki: Publications of the Finnish Artificial Intelligence Society.

Kaipainen, M. (1995). "Arguments for Ecomusicology." In P. Pylkkänen and P. Pylkkö, eds. *Proceedings of the 1995 International Symposium on New Directions in Cognitive Science.* Saariselkä, Finland. Hakapaino, Helsinki: Publications of the Finnish Artificial Intelligence Society.

Kohonen, T. (1984). *Self-Organization and Associative Memory.* Berlin, Germany: Springer-Verlag.

Laske, O. (1988). "Introduction to Cognitive Musicology." *Computer Music Journal* 12(1):43–57.

Laske, O. (1995). "Four Uses of Self in Cognitive Science: The No-Man's Land Between Mindware and Mind." In P. Pylkkänen and P. Pylkkö, eds. *Proceedings of the 1995 International Symposium on New Directions in Cognitive Science.* Saariselkä, Finland. Hakapaino, Helsinki: Publications of the Finnish Artificial Intelligence Society.

Leman, M. (1990). "Emergent Properties of Tonality by Self-Organization." *Journal of New Music Research* 19(2–3):85–105.

Leman, M. (1991). "The Ontogenesis of Tonal Semantics: Results of a Computer Study." In P. Todd and G. Loy, eds. *Music and Connectionism.* Cambridge, MA: MIT Press, pp. 100–127.

Lerdahl, F., and R. Jackendoff (1983). *A Generative Theory of Tonal Music.* Cambridge, MA: MIT Press.

Lord, A. (1960). *The Singer of Tales.* Harvard Studies in Comparative Literature 24. Cambridge, MA: Harvard University Press.

Louhivuori, J. (1988). *Veisuun vaihtoehdot: Musiikillinen distribuutio ja kognitiiviset toiminnot* [Alternatives of Hymn Singing: Musical Distribution and Cognitive Processes]. English Summary. Acta Musicologica Fennica 16. Jyväskylä: Suomen Musiikkitieteellinen Seura.

Louhivuori, J. (1990). "Computer Aided Analysis of Finnish Spiritual Folk Melodies." In H. Braun, ed. *Probleme der Volksmusikforschung.* Bern, Switserland: P. Lang, pp. 312–323.

Louhivuori, J. (1992). "Kognitiivinen musiikkitiede—musiikkitieteen uusi tutkimusparadigma?" ("Cognitive Musicology—A New Research Paradigm in Musicology?"). *Kognitiivinen musiikkitiede.* Jyväskylän yliopiston musiikkitieteen laitoksen julkaisusarja A: tutkielmia ja raportteja 8, pp. 25–44.

Meyer, L. (1956). *Emotion and Meaning in Music.* Chicago: University of Chicago Press.

Stern, D. (1985). *The Interpersonal World of the Infant: A View from Psychoanalysis and Developmental Psychology.* Yew York: Basic Books, Inc.

Sundberg, J. (1972). "Naturvetenskaplig metodic i musikforskning." *Svensk Tidskrift für Musikforskning* 7:103–114.

Sundberg, J., and B. Lindblom (1975). "Generative Theories in Language and Music Descriptions." *Cognition* 4:99–122.

Sundberg, J., and B. Lindblom (1976). "A Generative Theory of Swedish Nursery Tunes." In G. Stefani, ed. *1975 Proceedings of the 1st International Congress on Semiotics of Music.* Belgrade, October, 1973. Pesaro: Centro di Initiativa Culturale, pp. 111–124.

Toiviainen, P. (1996). "Optimizing Auditory Images and Distance Metrics for Self-Organizing Timbre Maps." *Journal of New Music Research* 25(1):1–30.

Toiviainen, P., M. Kaipainen, and J. Louhivuori (1995). "Musical Timbre: Similarity Ratings Correlate With Computational Feature Space Distances." *Journal of New Music Research* 24(3):282–298.

Zadeh, L. (1978). "Fuzzy Sets as a Basis for Theory of Possibility." *Fuzzy Sets and Systems* 1:3–28.

Part III

Composition and Cognitive Musicology in Practice

A Composer's Cognitive Musicology
Nico Schüler

Translated from the German by Nico Schüler and Otto Laske

OL = Otto Laske
NS = Nico Schüler

NS: Your academic and artistic work is so extensive—it extends from old languages to sociology, philosophy, musicology, especially cognitive musicology, composition, poetry, computer science, and on to artificial intelligence research and psychology. Here, we will have to restrict ourselves to cognitive musicology and composition. Would you mind outlining your development with regard to very positive or very negative impulses for your theoretical and compositional work?

OL: In retrospect, it is hard to clearly distinguish positive or negative influences, given that they are often both. However, perhaps the following was negative: I began to play the piano at the age of nine. When I was eleven, a nasty uncle who was my teacher told me that I lacked musical talent. As a consequence, I gave up piano playing and began to write poetry two years later. It took me thirteen years to come back to music. Luckily, I never really lost contact with music; my sister was an excellent pianist, and so I heard live music all through my adolescence. Throughout this time, however, music did not appear to me as a medium in which I could reach the immediacy of lyrical expression.

Very positive and important were my studies with the founders of the Frankfurt School of critical theory. I went to Adorno's and Horkheimer's Hegel seminars for seven years. There, every sentence of Hegel's logic was interpreted word for word. Sometimes we didn't interpret more than five sentences in two hours. This practice has influenced my thinking enormously, I think. It might sound odd, but for me, there is an important relationship between Hegel and artificial intelligence (AI). The emphasis in Hegel's philosophy as well as in AI is on the understanding of mental processes. The goal is to understand what drives the process, how the process is structured.

One of the most influential events was definitely my meeting with Gottfried Michael Koenig in Darmstadt in 1964. My education didn't end with my Ph.D. in 1966. Since 1964, I wanted to study computer music. The reason for this desire was my encounter with G. M. Koenig, a German composer from Magdeburg, who lived in Cologne in those days; he later moved to Utrecht to become the director of the Institute of Sonology. In 1964, Koenig gave a lecture on composing with computers. His ideas at that time evolved into "PROJECT 1" in 1967. I was immediately fascinated, and I thought, "You must study computer music, if not with Gottfried Michael Koenig, then in the United States." Everyone knew that computers were accepted there. I wanted to study at Princeton University, but the Fulbright Committee decided otherwise. Instead, I went to New England Conservatory, Boston. There, I couldn't study computer music; and so I went my own way in doing this, initially working at Brandeis University due to the kindness of Alvin Lucier. In 1969, Koenig invited me to come to Utrecht. I went there in 1970 and remained until 1975. (The education in Utrecht—that was education!) It was truly transformative, not just skills training. I learned the classical electronic music studio, as well as programming, studied computer music and taught music. At that time, the Institute of Sonology (later superseded by IRCAM) was the biggest and probably the best-equipped studio in Europe. While in Utrecht, I held a fellowship of the German Research Council *(Deutsche Forschungsgemeinschaft)*. The marvelous thing was that I was given the opportunity to teach my own theories, and that I could conduct my own experiments. (I didn't teach much—approximately four hours a week.) The second positive thing was that the Institute was wholly international. There were very bright students from Canada, the United States, many from Italy and France; strangely, there was almost nobody from Germany. The language of instruction was English.

In Utrecht I worked out the basic notions of my approach to cognitive musicology and, with the aid of Barry Truax, developed basic tools such as OBSERVER.

NS: But you had previously studied musicology!

OL: It is odd, isn't it, that I did not mention that. I studied musicology between 1960 and 1966. Philosophy was my major. Musicology was my first minor subject, the second one being English and American literature. Between 1960 and 1966, I sat in seminars by Osthoff, Hoffmann-Erbrecht, and the medievalist, Gennrich.

NS: Did traditional musicology in some way inspire your later approach to cognitive musicology, aside from composition, or were you directly stimulated by your philosophical studies?

OL: This is a very interesting question. I think it was more the distaste for traditional musicology than any positive stimulation that created this line of thought. It wasn't directly philosophy either. I felt the artist was being misrepresented by musicology. It was also my interest in compositional processes and in computers. At that time, I saw philosophy as a problem-posing device—a science that cannot solve problems, only pose them. I saw in AI a continuation of philosophy, but with the difference that AI seemed to be a problem-solving device.

I wanted to get away from mere problem posing (however important) to a discipline that could tackle and solve musical and musicological problems. This has much to do with the influence on me of Nicolai Hartmann, the German philosopher. I studied with one of his pupils, Bruno Liebrucks, in Frankfurt. Hartmann always distinguished treatable from untreatable problems in philosophy. (For him, there were problems that were treatable, and others, which were not.) I was interested in treatable problems, not in speculation. The philosophies I knew couldn't offer me this, and so I decided to go to another discipline; and I went to artificial intelligence, more generally, cognitive science.

It might be important to say that in my Canadian years (1968–1970) I wrote a voluminous work entitled "On Principles of Ordinary and Artistic Communication." It was never published, and I think it got lost in my travels. This monograph is the basis of all my later theories. I was initially influenced by information theory and semiotics. Later, I became acquainted with Chomsky and Pierre Schaeffer. Pierre Schaeffer, the founder of *musique concrète,* was an engineer but also a composer. He wrote a marvelous book, which I still admire, and which unfortunately has never been translated into English: *"Traité des objets musicaux."* Essentially, in that book Schaeffer defined what I came to call sonology.

I was impressed by Chomsky's work. In the late 1950s he made the distinction between linguistic competence and performance. This distinction shows up in my first work on musicology entitled "On Problems of a Performance Model for Music" [1972]. The second work, one year later, was the "Introduction to a Generative Theory of Music" [1973] which dealt more with competence. Both of these monographs derive from Chomsky's work, but also from that of Pierre Schaeffer. P. Schaeffer wanted to understand how we humans interpret sound. He distinguished between *objets sonores* and *objets musicaux.* Essentially, he investigated *objets sonores.* To him, *objets sonores* were something that could be taped, replayed, and edited—something which to understand entailed disregarding the sound source. Schaeffer wanted to grasp the sound itself, irrespective of the source. This intention is usually called phenomenological. Schaeffer thought that music theory had always dealt with notation, while acousticians had investigated physical sound sources. But nobody had investigated the sound itself, irrespective of its notation and the manner of its production. So Schaeffer worked out a phenomenology of sound, which he called *acoulogie. Acoulogie* had to do with the sound itself, irrespective of its source and its notation. *Acoulogie* deals with ideas, the mental shaping of sound, and thus with listening, not hearing. Now, this approach followed Husserl's phenomenological reduction, where one only deals with the mental object, regardless of its objective existence, which in our case is the sound. Schaeffer put the actual sounds "into brackets" *(epoché)*. He aimed to understand the human *intention d'entendre* as a basis of a theory of listening, going beyond a mere theory of perception. He saw clearly that we wouldn't have a theory of listening even if we had a perfect theory of perception or hearing, because perception or hearing are only two of the many components of listening. Listening is a more complicated process, involving mental representation and imagination, thus problem solving. Being in the French tradition, Schaeffer was not primarily interested in the actual process of listening; he was rather interested in the types and classes of *objets sonores* that were made possible by listening. He only speculated about the process of listening.

NS: We will come back to this later. For now, I'm interested in the main reasons for your emigration to the United States.

OL: I emigrated to America for several reasons: First, I had fallen in love with an American woman; second, I wanted to study computer music; . . . and third, I was sick and tired of Marxism and the Frankfurt School. I just had to leave! When the ship took off from the Bremerhafen pier, European history fell off my shoulders like a huge burden. It was simply gone. And my arrival in America was a totally new beginning for me. At thirty, I began my life once more, as if I had not lived before.

NS: You have spoken about some of the important elements of your approach to cognitive musicology. It seems to me that you came upon your cognitive musicology on account of your interdisciplinary studies, ending up with a discipline very different from traditional musicology. In detail, what counterarguments to traditional musicology do you propose?

OL: Initially, I was totally opposed to traditional, historical as well as systematic musicology. I didn't want to hear of either. I had to create a space for something new. By now, I think that cognitive musicology is not so much opposed to, as it is an enrichment of, traditional musicology. Cognitive musicology is the attempt to develop a different perspective, complementary to traditional musicology in that it does not focus on the end result of musical processes alone, but the processes that lead to such results. I don't mean musical processes in the macrohistorical sense, but in the microhistorical sense, that is, the processes by which an individual actually makes music. The psychological and epistemological bend of my thinking shows up here—the fact that I am a cognitive scientist. In the center of the cognitive musicology (as I understand it) stands the music-making individual, or the music-making group. Therefore, the emphasis is on the "making," the *poiesis,* the process—either with or without computers. Computers are only a good medium to hold on to and monitor processes and thereby make them analyzable. My main argument has always been that the discipline as we know it is one-sidedly oriented to end results, and then only to end results that are representable in some notation (which is a subset of a subset of *musics*).

NS: The issue of notation is certainly also a reason for your greater closeness to ethnomusicology, isn't it?

OL: Yes, that is so. Ethnomusicologists are dealing with living musicians from other cultures. Therefore they cannot take notation for granted; they have to reflect upon their own activities so as not to describe another culture very incorrectly. In ethnomusicology a lot of self-reflection and self-criticism is required to understand the music from the natives' point of view. There's also more of a closeness to the process of music making; there are reflections on the relativity of cultures. This is the reason I have oriented myself less to musicology and more to ethnomusicology.

Then there is a crucial epistemological difficulty in traditional musicology, namely, the attempt to draw conclusions from an artifact, a frozen end result of a process (not only the composer's, but in addition to that, one of the musicologist's own doing). The musicologist looks at notation, then he proceeds to equate this notation with the work in question, that is, with his own listening and intention. And finally, he asks how this work has been produced, either in composing or in the historical process the composer was part of. That is to say, the musicologist proceeds backwards, engaging in what I've called knowledge engineering in reverse. While it is possible to do so, this is methodologically a very, very limited way of working. This approach disregards the developmental and historical rootedness of the musicologist's thought process, as if the musicologist lived in a timeless sphere, and as if it wasn't the musicologist who is generating the music he purports to describe based on his own process in the here and now. And this thought process is not part of the description of the music but is taken for granted. This backward conclusion is limited at best, or is outright faulty. You cannot conclude from a product to a process. You can find some traces, on account of which you can formulate hypotheses about the process. To do so is an important enterprise. Therefore, I see traditional musicology as a hypothesis-forming enterprise, a science that formulates hypotheses which by itself it cannot either prove or disprove. To do so, musicology needs cognitive science.

NS: Is all music-historical research therefore pointless from the vantage point of cognitive musicology?

OL: Not at all. It's a question of the relative importance of this research within the broader scope of musicology as a cognitive discipline. A theory of historical thinking doesn't exist. If it did, we would probably find that historical thinking about music is a very, very complicated process. We perform this process as a listener, as an analyst, as a composer, as an historian, and last but not least as a human being. And these roles aren't usually distinguished. In traditional musicology, we do not make much of a distinction between music analyst and musicologist because so far musicology has been based on music analysis. (Unfortunately, this music analysis has its own implicit theory of creativity, which has never been critically investigated and today is totally outdated.) In my view, you cannot base music theory on the analysis of individual pieces of music. The trouble with traditional music theory is that, when proceeding historically, the musicologist impersonates a music analyst, music historian, and a music listener at the same time, and then in addition to that, he impersonates the composer, aiming to formulate hypotheses about him. As a result, he brings together, and mixes, a large number of different tasks (historical reconstruction, listening, analyzing, composing) thereby impersonating an ideal, not a real, musician. And that brings me to a very important point. Cognitive musicology deals with music as a task that humans like to carry out, an action they engage in. Music is not only something humans understand, but something they *do.* And it is this real-time process of making, this *poiesis,* that I as a musicologist am interested in. The historians (who are of course not stupid) know that they can't supply anything in this regard. They tend to neglect the element of *poiesis* or pay lip service to it; they are only looking for the *aisthesis.* Following Jean-Jacques Nattiez, we should distinguish between three poles: the *poiesis,* the *aisthesis* and the neutral pole. The *aisthesis* has to do with listening, perception; *poiesis* has to do with making, including that of musical analyses; and the neutral pole, for Nattiez the semiotician, is the structural description of a work on the basis of interpreting notation. Nattiez gave a very sensitive and good description of these three poles in his book *Fondements d'une sémiologie musicale,* published in 1975. I wrote a critique of it at the time, and he wrote back that he felt I was the only one who understood his book completely. In Nattiez's view, traditional musicology is unilaterally focussed on *aisthesis.* The semiotician Nattiez refocused on the neutral pole and the *aisthesis,* and also played a little bit with the *poiesis.* But I reproached him then as I do now, for not having gone far enough. Nattiez did not take music making as *poiesis* seriously.

NS: How, for you, does music, especially composition, relate to musicology?

OL: I really make no distinction between music making and musicology. To pursue musicology is for me a kind of music making, and therefore is one of the topics of research in cognitive musicology. Cognitive musicology should also develop a theory of *music,* but must do so on the basis of understanding its own activities; it must develop theories of what music analysis is, what historic thinking about music is, and what the process of traditional musicology is (or has been). To the extent that they have ideas about music, every composer and listener is also a musicologist, although without specialized historical knowledge. And music theory is not something that only exists in academia. Everyone has a music theory, even a child. In AI, we speak of a common-sense or pop theory (popular theory)—an informal theory, and I am not convinced that informal theories (which are rarely verbalized) are worse than the verbalized theories of academic musicians. I rather believe that the ordinary listener—let's say, the trained listener, the cultivated listener—is closer to the music than the musicologist, because he is not led astray by theoretical school prejudices. He is closer to the object, in the sense Schaeffer wanted to be. The ideological restrictions of the term "music theory" to that which music theorists are producing, and to the rules of the theory of harmony and counterpoint, are simply absurd. We all have music theories. Without music theories we could not listen to music, and we could not compose. And it is actually these informal common-sense music theories that I would like to understand—because that is where musical competence gets stored! What the music theorists know better than the layman, the listening layman, is really not at all very specific to music. It has rather to do with influences stemming from psychology and anthropology and the sciences generally that are presently fashionable, in vogue, in musicology. The musicologists always have a particular nonmusical science that they adore at the moment, and that then influences their jargon as well as the form their theory takes. But on account of these, musicology does not necessarily become any richer. Even AI could be just a fashion; it's too early to decide that. I have some hope that AI is more than a fashion, or at least cognitive science (in the European rather than American meaning of this term).

In the last fifty years, musicologists have admired and tried to adopt different sciences: physics; information theory; computer science; existentialism; phenomenology—it's endless. All these fashions! Semiotics was important, particularly on account of Nattiez. Musicology has always had the problem that it has not believed in itself. It had always behaved as if the task were to imitate other sciences and this has been detrimental to its development as a science. It has lacked a voice of its own, and I have very much wanted to give it such a voice. So, after a hundred years of being busy like a bee, musicology is still in its infancy as a science; it hasn't found its own voice; it is still looking to other sciences that could help it somehow. Adler already spoke of *Hilfswissenschaften* [auxiliary sciences]; it was he who made the distinction between historic and systematic, as if the historians were not systematic and the systematicians not historical! The question for me has always been: What is the heart of a systematic musicology? What could that be, if it is not physics or acoustics? I think that it is cognitive science, and hopefully not because I'm looking for a fashionable *Hilfswissenschaft,* but because cognitive science, including neuroscience, deals with knowledge representation and process description. And these are two fundamental issues in musicology.

The computer program is actually the first medium invented to describe processes precisely. And knowledge representation is the first attempt to describe human knowledge precisely on the basis of logic—and that has its severe limits. The task would seem to be to describe knowledge in such a way that it cannot only be "understood" but also be empirically tested. A computer program is a text, but it is an executable text. The program runs, it is doing something, and what the program fails to do is precisely something one has failed to understand and encode. There's an intricate connection between program and theory. Can a program be a theory? Or *is* a program a theory? Say you have collected empirical data about how some child composes a melody using electronic sounds. You have made a protocol analysis of the child's process on the basis of how the computer has documented the child's interactive work on a synthesizer. Then you try to write a program to simulate what this child has done over a thirty-minute period. You give the program the same "input" as you gave to the child. The task of your program is now to replicate what the child has done, in order for you to ascertain, by what the program puts out, whether you have understood the child's process. If the program's output is completely different from what the child has produced, then we can say our program is not a sufficient theory of the child's process; it is thus not a complete theory of it. If, however, the program should produce an identical or similar melody, regardless of the procedures it uses, would we then be able to say that we have "explained" the child's process? I am not sure. This question of whether a program is a theory: is it decidable or is it a spurious question? To write a program at all, you already have to have a theory. In this sense a program embodies a theory; the program represents a point of view. However, that does not make the program a theory in the strict sense. Rather, the program and its output require further interpretation. Perhaps this issue is a bit too esoteric for this conversation; we could discuss it for very long. . . . This difficult issue also concerns AI-and-music research, not just knowledge acquisition studies (to which I have referred above). If you write an AI program, can you maintain that you are formulating theories? Are these theories? Anyway, each program is based on an informal theory. So you can always check whether the program does what you expect of it, on account of your having written it. Then you can evaluate the distance between what the program puts out and the envisioned goal state. How near or far are you away from a complete understanding of the process as shown by the generated output? Here we are not speculating; we are measuring distances from a goal state, whether exemplified by a human product (as in knowledge acquisition) or not. So, in a way, the musicologist works like what Marvin Minsky would call a difference engine.

NS: Since the middle of the 1970s you have dealt intensively with the problem of "AI and music." Is it knowledge representation and process description that have convinced you that AI provides a promising approach to systematic musicology?

OL: Yes, it is the fact that the topic in AI is knowledge representation and process description. In my view, that is exactly what cognitive musicology today needs—new descriptions of music processes as knowledge processes. To be able to describe knowledge processes, you must find a way of representing knowledge in an encoded form. You have to settle on a particular knowledge representation. Without a decision about knowledge representation you cannot write programs. In AI, creating programs is the way of doing cognitive musicology. In this field, we work on the basis of formal languages, not natural languages. Traditional musicology lives in the medium of natural language; it may use as many formulas as it pleases, it is always natural language, whether in writing history or acoustics. However, acousticians already pass over into mathematical language, thus formal language. AI, by contrast, is totally bound to formal languages (programming languages). And that is a powerful difference, in the sense that natural languages are unable to explicate musical knowledge. We cannot translate music into a natural language. If we could, we would not need music, we could make everything with and in language. The fact that humans make music points to a limit of natural language. It shows that humans want to express something that cannot be articulated in natural language, except perhaps in lyric poetry. Therefore, music is not really congenial with language but with poetry.

NS: How do you see linguistics and musicology relating to one another?

OL: In the early 1970s, I criticized the idea that one could simply adopt linguistics as a *Hilfswissenschaft* in musicology, that we could design a musical grammar. This idea is simply too naive since it is not natural language but poetry that is similar to music. If we associate music with language at all, then we should at least associate music with poetry. Poetry works in the medium of natural language, but, so to speak, against the grain of it. The problem is whether there exist meaningful equivalent relationships between natural language and music. Is there something in music that everyone understands as a native speaker does? Is there a musical competence shared by everyone just as all native speakers of a particular language share a particular linguistic competence? That brings us to the distinction between competence and creativity. Assume that everyone has musical competence. What distinguishes musicians from nonmusicians, as well as from each other, is that they also manifest musical creativity to various degrees. For that reason I have always distinguished competence from creativity. Musicology, in my view, has committed a colossal error in that it has mixed up the two. Musicology has tried to formulate a theory of musical competence (referred to as music theory) that is based on the analysis of individual works of music. However, individual musical works are results of both creativity and competence, not of competence alone. Therefore, the attempt to establish a music theory based on individual works of music is like trying to formulate a French grammar on the basis of poems by, say, Mallarmé. Has anybody had the absurd idea of formulating a theory of the French language, or of French grammar, on the basis of poems by major nineteenth-century poets, such as Baudelaire or Mallarmé? No. So why should the idea of formulating a theory of music competence on the basis of works by major nineteenth-century composers, such as Beethoven or Brahms, be any less absurd? From my point of view, a music theory is a theory of competence. A theory of creativity is a different thing altogether; it is much more complicated, because one must already have a theory of competence, in order to conceive of creativity. Otherwise, one must develop a solid theory of creativity not confined to music, as Howard Gardner has done, for instance. But musicological theories have always tried to get away with mixing and merging competence and creativity, without committing themselves to either, and therefore have rightfully never gained scientific legitimacy. Cognitive musicology, therefore, cannot continue this dance! If a musicological theory wants to be scientific, it must commit itself to either competence or creativity; it cannot mix and merge the two, or reduce one to the other, for it must eventually do justice to both.

I have formulated these ideas very casually.

NS: Which subjects should a developing musicologist of today study to be prepared for taking on the tasks of the ending twentieth and beginning twenty-first centuries?

OL: That is a crucial question. For me, the musicologist is a knowledge engineer who tries to understand, document, analyze, and model the musical knowledge of living musicians. In this work he might be stimulated by hypotheses of historic musicology, among other disciplines. I would think a cognitive musicologist should first study composition, or at least be a very good musician; second, cognitive science, particularly AI and neural networks; and third, cognitive and developmental psychology. Cognitive science is a hybrid domain between psychology, philosophy of mind and AI. Developmental psychology is a relatively new discipline dealing with an individual's life history. Of course, knowing as much ethnomusicology as possible is a help, too.

I don't believe that somebody loses much if he has never heard about historical musicology, except when he is interested in products of people who have made music in other centuries. Such knowledge can be very important for a broad, historically sensitive, theory of competence. Don't forget; for me, traditional musicology, whether historic or systematic, is an attempt to formulate hypotheses about musical competence. Only musicologists, people who are really musicians, and who have an analytical understanding of music can do that. Scientists coming from AI or psychology cannot formulate adequate hypotheses about music or musical competence because they are not musicians. You can turn a musician into a cognitive scientist, but you cannot turn a cognitive scientist into a musician. People who pursue musicology must be musicians first of all. That is a big problem in cognitive musicology, since currently many people in this domain are engineers dabbling in music, but not musicians. AI began with people who were computer scientists and programmers. We have seen that this does not suffice for musicology. The leading people working in AI and neural networks today are those who have studied other disciplines, and therefore are at home in a particular specialty, and who absorb computer studies into their thinking. The dull people in cognitive science are simply computer scientists. And for that reason I would make the suggestion that a contemporary musicologist be a musician first, and that he study cognitive science and cognitive (if not also developmental) psychology.

NS: Don't you thereby go too unilaterally toward the side of the process, ignoring the music product?

OL: Yes, but only out of despair, because of the enormous difficulties I have found in developing a theory of product and process simultaneously. I have always aimed for a theory of both process and product. I am convinced that the product contains the process. But you cannot read the process out of the product after the fact. You can understand product and process simultaneously only if you observe the process as a process that leads to this product. This product can only be a product of living musicians, because as soon as the musicians who produced it live no more, you can only speculate about the process. You can't even find out the process from reading Beethoven's sketchbooks; you can perhaps formulate interesting hypotheses about this process. Now, that has already been done, but without fantastic results and without a true chance of verifying the hypotheses.

It is a philosophical issue that a human product is not transparent to the process by which it was created. Musicology has never grasped this issue. If the product only exists as an end product, cut off from the process that generated it because the process falls into history, then the product is like a rune, regarding which you can formulate interesting hypotheses, but on account of which you cannot understand the product in depth. I therefore concluded that if you study products of living musicians by simultaneously observing and analyzing their process, you have a better chance of understanding their process.

It is important to me that you don't go away with the notion that I'm possessed by the process as others are possessed by the product. Like all musicologists, I always wanted to have a theory of both, only I was looking more on the side of the process. But the real mystery is in the link of the two. In this context, there is a relationship between the process/product issue and what we call self-identity. Every person creates, in a certain way, his own identity. It is very hard for us humans to understand the process by which we have become the product that we are. If we could easily do that, we wouldn't need psychiatry or developmental psychology. (This is the source of my new interest in both of these areas.) Somehow, it is a mystery of human thought how product and process cohere. After having explored the musical product for a hundred years now, perhaps we should devote the next century to understanding the varieties of musical process. And thereafter we could possibly begin to consider the relationship between process and product more astutely.

NS: A final question regarding musicology: You left Germany because you didn't see opportunities for a cognitively thinking composer who is also a musicologist. Is it true that German musicology has not changed fundamentally yet, even though much time has progressed? What possibilities do you see for a future German musicology?

OL: These questions carry with them a number of assumptions I will have to comment on. First, I didn't leave Germany because I didn't see opportunities for myself as a musicologist but, as I have said, in order to study computer music. The urge to become a musicologist only arose through my experience of electronic and computer music. And what I then remembered from my studies in German musicology showed me that there was no way to build a direct bridge between what I had been taught and what I saw before me begging for answers.

So, being aware of Nietzsche's dictum that one cannot honor one's teachers by imitating, but only by surpassing them, I decided to strike out on my own, dealing with the musicological issues posed in the experimental studio. In other words, I followed my experience as a composer, hoping to renew musicology.

Second, as you say, twenty-five years have elapsed, and it seems as if not so much has changed in musicology. Here I speak of the domain in general, not only German musicology. My impression is that my writings have had a greater influence, so far, on acoustic ecology [Truax, in this volume] and ethnomusicology [Bel, in this volume], than on traditional musicology. As we know, up into the '50s, musicology in the United States, and perhaps everywhere, was heavily influenced by the musicological tradition of the German-speaking part of Europe, especially Austria and Germany. There was this distinction made by Adler between systematic and historic musicology that never quite made sense to me, especially considering Webern and the consequences of his approach.[1] And also, the musicological establishment has too much to defend to give up easily, especially since their rewards are diminishing.

NS: How do you see the future of German musicology? Also, what wishes do you have for it?

OL: I don't think there is a special mission for German musicology, except perhaps to become more international. Judging from my experience in the '80s, when I tried to gain a foothold in Germany as a musicologist, the German musicologists and musicians were not ready for me. Rather, they fought me with teeth and claws, unwilling to take the risk of letting Laske profess his musicology. Frankly, I think they passed up an opportunity of having a multilingual musicologist familiar with the German, French and American traditions bring some new ideas into their shop.

Now, as to musicology *tout court*, as far as I can see today, in 1993, there has been an increasing institutional need to legitimatize research by working with computers. However, in the fewest cases has one changed the direction of one's thinking, that is, product-oriented analysis. In my view, musicologists are making the same error that has been made in AI-and-music research, where one believed it would suffice simply to "apply" AI to music without further ado. Most musicologists still seem to believe that one can simply take over AI and cognitive science, or neuroscience, notions and go on doing musicology as usual.

NS: Can you say a little more explicitly what you mean?

OL: Sure. You see, the much larger task is to rethink AI (including network theory) on the basis of musical thinking. We ought to generate new problems in AI and neuroscience on the basis of thinking in, and about, music, as I did when using notions of psycholinguistics, developmental psychology, computer science, and AI in the '70s and '80s. (If I were working in musicology today, I would probably work in neuromusicology). We cannot simply adapt existing sciences to music. We can invent a new musicology only in the sense that we invent a new

AI and neuroscience, namely, one that does not limit itself to logical processes with respect to present-day programming languages, but which knows something about common sense, contextual embeddedness (task environment!), and creativity.

NS: What do you think has historically been musicology's greatest nemesis?

OL: I would say the *Hilfswissenschaften* taking over the musicology that called them to its aid. The so-called *Hilfswissenschaften* have opened the door to fashions, which today are cognitive science and neuroscience. If we do not know what we are looking for in musicology, then no *Hilfswissenschaft* will help. For twenty-five years, I have tried to formulate new goals and new tasks for musicology, in such a way that we can work with computers. I have been problem solving and task oriented in my musicological research, and have seen that as the preferred way to renew musicology as a science. And so my wish for the new musicology, not just the German, is for it to give up looking for fashionable subjects through which to legitimate their undeveloped thinking. (I realize, of course, that new *Hilfswissenschaften* can be a vehicle of discovery, as they were for me, but one has to prove true discovery by going beyond the aids.) Instead of hankering for respectability, as musicologists have always done, they might want to try to find new goals on the basis of thinking in and about music.

NS: What would you say is required to find such goals?

OL: I think we need to ask: What is musicological thinking? We need to develop a theory of musicological thinking. The only one, to my knowledge, who has worked in this area is my colleague Bernard Vecchione in Aix-en-Provence, who is striving for a theory of musicological thinking—in other words, *Grundlagenforschung* (analyzing one's own way of working)!. Vecchione sees clearly, I think, that as long as one has not understood how musicological thinking in particular tasks is structured and thus does not have a theory of it, one cannot set new goals in musicology. Take for instance Charles Seeger, the great American musicologist, who on the basis of insight into musicological thought pointed out the deficit in process thinking in musicology, especially systematic musicology, and the poverty of thinking from the composer's vantage point. That was setting new goals!

NS: You have spoken of the relevance of composition theory and the composer for cognitive musicology. Composition theory plays a very important part in this interdisciplinary field. What part does composing play in your life?

OL: In my life, the composer and the lyric poet always had to live beside each other. However, until recently they didn't really live *together*. I began to write poetry in German in 1950 and have written in English since 1968. Only last year have I really brought my own poetry and music together in my composition.

I became a musicologist because I am a composer with theoretical interests, like my teacher T. W. Adorno. Since 1970, I have worked with computers in composition, six years after I started composition "by hand." The computer has had a strong influence on me as a composer, in that it has forced me in interaction with it to think about my process. I haven't written programs for composition myself, but rather have used other people's programs (Koenig, Xenakis, Truax). But I have nonetheless thought very much about the process of compositional thinking. As a composer, I am interested not just in the product but in my own compositional process, which includes the listening process. My expertise in electroacoustic music made with the aid of computers has led me to explore the musical process. As a composer, I became critical of the view that one can base a theory of music on the listening process, because listening has more to do with understanding music than with making music. And as I have already said, for me music is a making as much as an understanding. Both are, of course, very closely linked. However, by writing instrumental and electroacoustic music at the computer, you can now reflect on your music making, *poiesis,* as a doing in real time, and you can document and trace your process more effectively than in previous times. The empirical tasks I have explored in cognitive musicology have mostly been oriented to composition. Take for instance the OBSERVER program through which I have explored the development of music-syntactical thinking of children between the ages of seven and twelve (1972 to 1977), and later the PRECOMP program (1988 to 1992) through which I have explored how mature composers think in interpretative composition. I have also written an extended study on music analysis, which deals with the real-time process of analysis of Debussy's *Syrinx* by advanced (graduate) students. Based on empirical material regarding what students analytically find in this piece through listening and reading notation, I have written an essay, entitled "Keith" (after a brilliant student composer), that is a theory of music analysis. My question in this essay is: What would a computer program have to know to pursue a music analysis of *Syrinx*? In "Keith," I conceive of music analysis as a discovery process that generates new concepts and conceptual linkages between them, in a search based on systematically derived examples.

But I don't want to digress from your question. I am arrogant enough to believe that if anyone understands music, it is the composer. Everyone else can also understand music, but secondhand, so to speak, by listening. The composer is at the source. And thus I find it vital that this compositional knowledge should enter musicology. Today one deals with remarks of composers about music too anecdotally. If Ligeti, Feldman, or Stockhausen write about their music and their composing, then the musicologists, above all the German ones, look upon this as a part of the composer's style or biography. It is indeed a part of their biography, but in my view we should take these anecdotal remarks of composers about music much more seriously. We should develop a theory of these remarks as Walter Benjamin [the literary critic of the Frankfurt School] might have done. Because composers are at the source. They determine what music is, at least to the extent that their work wins acceptance. Composers don't usually really worry about what music is; they write because they must. If people feel what has been written is music, composers are happy. If they don't feel it is music, then composers hope it will be seen as music in the coming decade. The composer "makes." In society, music is an idea. "Music" means something that is acceptable, something one can understand as music, now, at this moment. But no one knows what the situation is going to be in ten or twenty years from now. We don't know who the really important composers of this century are. We only believe to know. In any case, compositional knowledge is surely lacking in musicology.

NS: Which compositional techniques and which computer programs do you prefer to use?

OL: I have mostly worked with programs by G. M. Koenig, in particular, a program for interpretative composition, PROJECT 1. Another of Koenig's programs, PROJECT 2, which is for what I call stipulatory composition, is a completely different process. But one can of course mix the two, something I might try in the future. I have also used Xenakis' ST 10, a very interesting program. But I'm not interested in programs or machines that turn out compositions. Rather, what has always interested me are machines that allow and invite reflection about the compositional process and that simultaneously lead to a compositional product. I like machines capable of functioning as the composer's "alter ego," with which a composer can converse about his own process. And today, after thirty years' work, we have such programs even in the electroacoustic domain (e.g., Scaletti's KYMA).

NS: How do you see your compositional future, on the one hand, and your scientific future, on the other?

OL: I cannot predict. . . . If I could do what I wanted, I would let science be science, and only concern myself with composition and poetry—that would be my ideal life in the future. But because you cannot live from art making, at least not in this country where most composers earn their money outside of music, research is a way of earning a livelihood. But I am also on my way to becoming a clinical neuropsychologist, a career I initiated at Harvard working in developmental psychology. I have new research goals, such as bringing cognitive science and psychiatry together. I believe that cognitive science has developed ideas that can advance thinking about mental illness and human development and issues in creativity. For somebody who doesn't know me, it must be very difficult to see how all these things cohere. The key for me is and has always been epistemology. In everything I have ever done—composing, writing poetry, doing philosophy, musicology, AI, etc.—the question for me has always been: What is knowledge in this domain, and how can I know myself and the world? And that is really the link that holds all the different disciplines I am interested in together. However, reflection on how and what we know is not the same in poetry and in music or in science. I am probably at heart an epistemologist, and whoever understands that thereby has an entry point into my work. And as far as my artistic career goes, a main goal for me is to further the tone poem, in which my poetry and music come together. A further goal is to make my nearly sixty-five compositions, half of which are electroacoustic and half of which are vocal and instrumental, more known than they already are. Especially my purely vocal music, much of which has remained unperformed.

NOTE

1. Laske is here referring to the view held by Webern and his followers (Boulez, Stockhausen, etc.) that the compositional process and the completed work are of equal importance. Since these influential composers gave credence to this view, Laske questions the distinction many musicologists make between research concerned with individual compositions (i.e., historical musicology) and research into compositional processes (i.e., systematic musicology). He asserts both areas are essential for an adequate understanding of music.

9

Furies and Voices: Composition-Theoretical Observations
Otto Laske

I am interested in the question of how the control structure of a compositional process determines the form of the musical work the process produces, and in the impact of working with computers in composition on answers to this question. In this context, I take computer programs to be objectivications of selected parts of the composer's own knowledge. I conceive of such programs as the composer's "alter ego," without which he remains bereft of the benefit of externalized dialog. My view is that dialog with oneself in art making is crucial, and that computer programs, rather than being simply tools for achieving results, are dialoguing tools. Moreover, I consider them more as works of art than as tools. This entails that I don't believe in any linear progress in developing such programs, or in the merit of particularly "intelligent" programs. For me, a "stupid" program that makes a composer "intelligent" is more valuable than an "intelligent" program that hinders him from finding his own voice. The latter often happens only through conflict, and is based on resolution of conflict through dialog. In short, I am interested in the dialectic potential of programs for composition through which the composer is provoked to find himself. By "finding oneself," I mean being able to assess one's knowledge, the limitations of one's knowledge, and being able, therefore, to make a competent judgment as to which tasks should be handled by the program and which by the composer, as well as strengthening one's own capability of experimentation and unlearning. (I find habits and scripts pernicious.)

In "Composition Theory: An Enrichment of Music Theory" (Laske 1989), I noted a compositional paradigm shift from example-based to rule-based composition in twentieth-century music, and outlined three pure prototypes of rule-based composition in the arts: interpretive, stipulatory, and improvisational com-position. In interpretive composition, the composer interprets materials gener-ated by a computer program according to rules (Laske 1990). When working in a stipulatory fashion, the composer himself stipulates rules for generating syntactic structures or sonic repertories. Working improvisationally, the composer ac-cesses his results in real time, on the fly. The point was not that these approaches are exclusive of each other but rather that they tend to merge, for which reason composition is a process difficult to understand. In contrast to example-based composition, rule-based approaches enable composers to choose not only their materials but their mental process as well. Composers who do not choose their process consciously, but leave the choice to their memory (i.e., habit) or to ma-chines, would seem to lose a large part of the creative potential of computer pro-grams for music.

In order to understand cognitive processes of composition empirically, I find it important to distinguish example-based and rule-based composition (or, to speak in the jargon of artificial intelligence, case-based and constraint-based reasoning), as shown in Figure 9.1. Most of pre-twentieth-century Western music is example based, meaning that in their work, composers relied on their memory of heard examples of music—whether music of authors they studied, or their own music—in creating new works. By contrast, much of twentieth-century mu-sic is based on rule systems, or rather, on constraints. Rule-based composition is an approach to composition one can also observe in fourteenth-century (Machaut) and seventeenth-century (Bach) Europe. While example-based com-position leads to personal scripts ("Brahms's piano style"), extended use of rule-based composition ultimately leads to habits, and thus also to scripts (as indi-cated by the arrow pointing to the left in Figure 9.1). Composition-theoretically, however, there are significant differences between example-based and rule-based

Figure 9.1
Paradigms of rule-based composition

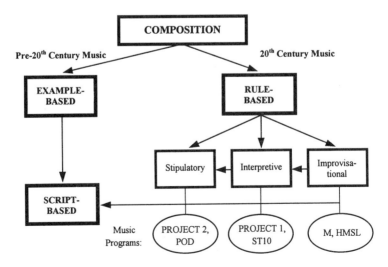

scripts. Example-based scripts are based on listening experiences, while rule-based scripts are based on experiences of one's own (or somebody else's) compositional processes—that is, on remembered strategies. Whether these different scripts get related in a compositional process depends on the composer, who is in charge of how to use his memory. From this vantage point, the use of computer programs in composition is based on a decision by the composer about how to deal with his own memory, or past life. The composer must decide whether to hold on to sonic memories and make them the basis of his works, or whether to avoid such memories, letting algorithms dispossess him of them. Music is thus ultimately a cognitive and anthropological, not a merely musical, fact; it is inseparable from a choice of how to live and what to value.

My recent composition *Furies and Voices* (1989–1990) is an example of rule-based composition. Commissioned by the Centre for the Arts, Simon Fraser University, Burnaby, British Columbia, this work was made in a studio unknown to me, with the aid of Barry Truax's program environment for granular synthesis (Truax 1988a/b; Roads 1985, 1978; Xenakis 1971; Gabor 1947). Making this composition presupposed learning a completely new *task environment (see the glossary for terms preceded by *), since my memory was not there to guide me, except for a very general memory of how programs work. For this reason, the task environment, usually taken for granted in descriptions of compositional processes, its structure, as well as the process of learning it, had a direct influence on the emerging composition. After some orientation and experimentation, I decided to proceed in a top-down (stipulatory) manner, being nevertheless in constant and immediate touch with sonic results. In this experimental situation, I had ample occasion for observing the cognitive influence of a programmed task environment on the emergence and refinement of compositional ideas.

The task environment for computer-aided composition at Simon Fraser University is characterized by the fact that much attention has been paid to the need of a composer to choose his mental process for a particular work. In the university's studio, the composer can use his visual imagination in producing high-level designs of compositions (called *tendency masks*) and hear them almost instantaneously, in realizations based on three different acoustic models: waveform synthesis, frequency modulation, and digital sampling. This cognitively rich environment has several important composition-theoretical consequences:

1. Designs, such as *scores and *tendency masks, are not necessarily note based (thus local, based on an instrumental model of music), although the direct generation of scores is possible
2. Designs can be instantaneously evaluated in terms of sonic outcomes
3. The sonic realization of designs can be improvisationally altered in real time, thereby transforming them into frameworks for improvisation
4. The composer can merge different design approaches (as distinguished above) in producing a work

By manually intervening in the machine realization of a design, the composer is able to interpret designs stipulated by him in a top-down manner. Beyond that, he can rehearse performances of a design by formulating improvisational rules, thus merging all three rule-based approaches (i.e., interpretive, stipulatory, and improvisational). For me, this capability is the hallmark of a cognitively creative environment.

LEARNING THE TASK ENVIRONMENT

The task environment at Simon Fraser University is a software and hardware environment for *granular synthesis linked to an analog/digital sound studio for recording and mixing. These two parts of the studio are linked by A/D/A converters and an 8-channel (analog) tape recorder.

As shown in Figure 9.2, resources for structure definition and sonic specification are equally rich, especially since all sonic options can be used with all structural ones. As indicated by the arrows to the left of Figure 9.2, there is great flexibility in choosing a particular level of the structural hierarchy, since the real-time performance of tendency masks, scores, and *ramps can, at any time, be improvisationally altered by using manual controls. (For instance, a mask, when executing, can be interrupted and changed during the performance of one of its segments.) For this reason, stipulatory approaches to composition, which otherwise would be quite austere, can be effortlessly combined with improvisational ones. Abstract designs can be debugged using real-time feedback, and sonic definitions can be tested in the framework of high-level syntactic constructs.

As to sonic resources, there are two distinct palettes: one for waveform and FM synthesis (both using waveform repertories); another for three kinds of *sampling, differentiated according to *sampling speed (fixed, continuous, vari-

Figure 9.2
Compositional resources in Truax's granular synthesis system

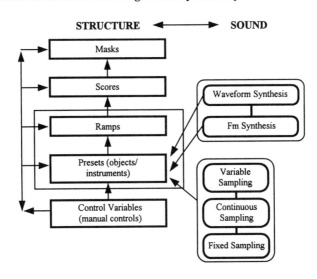

able). As a consequence, in the sonic domain, there exists a hierarchy of degrees of generality of design that is comparable to, although not as differentiated as, the options available in the syntactic domain.

Upon entering the studio, a novice gets into the succession of tasks diagrammed in Figure 9.3. The compositional process, including the learning process, comprises eight steps:

1. Learning the available software and the peculiar control variables of its interface(s)
2. Learning to define sound objects (called *presets) by way of sonic feedback and to define higher-level syntactic constructs (*ramps, *scores, *tendency masks)
3. Deciding on a planning method by which to solve the composition problem abstractly, without recourse to concrete goals and operators, by specifying the principal goals to be realized
4. Having decided in favor of one of the strategic planning options, deriving the *problem space for that option. This entails becoming aware of the required objects, operators, and subgoals to be employed

Figure 9.3
Task structure in *Furies and Voices*

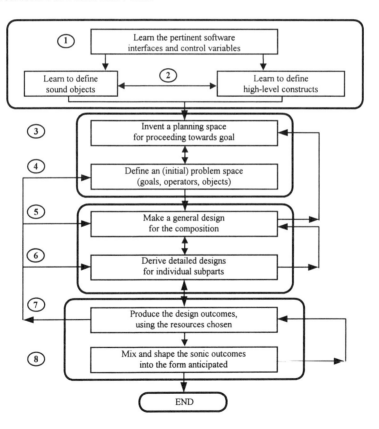

5. Making an overall design for the planned composition (musical form)
6. Deriving detailed designs for individual parts of the composition
7. Realizing the designs made, that is, producing the syntactic resources needed, as well as their auditory outcomes
8. Mixing and shaping the obtained auditory material into the form preconceived by the design, with as much of a possibility of revision as time permits

Considered from an artificial intelligence point of view, these tasks fall into five categories: learning, planning, design, analysis, and synthesis, where analysis pervades the other four categories to various degrees. Of these, the Simon Fraser University environment strongly supports design and production tasks and, to a far lesser degree, planning and learning tasks. Analysis tasks are largely unsupported.

Planning and design overlap in many ways, since decisions at all levels are influenced by notions of musical form, and vice versa. There is a frequent overlap between production and planning and production and design, since the experience of sonic outcomes often necessitates revisions of procedure or form, depending on the present state of the goal pursued. The interdependence of planning and actual problem solving is a subtle and complex affair; *problem spaces are revised frequently during the compositional process, meaning that the relevant operators and goals are revised, which may lead to changes in planning. The opposite, changes in planning that result in problem space revisions (such as the adoption of a different sequence of subgoals, or of different subgoals altogether) are equally frequent. Especially intricate is the progression from planning to design. This progression involves a mental leap leading from the analysis of options and steps to the synthesis of a model of materials (including one's own scripts). Within design itself, general and detailed design activities have close connections, and important mutual repercussions (such as when the specification of an individual subpart of a composition necessitates changes in its overall form, or vice versa).

More concretely, defining the sonic resources and the high-level constructs meant to embody them are interdependent processes during production. The kind and degree of interdependence between these definitions and their embodiment is a function of the compositional approach taken, which is basically a matter of planning. There are two extremes—working from perception (sound), and working from conception (syntactic structure)—with a corresponding difference in the use of human memory (i.e., sonic memory or rule memory):

1. the acousmatic approach (Schaeffer 1966), in which the choice of sound materials determines the choice of high-level syntactic constructs, and
2. the abstract-syntax approach in which decisions about structure predetermine or constrain the choice of sonic materials.

An approach intermediate between the two listed above is the incarnated-syntax approach that starts with a structural design and employs sound materials for optimally articulating the design. In this approach, both the sonic and the structural aspects of composition have equal weight.

From the point of view of present-day artificial intelligence research, most of the composition tasks outlined above are beyond state-of-the-art methodologies, constructs, and tools (Kobsa et al. 1990, Kodratoff and Tecuci 1988, Roads 1989, Ames 1987). There are two main reasons. First, the composition of music is based on material that includes the composer's own personality and his interpretation of life experiences, and is inseparable from story-telling and self-dialog (Laske 1990). Second, the composition of music as a mental process is based on the constant reevaluation of its own history; and tools for tracking mental history intelligently and effectively, on the basis of a constantly updated data base of one's past decision making, are practically nonexistent.

Less pervasive reasons abound. Knowledge acquisition, in music practically nonexistent, has been largely restricted to diagnostic tasks, while synthesis tasks such as composition and management, except for strictly technical (e.g., VLSI) design, have remained largely unexplored (Schreiber et al. 1988). Planning has been well researched, but expert systems capable of well-founded decisions regarding alternative strategies are just beginning to emerge. In user modeling, plan recognition by machine is in its infancy, and machine learning is more of a hope than a reality.[1] Also, systems that do not simply accomplish predefined tasks but generate higher-level tasks based on newly synthesized ideas and an assessment of the merit of previous solutions in light of a complex goal are hard to come by. Object-oriented composition environments, however beneficial, still deal primarily with syntactic issues in composition, being tongue-tied when it comes to materials of a sonic and timbral nature, and their link to syntactic solutions (Pope 1989). For this reason, musical composition, especially in combination with the acquisition of action knowledge (not just speech knowledge) from experts, remains a promising topic for artificial intelligence research. Nevertheless, AI and music papers are often regarded with suspicion by peer reviewers—most of whom are not themselves musicians—because of the prejudice that they are "soft science." But this may be about to change.

FORMULATING A COMPOSITIONAL PLAN

In composing *Furies and Voices*, a strategic turning point was reached when I realized that I could not go the acousmatic route (starting from the definition of sound objects) but needed to concentrate on high-level conceptual constructs, owing partly to prior experience, partly to time constraints. Thereby, I adopted the incarnated-structure approach that starts with a structural design and proceeds to embodying it in sound by way of experimentation (constraining it to within reasonable limits). In this process, I decided to construct a solution in very general terms before working out any details. This led to the definition of a sequence of subgoals of the overall compositional goal, as depicted in Figure 9.4. This goal structure provided me with a planning method in terms of which the total compositional problem could be explored and solved abstractly before dealing with all of its details. The goal structure imposed a directionality on the search for solutions to all of the subproblems. Before solutions to each subgoal

Figure 9.4
Planning space for *Furies and Voices*

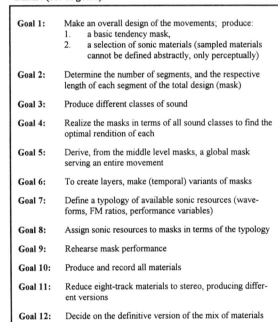

PROBLEM:

Given: a sound synthesis environment incorporating three acoustic models (WFS, FMS, SAM), all available under granular synthesis,

Create: a composition comprising movements that differ in character, texture, and tone color, and manifest differences in speed and complexity of layering.

PLAN (set of goals):

Goal 1:	Make an overall design of the movements; produce:
	1. a basic tendency mask,
	2. a selection of sonic materials (sampled materials cannot be defined abstractly, only perceptually)
Goal 2:	Determine the number of segments, and the respective length of each segment of the total design (mask)
Goal 3:	Produce different classes of sound
Goal 4:	Realize the masks in terms of all sound classes to find the optimal rendition of each
Goal 5:	Derive, from the middle level masks, a global mask serving an entire movement
Goal 6:	To create layers, make (temporal) variants of masks
Goal 7:	Define a typology of available sonic resources (waveforms, FM ratios, performance variables)
Goal 8:	Assign sonic resources to masks in terms of the typology
Goal 9:	Rehearse mask performance
Goal 10:	Produce and record all materials
Goal 11:	Reduce eight-track materials to stereo, producing different versions
Goal 12:	Decide on the definitive version of the mix of materials

were explored, plans specific to solving each of the subgoals emerged. At that point, the *problem space associated with each subgoal, which contains the objects and operators needed to solve it, as well as the knowledge states relevant to it, could be worked out in detail (Newell and Simon 1972:428–431).

Among the goals entailed by the planning method chosen, three are most significant:

1. Two-pronged approach to form: Goal 1 implies that some parts of the form are to be *mask (thus structure) determined, while some are not (use of variable sampling of acoustic materials). The basic approach is nevertheless a type of stipulatory (top-down) composition.

2. Interlayer and intermovement relationships: Goal 5 stipulates that one of the (four) sequential submasks of a layer is to serve as material for a higher-level mask spanning an entire movement (either the same, or another movement). Goal 6 specifies further that temporal variants of both sectional and movement masks are to be derived so as to produce four different (pair-wise related) layers of material.
3. Use of sonic resources for the purpose of structure articulation, not as an end in itself: Goals 4, 7, and 8 subordinate the use of sonic resources to the articulation of stipulated mask structures, thereby endorsing the composer's incarnated-structure approach.

PLAN REALIZATION: MAKING THE DESIGN

Figure 9.5 shows the overall design for *Furies and Voices* that underlies the specifications in Figures 9.6 to 9.8. The design has the form of a virtual *mask that never sounds but provides the blueprint for all (twleve) specific designs (masks) used, shown together in Figure 9.8. The spatial shapes of the mask (Figure 9.5) define value selections from parameter repertories for duration, modulation index, and frequency, while amplitude and delay are sketched out independently (underneath). The shapes also stipulate the real-time length of each of the submasks (I, II, III, 1-4), and the general direction of parametric development throughout the composition. In working out specific designs, each segment of the virtual mask is itself turned into a set of five submasks, one for each of the five parameters of granular synthesis, as shown by example in Figure 9.7. (The modulation index parameter is not always used.) Some of the segment masks

Figure 9.5
Virtual mask (basic design) for *Furies and Voices*

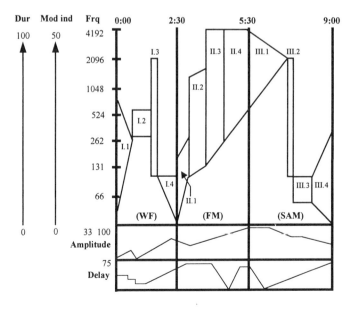

shown in Figure 9.8 were extended to movement masks, and temporal variants were created for them. Consequently, four kinds of masks came to be used in the piece:

1. the virtual mask serving as a general design (Figure 9.5)
2. the sectional masks (four for each of one or two upper layers, systematically derived from segments of the virtual mask (Figure 9.8, upper layer)
3. the movement masks, derived by time stretching of a particular sectional mask (for example, O41→EIN, Figure 9.8, lowest layer)
4. the variant masks for the middle two layers that were overlaid to create each movement's total texture (layers two and three, Figure 9.8)

This way of working led to a kind of *talea-based composition similar to that practiced in fourteenth-century French motets (e.g., by G. de Machaut). In this type of composition, one uses taleae, namely, fixed sequences of durations repeated throughout a composition, as form-defining elements. In the present case, some of these elements (masks) are themselves temporal variants (expansions, variations) of other elements (a device that appears in contrapuntal works of the Low Countries in the fifteenth century—e.g., in works by Dufay and Ockeghem.)

Note that five masks, one for each synthesis parameter, need to be superimposed to define a sectional or movement mask. This necessity leads to a kind of "parametrical counterpoint," where not voices in the traditional sense, but parametric value sequences are mapped onto each other. An example of such parametrical counterpoint is shown in Figure 9.7, where the five parametrical masks defining mask "EEN" are shown in their superimposition. (For the function of mask EEN within the entire composition, see Figure 9.8.)

Each of the individual masks defined in *Furies and Voices* has a predetermined number of segments of a certain duration (in seconds) that make up the total mask. To derive all sectional and movement masks from the virtual mask, the composer needed to stipulate the number of segments and their real-time lengths for each mask. These stipulations are shown in Figure 9.6. Figure 9.7 instantiates the fourth column of values in Figure 9.6 (segment I.4), which were originally embodied in mask O41, but then were time stretched to yield mask EIN (of which mask EEN is a variant).

In Figure 9.6, underneath the syntax tree summarizing the transformations of the virtual mask, there are two integer tables listing, in the rows, specifications for each of the five principal synthesis parameters:

1. frequency (in the sampling mode interpreted as *offset between grains),
2. *grain duration,
3. modulation index (for FM, where applicable),
4. amplitude, and
5. *delay.

The columns of the table define the sequence of the twelve compositional sections, from I.1 to III.4. The first (upper) table specifies the number of segments each sectional mask is to comprise. The second (lower) table (for which only a single example is given) determines the time, in seconds, of each of the segments

Figure 9.6
Derivation of individual mask segments

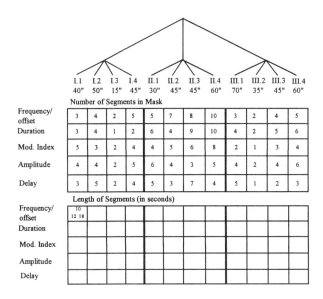

	I.1 40"	I.2 50"	I.3 15"	I.4 45"	II.1 30"	II.2 45"	II.3 45"	II.4 60"	III.1 70"	III.2 35"	III.3 45"	III.4 60"
Number of Segments in Mask												
Frequency/ offset	3	4	2	5	5	7	8	10	3	2	4	5
Duration	3	4	1	2	6	4	9	10	4	2	5	6
Mod. Index	5	3	2	4	4	5	6	8	2	1	3	4
Amplitude	4	4	2	5	6	4	3	5	4	2	4	6
Delay	3	5	2	4	5	3	7	4	5	1	2	3
Length of Segments (in seconds)												
Frequency/ offset	10 12 18											
Duration												
Mod. Index												
Amplitude												
Delay												

of the sectional masks. These specifications were derived intuitively, but could equally have been generated by rule. The number of mask segments varies between one and ten, the length of segments, in seconds, between five and twenty-five.

In Figure 9.7, frequency, duration, and modulation index are shown in terms of fields (outlined regions), while the other two parameters (amplitude and delay) are shown as single, dashed lines. In the figure, durations (shown in the

Figure 9.7
Parametrical counterpoint in *Furies and Voices* (in movement mask "EEN" [3:10])

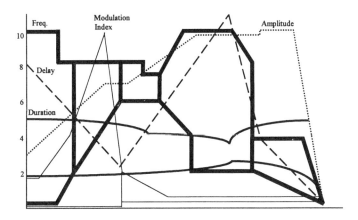

horizontally extended region demarcated by curved lines in the lower half of the diagram) are fairly short, thus entail dense textures. Delay (— —), begins quite long (i.e., detached textures), becomes short (fused textures), and then reverses its course, ending even shorter. Amplitude (··········), steadily rises, falling abruptly at the end. Frequency (defined by fields with a thick outline) starts with a very broad field encompassing almost the entire frequency range, narrows toward the middle of the mask, then suddenly widens again, only to end in the very low registers. Modulation index rises to a maximum during the first third, then falls precipitously. These outlines can easily be heard in the first movement of *Furies and Voices*.

Masks for each of the principal five parameters are overlaid in each resulting (sectional or movement) mask. These stipulations embody the contrapuntal rules according to which individual musical parameters are mapped onto each other. By using the tables in Figure 9.6, twelve movement masks were defined, four for each of three movements. (As shown in Figure 9.8, two of them were not used, but were replaced by structures generated by variable sampling.) In terms of relating Figures 9.5 and 9.6, all of the stipulations found—for example, in Figure 9.6 under I.1—are embodied in mask 011 of movement I shown in Figure 9.8. Of this sectional mask, the composer created four variants (012 to 015), but used only the last one (015).

According to goal 5 (see Figure 9.4), some of the segment masks serve as prototypes for masks spanning an entire movement. According to Figure 9.8, mask 041, for instance, is expanded to yield mask EIN (and its variant, mask EEN) in the first movement, while masks 081 and 071 serve as prototypes of masks for the second and third movements (ZWO and DRI), respectively. In accordance with goal 6, temporal variants were created of the twelve sectional masks (011 to 121), some of which were actually used (see Figure 9.8). The ini-

Figure 9.8
Syntactic structure of *Furies and Voices*

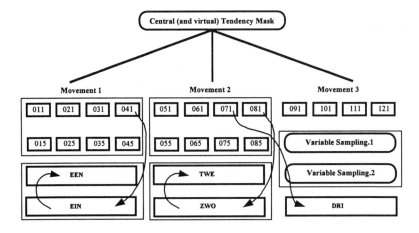

tial idea of sounding the virtual mask itself (Figure 9.5) as a fifth layer spanning all movements of the composition, was abandoned on perceptual grounds.

INSTANTIATING THE DESIGN: PRODUCING THE FORM

In the sonic domain, the resources that had accrued from real-time experiments consist of the elements depicted in Figure 9.9. As shown, the resources are of four kinds: waveform sets (A), FM ratio sets (B), fixed samples (C1), and variable samples (C2). Of these, (A) is used in the first, (A) and (B) are used in the second, and (C1, C2) as well as (A) and (B), in the third movement. All sonic resources are influenced by control variables, their use being subject to real-time intervention during performance (improvisational composition).

The actual use of sonic resources in the three movements of *Furies and Voices* is shown in Figure 9.10, the orchestrational analog of Figure 9.8. As can be seen by comparing Figures 9.8 and 9.10, in the first two movements, related scores (e.g., 011 and 015) are often sounded in opposite ways (e.g., smooth vs. metallic tone colors), while in the third movement, two different modes of sampling are combined with FM synthesis in the upper layer. There are links between sonic resources used in movements 1 and 2, as well as between movements 2 and 3. The four layers of each movement are further differentiated by the use of different performance variables, such as manual changes in the delay,

Figure 9.9
Typology of sonic materials for *Furies and Voices*

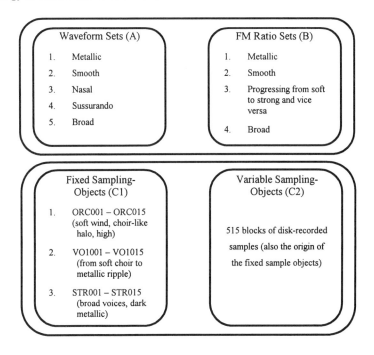

Figure 9.10
Orchestral palette for *Furies and Voices*

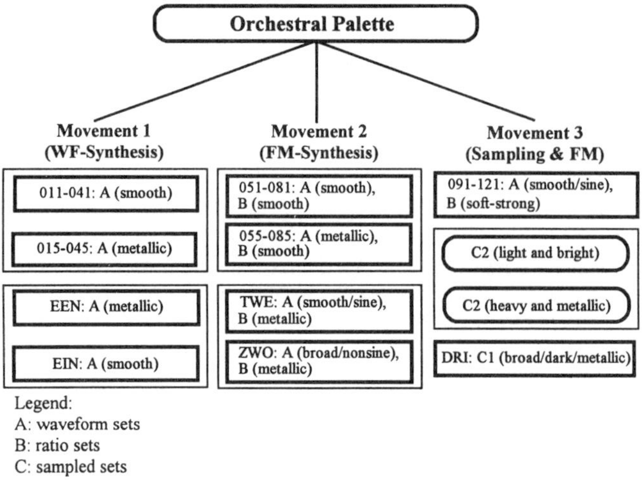

Legend:
A: waveform sets
B: ratio sets
C: sampled sets

duration, and frequency parameters. Especially in movement 3, the FM synthesis voice is crafted in terms of the sampled materials; it was substantially revised from its original form, and was treated almost improvisationally. Because of time constraints, a similar treatment of materials used in the first two movements had to be foregone.

In a postprocessing phase in the composer's own studio, various registrations of the end material generated at Simon Fraser University were produced over several months (1989–1990). This prolonged working period guaranteed a distance from the raw compositional result that is unattainable immediately after its production. Also, postprocessing showed the relevance of analog means for the definitive shaping of a computer-generated composition—the need to subordinate the work computers can do to one's own hands, and to the final arbiter, the mind's ear. Having forgotten its strategies, memory was free to pay attention to the composition on its own terms, and esthetic judgments became possible where only technical ones were present before. Viewed in retrospect, what Ignace Meyerson called *l'instauration* (Meyerson 1949, Vecchione 1990), the process—by which a work is conceived, produced, distributed, received, and analyzed—came to be seen as being of an importance equal to that of the work itself. This marriage of the work and the process that generated it may remain, despite of all analyses, an anthropological and musicological mystery. To explore this linkage would seem to be the supreme task of any musicology.

CONCLUSION

In commenting on the process that led to *Furies and Voices*, I hope to have demonstrated the following:

1. The incorporation of programmed "intelligence" (rule sets) into human problem solving, made possible by computer programs
2. The complexity of compositional expertise as woven together from strands of learning, planning, analysis, design, and production/monitoring
3. The interleaving of different kinds of tasks
4. The relevance of the strategic use of memory as the composer's "inner task environment"
5. The cognitive benefits of a task environment in which diverse, even opposite, approaches to composition can be pursued and merged
6. The interdependence, as well as subtle linkage, of work and process
7. The musicological and anthropological challenge of understanding how the form of a musical work derives from the control structure of the process that generates it

With regard to research on composition theory in the field called AI and Music (Roads 1980), it is my view the most promising approach to understanding the process of composition lies in actually building artificial composers. Such programs will show in due time that neither syntactic nor emotional constraints on decision making alone suffice to make compositional processes explicit. What seems to be needed is a way of simulating the dialogue of a composer, both with himself and with his materials (Farrett 1990). Needed as well is a way of rendering the constraints composers use in formulating "musical pseudo-stories" (Laske 1986, 1990), that is, high-level semantic notions that lead a composer to develop textures, and let them follow one another in a peculiar, idiosyncratic way. Constructing artificial composers presupposes extensive knowledge-acquisition studies, in which living composers communicate their knowledge. This can readily be done in two ways: by concurrent reports in which composers speak about what they are doing at a particular moment during their process, and by retrospective reports on their process. For such studies, the already sizable repertory of programs for computer-aided composition is an indispensable aid (Bel 1990, Laske 1992).

NOTE

1. Editor's comment: The reader is reminded that this chapter is a reprint from 1992. More recent discussions regarding machine learning can be found in chapters 6 and 7 in this volume.

GLOSSARY

Acoustic model: A model of digital sound synthesis that is based on (psycho-)acoustic theory, such as waveform synthesis, frequency modulation, waveshaping, or *granular synthesis.

Delay: In the context of *granular synthesis, the delay between consecutive grains; semantically, a parameter giving rise to differences in texture (fused/detached) and rhythm.

Grain duration: In the context of *granular synthesis, the duration of an individual grain of sound (measured in milliseconds); semantically, a parameter giving rise to differences in texture (sparse/dense) and apparent speed, as well as timbre.

Granular synthesis: A model of sound synthesis first proposed by Gabor, Xenakis, and Roads according to which sound is produced by way of a large number of small sonic grains lasting on the order of ten to twenty milliseconds.

Mask: A two-dimensional quantitative representation of the temporal evolution of one or more musical parameters over time. The mask design is used to define the structure of a compositional section (sectional mask), movement (movement mask), or entire composition (basic design mask, virtual or sounding). Masks can be overlaid to form layers.

Offset: The temporal distance, measured in number of samples, between the virtual start of a stream of sound samples and any individual grain within the stream.

Preset: A sound object defined according to a particular acoustic model which serves as instrument of tone color.

Problem space: A more or less formal representation of the objects, operators, goals, and knowledge states associated with a particular well-defined problem; a term introduced by Newell and Simon (1972).

Ramp: A pattern of temporal change in a grouping of sonic parameters determining rate of change.

Sampling: The conversion of continuous sound (in analog form) to discrete digital samples manipulable by a computer program.

Sampling rate: The rate of sampling (per second) that correlates with changes in pitch.

Sampling speed: The speed of movement through a sample stream which amounts to a time expansion of the sound with no changes in pitch (a ratio of 999:1, for example, results in an expansion of one second of sound to sixteen minutes). In Truax's software, there are three types of movement through a stream of samples: fixed (size of stream samples is fixed), continuous (continuous movement through the samples), and variable (specified by an off:on ratio, where the rate of 0:1 produces normal movement through the samples, while 50:1, for example, results in 50 ms of no forward movement through samples for each 1 ms of forward movement).

Score: A two-dimensional, computer-generated, and computer-executable matrix (text file) whose rows list musical events and whose columns define the events' attributes, such as frequency, starting time, object (instrument) number, and dynamic level.

Talea (plural taleae): A fixed sequence of note durations serving as a time scheme in the composition of fourteenth-century French motets, above all by G. de Machaut.

Task environment: The social and physical habitat, or niche, in which a composer works, including his inner task environment (personal scripts, conventions, habits, and aesthetics).

Tendency mask: A high-level syntactic construct originally defined for instrumental music by G. M. Koenig (PROJECT 2, 1970) and adopted in Truax's POD systems, which defines, for each parameter, the range over time from which average values are randomly selected. In Truax's granular synthesis environment, a tendency mask is translated into *presets (objects) and *ramps.

REFERENCES

Ames, C. (1987). "Automated Composition in Retrospect: 1956–1986." *Leonardo* 20(2):169–185.

Bel, B. (1990). *Acquisition et représentation de connaissances en musique*. Ph.D. diss., Faculté des sciences et techniques de Saint-Jérôme, Université Aix-Marseille III, Marseille.

Farrett, P. (1990). *Intentional Composer: A System for Acquiring Creative Design Knowledge*. Ph.D. diss., Department of Computing and Information Science, Queen's University, Kingston, Ontario, Canada.

Gabor, D. (1947). "Acoustical Quanta and the Theory of Hearing." *Nature* 159(4044):591–594.

Kobsa, A. et al. (1990). "Bericht über den 2nd International Workshop on User Modeling." *K.I. Zeitschrift* 3(90):26 ff.

Kodratoff, Y., and G. Tecuci (1988). "Learning at Different Levels of Knowledge." In J. Boose, B. Gaines, and M. Linster, eds. *GMD-Studien 143*. Birlinghoven, Germany: Gesellschaft für Mathematik und Datenverarbeitung.

Laske, O. (1986). "Toward a Computational Theory of Musical Listening." In F. Vandamme, J. Broeckx, and H. Sabbe, eds. *Proceedings of the 1983 International Conference on Music, Ratio, and Affect*. In *Communication and Cognition* 18(4):363–392.

Laske, O. (1989). "Composition Theory: An Enrichment of Music Theory." *Interface* 18(1–2):45–59

Laske, O. (1990). "The Computer as the Artist's Alter Ego." *Leonardo* 23(1):53–66.

Laske, O. (1992). "The OBSERVER Tradition of Knowledge Acquisition." In M. Balaban, K. Ebcioglu, and O. Laske, eds. *Understanding Music with AI*. Menlo Park, CA: AAAI Press, pp. 258–289.

Meyerson, I. (1948). *Les fonctions psychologiques et les oeuvres*. Paris, France: Vrin.

Newell, A., and H. Simon (1972). *Human Problem Solving*. Englewood Cliffs, NJ: Prentice–Hall.

Pope, S., ed. (1989). *Computer Music Journal* 13(2). [Issue devoted to object-oriented software.]

Roads, C. (1978). "Automated Granular Synthesis of Sound." *Computer Music Journal* 2(2):62–63.

Roads, C., ed. (1980). *Computer Music Journal* 4(1–2). Cambridge, MA: MIT Press.

Roads, C. (1985). "Granular Synthesis of Sound." In C. Roads and J. Strawn, eds. *Foundations of Computer Music*. Cambridge, MA: MIT Press, pp. 145–159.

Roads, C. (1989). *The Music Machine*. Cambridge, MA: MIT Press.

Schaeffer, P. (1966). *Traité des objets musicaux*. Paris: Éditions du Seuil.

Schreiber G., J. Breuker, B. Bredeweg, and B. Wielinga (1988). "Modeling in KBS Development." In J. Boose, B. Gaines, and M. Linster, eds. *GMD-Studien 143*. Birlinghoven, Germany: Gesellschaft für Mathematik und Datenverarbeitung.

Truax, B. (1988a). "Real-Time Granular Synthesis with a Digital Signal Processor." *Computer Music Journal* 12(2):14–26.

Truax, B. (1988b). "GSX.DOC: Software Documentation." Technical report. Centre for the Arts, Vancouver, B.C., Canada: Simon Fraser University.

Vecchione, B. (1990). "Méthodologie de la composition—Le raisonnement créateur." *Actes du colloque musique et assistance informatique*. Marseille: Laboratoire Musique et Informatique de Marseille (MIM), pp. 69–128.

Xenakis, I. (1971). *Formalized Music*. Bloomington, IN: Indiana University Press.

10

Creating Music as an Articulation of Prelinguistic Senses of Self (A Lecture)

Otto Laske

I interpret findings of my ethnographic studies on the childhood and adolescence of living musicians, poets, and visual artists. My interpretation leads me to the hypothesis that creating music, and art making generally, is an attempt to articulate prelinguistic senses of self, or modes of experience already mastered in infancy. I use the testimony of a visual artist, Lee, to come closer to the compositional experience of the tape music composer whom I see as a creator of *personal spaces*. The chapter is in three parts, A to C.[1] In A, I introduce the topic and some ethnographic evidence regarding artistic creation in adolescence. In B, I use findings from current infancy research for leading up to the hypothesis that adolescent art making is powered by a desire to (re)turn[2] to prelinguistic senses of self. Finally, in C, I draw some conclusions from this research for the concept of composition.

PART A

Introductory Remarks

In a recent paper, Barry Truax, reviewing changes in the notion of musical composition caused by the wide public acceptance of tape music as an artistic medium, calls the contemporary composer a "postliterary" artist. By this adjective he means to convey that the written sources of music less and less function as the source of the composer's inspiration and work. At least in Western culture, the long dependency of the composer on written music seems to be coming to an end. While this does not hold for every composer and to some extent remains a matter of personal choice, this situation suggests that in musical esthetics, perhaps too little attention has been paid to the composer's cognitive-emotional development from infancy to childhood and adolescence. I see it as one of the tasks of composition theory to replace the speculatively reconstructed dead composer of the musicological tradition by the observed (interviewed) living composer of studies in artistic development. For better understanding a composer's work, as well as understanding how an individual becomes a composer in the first place, some novel thinking about artistic development is called for.

Topic of Interest

As a composer and poet who is also a developmental psychologist, I have been interested in understanding how thinking in the arts develops over the life span. My recent interest has been in the metaphors by which composers, and artists generally, represent to themselves their own compositional processes (Laske 1993, 1994a/b). It is my view that the metaphors composers employ are in part derived from the medium they work in, and, in part, stem from their life history and the "meanings of enduring quality," or life themes (Noam 1988), by which individuals interpret their life history.

As indicated in Figure 10.1, I find the following issues of interest for ethnographic research in artistic development over the life span:

1. What are the metaphors a composer uses to represent to him/herself the compositional process he/she is engaged in?
2. What, if any, are a composer's pervasive life themes (biography) that provide continuity in his/her personal and artistic life?
3. How do metaphors relate to life themes and vice versa?
4. How is life history interpreted by the composer in terms of life themes, in particular, which of his/her *senses of self* (of which below) is predominantly involved in the artistic experience?
5. How are senses of self represented by the metaphors used to describe the actual compositional process?
6. How do the metaphors used by the composer influence and structure the actual compositional process?

In this chapter, I will outline a developmental framework for approaching these questions, both independently and in relation to each other. For this purpose, I will review some of my ethnographic research on the adolescence and young adulthood of poets, visual artists, and musicians. Through my research, I have formed hypotheses as to how compositional thinking may develop between childhood and adolescence and how, therefore, the psychological development of artists might differ from those of individuals who make up their audience.

The Notion of Self

The notion of "self" used in the title could be misleading. I am not going to speculate about what is a self. I am only going to ask you to accept, for the moment, the notion of self as a label for what one might also call personal identity and, by extension, stylistic identity.

Figure 10.1
The relationships holding between the artist's life history, biography, central metaphors, and actual compositional process

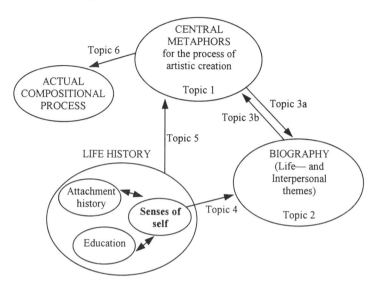

Rather than using the notion of self, I will use Daniel Stern's notion of "senses of self" (Stern 1985). A sense of self is a mode of perceptional-emotional experience. In current infancy research, this notion is used to shed light on what we know about how, during the first two years of life, an infant might experience the interpersonal, physical and social worlds. The important distinction here is that, while "self" is a metaphysical notion, "sense of self" is an experiential, phenomenological one.

Stern's Four Senses of Self

It is my hypothesis that, contrary to present theories of artistic development, much of the compositional experience of a mature artist is already mastered by the two-year-old infant. If this sounds like tiresome psychoanalytic speculation, it is only because we do not ordinarily think in developmental terms. As a consequence of our agenetic thinking, we have become accustomed to putting too much stock into the expertises and competences we as musicians learn at a later age. In terms of developmental psychology, those compositional expertises by themselves would be quite fruitless, or even impossible to acquire, were not their exercise based on a fundamental experiential matrix that, according to current research, is formed during the first two years of life. In harmony with the developmental credo, my emphasis will be on the transformations the infant's early experiences undergo over the life span, on how they become especially salient in adolescence, and on how an artist's adolescence prefigures his/her adult development.

Figure 10.2 is a diagram of Stern's hypothesis regarding senses of self, formulated by interpreting findings regarding the actually observed infant (in contrast to the speculatively reconstructed infant that has so far dominated the field of developmental psychology). As shown, Stern assumes that during the first two years of life, there emerges a succession of four distinct senses of self called the (1) emergent, (2) core, (3) (inter)subjective, and (4) verbal sense of self. What is remarkable about this formulation—at least in light of present self theories and theories of artistic development—is that the first three of these senses of self constitute an individual's prelinguistic experiences. As Stern puts it:

Infants do not attend to what domain their experience is occurring in. They take sensations, perceptions, actions, cognitions, internal states of motivation, and states of consciousness, and experience them directly in terms of intensities, shapes, temporal patterns, vitality affects, categorical affects, and hedonic tones. These are the basic elements of early subjective experience. Cognitions, actions, and perceptions as such do not exist. All experiences became recast as patterned constellations of all the infant's basic subjective elements combined. . . . This global, subjective world of emerging organization is and remains the fundamental domain of human subjectivity. It operates out of awareness as the experiential matrix from which thoughts and perceived forms, identifiable acts and verbalized feelings will later arise. (Stern 1985:67)

If Stern is correct, research in artistic development has so far been wrongheaded in that it has largely relied on adultomorph notions of how the perception and production of art develops in the child. In the adultomorph perspective, the purpose of studies in artistic development of children lies in understanding "how the

Figure 10.2
Stern's senses of self in infancy. (The box comprises Stern's three preverbal senses of self.)

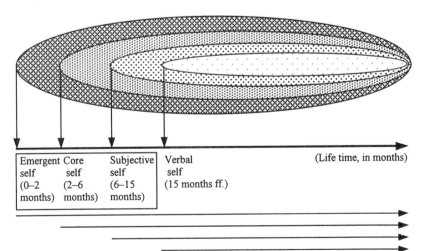

| Emergent self (0–2 months) | Core self (2–6 months) | Subjective self (6–15 months) | Verbal self (15 months ff.) | (Life time, in months) |

adult perceiver responds to and makes sense of the art form in question, how these perceptual skills develop in the child, and how the ability to produce the art form develops" (Winner 1982:11). Empirical research in infancy is now advanced enough to make us critical of adultomorph points of view. Below, I show in more detail what Stern's hypothesis entails in terms of a developmental theory of artistic composition. Let me begin by reviewing some of my findings.

Ethnographic Background

In ethnographic studies of poets (Laske 1993), musicians (Laske 1994a), and visual artists (Laske 1994b), I have tried to determine through open-ended interviews what it might be that sets an artist's adolescence apart from the more typical ways of experiencing teenage. A particularly striking occurrence in adolescence today, not only in the United States, is the intake of drugs by teenagers. Interestingly, drugs and music often go together, although perhaps more in the sense of consuming, rather than creating, music. If for adolescents music is a drug, what does that tell us about music, and why do some adolescents, whether or not they take drugs, begin engaging in a cultural symbol system such as music?

Allow me to share with you the testimony of a visual artist, Lee B., age fifty-four. Lee's particular interest is in creating what he calls personal spaces, whether by using architecture, design of interiors, photography, or video tape. Correspondingly, one might think of a composer, especially a tape music composer, as creating personal acoustic spaces.

Referring to his childhood, Lee says, "When I was a kid [of age seven]. . . I wanted to make something special that people would recognize, through which I would be in communication with mysterious others, the others that I thought existed who would understand, . . . environments wherein people could . . . contact the higher sensibilities that inside of myself were the way things should be" (op. cit.:6–7). Since age seven, Lee's lifelong urge has been to create imaginary spaces that he calls personal since they reflect his own sense of self and sensibilities (op. cit.:2–3):

I would build little paths in the woods, and then the people who were picking blackberries [would find] this little path beside the road. They would follow the path, and by that would go into my stream, . . . and when I got them in there, I realized, if I built a bridge across the stream, they would go across it, then I had them; . . . they would go through, and they looked at all the little things that I thought they would find pretty, . . . and then I'd dump them back out into the blackberry path. And I built little side paths along the way so they would have access to good berries, to motivate them, you know [laugh]. (op. cit.:39)

For Lee, adolescence stands out as a period in which the urge to create personal spaces manifested itself more imperatively and developed into a passionate interest: "that period when it started to become very clear that I had special capacities, with the compulsion to manifest them . . . and then, during that teenage, adolescence . . . was about coming out, letting it be seen to other people that you were not like them, breaking the agreement to conform."

Creating personal spaces, for him, is synonymous with dealing in preverbal realities. Now, in his middle adulthood, Lee sees making such spaces as an attempt to return to a state of oneness. He speaks most cogently about that state when conveying his view of why many adolescents take drugs:

It's my belief that a lot of adolescents take drugs because they intuit that there is a state of . . . being, of oneness that they want to reaccess, and they are not necessarily artists, so it hasn't occurred to them that they can restructure their space through metaphors, models, images, words, sounds, . . . and so they try to do it directly, . . . and they are of interest in regard to this question [of yours], whether there is this need to go back to the prelinguistic truth and reality, a relationship for life, and I think it very clearly establishes that there is. (op. cit.:7)

What Lee tells us in the above quotes is that, in his view, art making (1) is a way of making personal spaces, and (2) is based on a need, first imperatively felt in early adolescence, to reaccess a state of being he refers to as oneness. Lee also indicates (3) that what in his view sets adolescent creators apart from others is that they approach the return to prelinguistic realities indirectly, through metaphors, models, images, words, and sounds, rather than directly, through drugs. Lee views art making as an attempt to approach the longed for state of oneness indirectly, namely, by way of engaging in a symbol system provided by the culture the individual is part of.

Later in the interview, Lee uses the metaphor of the upstream wanderings of schools of salmon to express his notion of the universality of the need for a return to oneness (Laske 1994b:8). Art making, for him, is a way "to get to the space that all of us little salmons are swimming to, like we are all salmons swimming to the same home ground. . . . Some people are able to get back to that . . . spiritual space more readily, with less craziness [than I am myself]."

Instead of quoting a visual artist, I could just as well have chosen a musician. As a tape music composer, however, I find Lee's analogies and metaphors more apt than the usual literary talk musicians engage in when they speak of learning an instrument, mastering orchestration, or counterpoint. Lee suggests that artists have this in common: that they are engaged in creating personal spaces, whether architectural, acoustic, visual, kinesthetic, or metaphorical. For him, the creation of such spaces is synonymous with reaccessing prelinguistic realities. However differently artists might metaphorize their engagement with a cultural symbol system, the metaphor of a virtual space is a potent one, especially for tape music.

Below, I discuss the hypothesis that the need to reaccess prelinguistic realities constitutes a resurfacing of senses of self developmentally prior to the emergence of the verbal self at age two.

PART B

The Emergent Self

As shown in Figure 10.2, the four senses of self discussed by Stern emerge in succession, namely, from birth to two, to six, to fifteen months and beyond. Once they have emerged, they are coexistent over the life span, forming the fundamental domain of human subjectivity. Of these four senses of self the first to appear, between birth and two months, is the emergent sense of self. Stern characterizes this sense of self by two main categories: (1) amodal perception, and (2) vitality affect (in contrast to categorical affect).

Amodal perception is the capacity of the infant to translate information received in one sensory modality into another sensory modality. This seems to require an abstract representation, not of particular sounds, sights, or smells, but of global qualities of experience, such as shapes, intensities, and temporal patterns (Stern 1985:51). As Stern puts it: "While amodal perceptions will help the infant integrate potentially diverse experiences of self and other, a sense of an emergent self is concerned not only with the product but with the process of integration" (op. cit.:52). The infant's experiential process is one of composition as well as discovery (op. cit.:53): "Some properties of people and things, such as shape, intensity level, motion, number, and rhythm, are experienced directly as global, amodal perceptual qualities." According to Stern, between birth and two months, the infant is not only experiencing the result but, centrally, the process of integration. This process is one of composition (of self). In terms of the infant's affectivity, we are not dealing with categorical affects such as joy and sadness but with what Stern calls vitality affects whose expressivity he likens to that of a puppet show "where the puppets have little or no capacity to express categories of affect by way of facial signals. . . . It is from the way they move that we infer the different vitality affects from the activation contours that they trace" (op. cit.:56). Stern suggests that abstract dance and music are examples par excellence of the expressiveness of vitality affects (ibid.). This analogy seems to me to be particularly apt for tape music. In tape music, more than in music performed on instruments, the composer's and listener's attention is potentially freed from visual stimuli as well as acoustic sound sources. (As Pierre Schaefer would say, the experience of listening becomes acoulogical.) Therefore, musicians and their audience can focus on activation contours, whether they are auditory, visual, or kinesthetic. By its very nature, tape music takes the composition and perception of activation contours, and thus the engagement of vitality affects (S. Langer's [1942] forms of feeling), to another level of distinctness and autonomy.

The Other Prelinguistic Senses of Self

The subsequent sense of self to emerge in the infant, according to Stern, is the sense of core self which henceforth coexists with that of emergent self. This sense of self is based on the experience of (1) self-agency, (2) self-coherence over time and space, (3) self-affectivity, and (4) self-history. Self-history is based on recall memories that are not language based, but are preverbal. Self-affectivity is rooted in affects functioning as higher-order self-invariants. These invariants constitute the infant's preverbal identity and shape its capability of sharing feelings through attunement with others (Stern 1985:89).

Around the age of six months, what emerges is the intersubjective sense of self through which the infant becomes capable of emotional attunement to others. The infant discovers that other people have emotions, too, and that these can be shared without language. As Stern puts it: "While intersubjective relatedness transforms the interpersonal world, however, core-relatedness [and emergent self] continues. . . . The sharing of affective states is the most persuasive . . . feature of intersubjective relatedness" (op. cit.:125, 138). Importantly, the inter-subjective sense of self is centrally based on emotional attunement to others, especially caretakers. This sense of self is largely rooted in the ability of the infant to experience activation contours (first perceived through the emergent sense of self). In fact, intersubjective attunement through the shared experience of activation contours (such as eye and body movements) is a direct precursor of communication by way of language.

The Verbal Sense of Self

I would not have dwelled on each of these prelinguistic senses of self were it not that knowledge of them can serve as the background against which to appreciate the emergence of the verbal self. This emergence constitutes a major revolution in the infant's experience of prelinguistic realities which up to fifteen months have been the focus of its senses of self. The nature of the verbal revolution sheds much light on the specificity and function of the arts, all of which produce their effects on a prelinguistic level (even those that use natural language, such as poetry).

According to Stern, the infant's prelinguistic universe of experience suffers massive losses with the onset of verbal language, above all because verbal language enforces categorizations that are too impoverished to capture the richness of personal experience:

[Verbal] language can thus fracture amodal global experience. A discontinuity in experience is introduced. . . . The advent of language is a very mixed blessing to the child. What begins to be lost (or made latent) is enormous; what begins to be gained is also enormous. The infant gains entrance into a wider cultural membership, but at the risk of losing the force and wholeness of original experience. (op. cit.:176–177)

This not only holds with regard to private experiences, but with regard to interpersonal experience as well:

Language forces a space between interpersonal experience as lived and as represented. And it is exactly across this space that the connections and associations that constitute neurotic behavior may form. But also with language, infants for the first time can share their personal experience of the world with others, including "being with" others in intimacy, isolation, loneliness, fear, awe, and love. . . . Experience in the domains of emergent, core-, and intersubjective relatedness (i.e., pre-linguistic relatedness), which continues irrespective of language, can be embraced only very partially in the domain of verbal relatedness. (op. cit.:182, 162–163)

As a result there arises, in the child, a need for safeguarding realities that have been experienced in early infancy, most of which, after the advent of verbal language, go underground rather than finding their way into words. As Lee, the visual artist who spoke to us before, puts it:

Even up into . . . six [years of age], and sometimes more, a child still has a sense of personal reality wherein certain qualities are still in existence, even though they are not finding them very much in their environment, . . . they still find them enough, they don't give them up. They hold them in fantasy, they accept smaller and smaller proportions, they accept the illusion of them, the postponement of them, the belief that it will come somewhere, some other time, on their birthday, when grandma' comes, on the weekend, . . . they transfer them over into art, . . . into their dress, into other ways by which they get attention and acknowledgement. (Laske 1994b:9)

Hypothesis

Referring back to Lee's notion of the adolescent need to return to, or reaccess, prelinguistic realities, I would suggest that adolescence, for some, brings about a return to the prelinguistic senses of self first mastered in infancy, and that for an artist, this return is a central and lifelong endeavor. It is not a return to the same place, however, but an interpretation, thus a transformation, of earlier experiences by way of more sophisticated cognitive-emotional means. The return is an attempt to reclaim territory lost during language development since age two. In light of studies of artistic development in childhood, this return is moreover a way to exit from the so-called literal stage of artistic development that, during the period of seven to twelve years of age, tends to replace the artistic flowering of the younger child aged five to seven.

In developmental studies on children's art making and aesthetic perception, one speaks of the U-shaped curve of artistic development. By this one means that from age seven on, children tend to become preoccupied with obeying rules and following conventions in their artistic production. Therefore, as is depicted by the bottom line of the U-shape, children lose the freedom of experimentation that characterizes the five to seven year olds. As a consequence, only very few, so-called gifted individuals manage to sustain their interest in the arts beyond age twelve. This developmental fact raises the questions of (1) how these exceptional individuals manage to sustain their artistic involvement with a cultural symbol system (e.g., music), and (2) how the adult development of these individuals differs from those who do not recover from the devastations of the social contract of language use, and who, therefore, get stuck at the literal stage of aesthetic/artistic development.

How, then, is adolescent creativity to be accounted for? My developmental hypothesis is twofold. First, it is on account of two capacities that an individual can sustain the sense of prelinguistic realities, and therefore can make the effort of acquiring the expertise required to articulate these realities within a cultural symbol system (such as music). The two capacities I have in mind are the capacities for solitude and for holding passionate interests (Laske 1994b). The two are related. One could define solitude, with Modell (1993:127), as a state in which one is sustained by passionate interests.

In contrast to loneliness, solitude implies that someone is present. This someone has sometimes been addressed as "the muse." My guess is that an individual's prelinguistic experiences are fully capable of serving as the foundation for sustaining solitude and having discourse with the muse. In light of this hypothesis, gifted individuals are those who discover that through engagement in a symbol system, whether by using words, images, sounds, or other symbolic media, they can get away with *being themselves*, by negotiating their social acceptance through fashioning products of their imagination.

My second hypothesis is that the return to the prelinguistic sense of self in some, but not all, adolescents has to do with the individual's nascent interpretation of his/her life history in terms of themes, as diagrammed in Figure 10.1. (This hypothesis stands in opposition to cognitive-structural and life-phase theories of adult development and artistic development that I will not detail here.) Life themes are those meanings of enduring quality by which an individual, even unconsciously, understands his/her own life history in terms of semantic invariants determining much of what is essential in that individual's life. For Lee, for instance, the overriding theme of his life is that of "engagement" (Laske 1994b:4):

OL: If you had to use a single abstraction to identify the issue you were dealing with then, . . . in your early adolescence, what notion would you use?
Lee: In early adolescence? It might be the same thing as now, engagement.
OL: Engagement?
Lee: I think that'll do tentatively.
OL: So o.k., [engagement] with people?
Lee: No, with myself.

Lee speaks most articulately about the nature of this engagement when speaking of the failures he experiences in his art making at the present time:

The relationship with myself doesn't produce works, at this point, that are sufficiently . . . an encoding of a personal realization [such] that the decoding of it by another person would give them the experience of being in link with someone's personal experience . . .; so the work does not contain it yet. . . . That's what I am currently on right now [i.e., at age fifty-four], . . . turning these [experimental realities] into actual, engaged things that aren't just [theater] sets and props and illusions. (op. cit.:6)

Engagement, and making engaged things, then, is the life theme in terms of which this particular artist sees his adult development. I could give you other examples, elicited through interviews with poets and musicians, that show similar semantic invariants providing continuity in their lives (Laske 1993, Laske 1994a).

We do not at this point understand too well how the experience of prelinguistic realities (i.e., prelinguistic senses of self) during infancy and early childhood may be linked to the formation of life themes. One might suggest that artists maintain a better hold on prelinguistic senses of self than do other individuals. Let me restate one of Lee's earlier statements:

Even up into . . . six [years of age], and sometimes more, a child still has a sense of personal reality wherein certain qualities are still in existence, even though they are not finding them very much in their environment, . . . they still find them enough, they don't give them up. They hold them in fantasy, they accept smaller and smaller proportions, they accept the illusion of them, the postponement of them, the belief that it will come somewhere, some other time, on their birthday, when grandma' comes, on the weekend, . . . they transfer them over into art, . . . into their dress, into other ways by which they get attention and acknowledgement. (Laske 1994b:9)

The Case of Tape Music

Returning to Figure 10.1 from this vantage point, I think it would be interesting to discover what are the metaphors composers of music use to present to themselves their compositional process and to look for empirical links between such metaphors and the meanings of enduring quality (life themes) by which they interpret their life history. One might then find that musicians drawn to tape music articulate a different sense of prelinguistic realities than do writers of instrumental music (This is my third hypothesis.)

PART C

On the Concept of Composition

I have suggested that in developmental terms, artistic composition is a particular case of composition of self (modes of experience) by way of integrating different senses of self through engagement in a symbol system. In particular, it is the prelinguistic senses of self first mastered in infancy that are reaccessed by the artist. It is my hunch that the composition of art works, and the composition of self in infancy before the emergence of the verbal self, have many things in common. Both a piece of music and what, in this culture, we refer to as "self" are a work of art in that they are composed by the individual in question and are utterly unique. Composition in an artistic medium might therefore be seen as a symbolic activity by which the composition of self is enhanced over an individual's lifetime, in a way that is thought provoking, and possibly life changing, for other individuals sharing the artist's culture.

Developmentally, what matters is not that there is a return to infancy, as psychoanalysis would have it. One never steps into the same river twice. The challenge for a developmental aesthetics is, rather, to understand what are the transformations whereby the prelinguistic realities experienced in infancy are readied, across childhood and adolescence, to emerge into what our culture sanctions as art making and, relatedly, artistic creativity. In the domain of music, the developmental esthetics of tape music is an open field for future discoveries.

NOTES

1. Editor's Comment: This lecture was presented during the "Technology and the Composer" conference held in 1994 at the Bibliothèque Nationale de Luxembourg and, subsequently, at the University of Maryland at College Park. It is published here for the first time.

2. Editor's comment: By "(re)turn" Laske intends to articulate the appropriateness of both words—"turn" and "return"—in this context. See under heading, Hypothesis, on page 177.

REFERENCES

Langer, S. (1942). *Philosophy in a New Key*. Cambridge, MA: Harvard University Press.

Laske, O. (1976). "On Some Developmental Problems of Auditory Imagery." *International Review of the Sociology and Aesthetics of Music* 7(1):77–82.

Laske, O. (1993). "What has Poetry Writing Meant to You Over Your Life Time?" Unpublished manuscript, Harvard University Graduate School of Education.

Laske, O. (1994a). "Bryan: a Case Study in the Relationship of Psychosocial and Psychosymbolic Self." Unpublished manuscript, Harvard University Graduate School of Education.

Laske, O. (1994b). "Bargaining for Personal Space by Way of Creating it: the Dialectic of Psychosymbolic and Psychosocial Self." Unpublished manuscript, Harvard University Graduate School of Education.

Laske, O. (1994c). "What Artistic Development Tells About Adult Development." Invited paper, Ninth Annual Conference on Adult Development, Society for Adult Development, University of Massachusetts, Amherst.

Modell, A. (1993). *The Private Self*. Cambridge, MA: Harvard University Press.

Noam, G. (1988). "A Constructivist Approach to Developmental Psychopathology." In E. Nannis et al., eds. *New Directions for Child Development*, no. 39. [Title of volume: *Developmental Psychopathology and its Treatment*.] San Francisco, CA: Jossey Bass.

Stern, D. (1985). *The Interpersonal World of the Infant: A View from Psychoanalysis and Developmental Psychology*. New York: Basic Books.

Strauss, S., ed. (1982). *U-shaped Behavioral Growth*. New York: Academic Press.

Winner, E. (1982). *Invented Worlds*. Cambridge, MA: Harvard University Press.

11

The Newcomp Experiment
Curtis Roads

While many of the texts in this volume will undoubtedly traverse the abstract dimensions of Otto Laske's thought, another aspect of the man deserves highlighting, namely his central role on the ground floor of building the Newcomp arts organization. In its essence, this experiment stood for the power of collective artistic action as a response to the deeply rooted predicament of the arts in America (Miller 1944).

In the gray spring of 1980 I arrived in Cambridge, Massachusetts to take a new position at MIT. I knew no one in the area but had written down the name and address of Dr. Otto Laske as a contact. We had exchanged correspondence concerning an article he submitted to *Computer Music Journal,* of which I was the editor. I met him at his apartment on Commonwealth Avenue in Boston. As a researcher, I shared Dr. Laske's intense interest in making computer systems more "musically intelligent." As a composer, I was also curious about the Boston new music scene. At that time it appeared that the split between modern music and audiences was at its peak. In a Saturday evening concert at Harvard I witnessed a chamber orchestra performing to about a dozen people scattered sparsely in the cavernous space of Sanders Theater. Soon afterward a string quartet performed with great seriousness for three people in the audience, one of whom was the composer. Concert programs were dominated by compositions in an arid academic idiom. The presentations were drab and unimaginative, with little attention paid to theatrical realities such as stage lighting. Electronic music, if it was presented at all, was assigned a marginal role. I will always remember the spectacle of a highly publicized "mixed" (instrument and tape) concert featuring Luciano Berio. Sitting in the front row, maestro Berio had to lean out of his seat to adjust the volume knob of a power amplifier situated awkwardly on stage, since no one had bothered to arrange for the amenity of a mixing console. Connected to the amplifier were two thin-sounding loudspeakers at the rear of the stage. At the reception I approached the music director of this concert to politely suggest an improvement to their presentation of electronic music. He informed me bluntly that the electronic aspect was not a priority. The general attitude of the presenters seemed to be: "Who cares if you listen?"

It was in this atmosphere that Otto and I began to discuss the formation of a more creative and dynamic music association: the New England Computer Music Association (Newcomp). We found common ground in the vision of a more open and experimental view of new music, and in the integration of many art forms in performance. Indeed, as artistic codirectors, we later replaced the term "Computer Music" with "Computer Arts" to stress our mixed-media intersects.

With characteristic thoroughness, Otto attended to the details of the drawn-out legal arrangements. Our first concerts in 1981 took place in a renovated factory space called the Village Street Theater, operated by Otto's friend, the artist Be Allen. This fresh space projected well the new ambience we hoped to generate: brick walls, a high wooden ceiling, large glass windows, and for decoration, a gigantic crane hook hanging down from the center of the ceiling like a kind of Industrial Age chandelier.

We wanted to build a new audience. To this end we organized programs around innovative themes, such as "Computer Sound and Light Spectacle," "Live Computer Music and Dance," "European Computer Music," and "Computer Music and Poetry." (The interspersion of poetry and music is a wonderful combination, by the way, even though they are rarely heard in the same concert.) In the first two seasons we organized twelve concerts, including ten in the Boston area and two at the International Music Institute in Darmstadt, Germany. Publicity and theatrical aspects such as lighting had been mastered. We made posters, printed and mailed press releases, and did radio interviews.

Over time we learned many lessons about presenting music in the "real" world. One secret to concert programming is to intersperse diverse tendencies and media. Contrasts articulate the uniqueness of each work, and give the audience clear choices. A complex, cerebral work can be counterbalanced, for example, by lighter or more visual works. Far from detracting from the more serious music, lighter elements enhance the presentation by serving as transitions between more concentrated listening. A similar principle applies in the case of taped electroacoustic music. Audiences will devote full attention to a tape work provided that it is "performed" in concert over a multichannel sound system and sandwiched in between works with more visual elements.

We felt it was important to educate composers, other artists, and the public about the creative possibilities of computer media. To this end we organized summer workshops on computer music using space generously provided by Digital Music Systems in Boston. And from 1983 to 1990 Newcomp sponsored a major annual composition competition open to musicians from around the world.

The legacy of Newcomp is now history: sixty-five events, more than three hundred artists showcased, dozens of premieres, not to forget symposia, workshops, and the annual international competition. One might ask how all this activity was funded? Hardly at all. Newcomp was never particularly favored by the Massachusetts Arts Council, but we were grateful for the tiny annual grant they did provide. Artists need to create and will do so in the absence of incentive. But the organization of performing arts events and festivals—cultural animation as the French call it—cannot exist without funding. We quite depended on our grant for hall rental and publicity. The organization was fortunate to find good venues for many concerts, such as the auditorium at First Church in Harvard Square. Concerts were generally well attended, occasionally sold out, and audiences paid a donation. Many performers and visual artists contributed their time, and a network of volunteers offered valuable labor and counsel. I was always amazed at how Otto managed to rally diverse people to the service of Newcomp.

Newcomp required a great deal of personal time, and after six years of service to the organization I stepped down as artistic director to allow more hours for other projects. Otto carried on for several years. But political winds started shifting to the right in the late 1980s. The arts became the target of orchestrated political attacks. In this unhealthy climate, the budgets of vital arts organizations across America were greatly reduced, the victims of ignorance. Newcomp's funding went with it. Thanks largely to Otto's efforts, this collective energy had managed to survive for more than a decade. It was a noble experiment, and I hope it will serve as an example to future generations of creative artists.

REFERENCE

Miller, H. (1944). *The Plight of the Creative Artist in The United States of America.* Berkeley: Bern Porter.

Bibliography

Selected Works of Otto Laske
(1964–1998)

(In reverse chronological order, by category)

COMPOSITIONS

Music a Cappella

Des Menschen Seele gleicht dem Wasser (1987). 4 voices, SATB. Text: J. W. Goethe. 11:00 minutes. Composed using PROJECT 1.

Nachtstücke (1981). 12 voices, SATB. Text: O. Laske. 17:30 minutes. Composed using PROJECT 1.

Quatre Fascinants (1971, Revised 1992). 3 altos and 3 tenors. Text: R. Char. 7:45 minutes.

Tristis est anima mea (1968). SATB. Text: Liturgy. 3:00 minutes.

Kyrie Eleison (1968). 36 solo voices. Text: Liturgy. 12:00 minutes.

Motet (1964). SATB. Text: German Liturgy. 3:00 minutes.

Music for Solo Voice and Chamber Ensemble

Voices of Night (1985). Mezzo soprano and string quartet [no. 2]. Text: O. Laske. 13:00 minutes. Composed using PROJECT 1.

Vocalise (1982). Soprano, cello, and percussion. Text: O. Laske. 13:00 minutes. Composed using PROJECT 1 .

Ils sont heureux (1969). Baritone, trombone, and piano. Text: Guillevic. 4:50 minutes.

Klage (1968). Alto and cello. Text: O. Laske. 3:15 minutes.

Inçantation (1967). 2 sopranos, alto, tenor, choir 1 (altos), choir 2 (tenors), 2 trumpets, trombone, viola, percussion. 5:00 minutes (fragment). [Graphic score.]

De Aegypto (1965). Tenor, harp, horn, viola, and percussion. Text: E. Pound. 9:00 minutes.

Song (1965). Soprano and piano. Text: V. Millay. 2:50 minutes.

Instrumental Chamber Music

Organ Piece (in progress). Organ and percussion. ca 10 minutes. Composed using PROJECT 1.

String Quartet No. 3 (1997). 10:30 minutes. Composed using PROJECT 2.

Interchanges for Two Pianos [Piano Piece no. 3] (1986). 10:30 minutes. Composed using PROJECT 1.

Screening (1985). Flute and percussion. 15:00 minutes. Composed using PROJECT 1.

Atlantis (1983). Guitar, clarinet (or recorders). 11:30 minutes. Composed using PROJECT 1.

Reflections for Brass Quintet (1983). 2 trumpets, trombone, horn, and tuba. 10:30 minutes. Composed using PROJECT 1.

Perturbations (1979). Flute, clarinet, violin, viola, cello, piano, and 2 percussion. 13:00 minutes. Composed using PROJECT 1.

Monologue intérieur (1968). Horn and viola. 3:00 minutes.

Vienne la nuit sonne l'heure (1968). Clarinet, cello, and percussion. 5:15 minutes.

Woodwind Quintet (1967, revised 1972). Flute, oboe, clarinet, bass clarinet, and bassoon. 6:00 minutes.

How Time Passes (1967, version 2, 1969). Oboe, English horn, bassoon, 2 horns, 2 trumpets, trombone, tuba, and piano. 15:00 minutes.

Duet No. 2 (1967). Violoncello and piano. 1:30 minutes.

Radiation (1966). Clarinet, bass clarinet, soprano saxophone, 2 trumpets, 2 trombones, strings, and 2 percussion. 6:00 minutes.

Time Points II (1966) [Version 2 of String Quartet No. 1]. Double string quartet. 7:15 minutes.

Time Points I (1966) [Version 1 of String Quartet No. 1]. Double string quartet. 4:30 minutes.

Duet No. 1 (1965). Violoncello and piano. 1:30 minutes.

Music for Solo Instruments

Match for Piano [Piano Piece no. 4] (1989). Variable, e.g. 8:00 minutes. Composed using PRECOMP.

Immersion (1988). Saxophone. 13:00 minutes. Composed using PRECOMP.

Soliloquy (1984) Double bass. 12:00 minutes. Composed using PROJECT 1.

Fluctuations (1982). Flute. 9:00 minutes. Composed using Xenakis' ST-10.

Cantus (1970, revised 1976). Violin. 15:00 minutes.

Piano Piece No. 2 (1969, revised 1977). 7:00 minutes.

Piano Piece No. 1 (1967, revised 1977) 5:45 minutes.

Four Studies (1964). Piano. 6:30 minutes.

Music for Orchestra

Symmetries (1982). 3 Flutes, 3 clarinets, 3 oboes, 3 English horns, 3 bassoons, 4 horns, 3 trumpets, 3 trombones, tuba, 12 violins, 8 violas, 6 cellos, 5 double basses, harp, and 3 percussion. 11:00 minutes. Composed using PROJECT 1.

Music for Tape

TwinSister (1995). Text: O. Laske. 16:00 minutes. Composed using KYMA System.

Treelink (1992). Speaker and tape. Poem by Otto Laske. 14:15 minutes. Composed using KYMA System. Released on "Electro Acoustic Music V" CD (Neuma), 1996.

Hallucination (1991) [replaces *Mediation* of 1980/81]. 8:30 minutes. Composed using PROJECT 1 and CSOUND.

Furies and Voices (1989–1990). 10:30 minutes. Composed using PODX and DMX-DSP. Released on "Electro Acoustic Music VI" CD (Neuma), 1998.

In Memory (1988, revised 1991)[replaces *Strata*]. 8:25 minutes. Composed using PROJECT 1 and CSOUND.

La Forêt Enchantée (1987). 8:30 minutes. Composed using PROJECT 1 and DMX-1000/DMX-DSP.

Voie Lactée (1984). 11:15 minutes. Composed using PROJECT 1 and DMX-1000/DMX-DSP.

Terpsichore (1980). 14:00 minutes. Composed using PROJECT 1 and SSSP.

Message to the Messiah (1978, revised 1991). 16:30 minutes. Composed with Buchla Synthesizer as sound source using *musique concrète* techniques.

Brainstorms [*Structure IX*] (1975, revised 1990). 11:30 minutes. Composed using POD.

Objects and Spaces [*Structure VIII*] (1975, revised 1990). 12:00 minutes. Composed using POD.

De Profundis [*Structure VII*] (1974, revised 1990). Text by O. Laske. 16:00 minutes. Composed using Voltage Control Synthesis.

Eruptions [*Structure VI*] (1974, revised 1990). 19:45 minutes. Composed using Voltage Control Synthesis.

Structure V (1973, revised 1990). 18:00 minutes. Composed using POD.

Distances and Proximities [*Structure IV*] (1973, revised 1990). 16:30 minutes. Composed using POD.

Nature's Self [*Structure III.2*] (1972, revised 1990). 5:20 minutes. Composed using Voltage Control Synthesis.

Nature's Dream [*Structure III.1*] (1972, revised 1990). 8:30 minutes. Composed using Voltage Control Synthesis.

From Here to Infinity [*Structure II.2*] (1971, revised 1990). 11:25 minutes. Composed using *musique concrète* techniques.

Exorcism [*Structure II.1*] (1971, revised 1990). 6:00 minutes. Composed using *musique concrète* techniques.

Inner Spaces [*Structure I.2*] (1970, revised 1990). 7:10 minutes. Composed using *musique concrète* techniques.

Perpetuum Mobile [*Structure I.1*] (1970, revised 1990). 5:00 minutes. Composed using *musique concrète* techniques.

Abgesang [not preserved] (1967). Composed using voltage control synthesis.

CHOREOGRAPHY

Vitre (1973). Graphic Score. One or more dancers. Text by R. Char. Approximately 20 minutes.

Transitions (1967). Graphic score. 3 dancers, clarinet, bass clarinet, guitar, percussion, and vocal sounds by dancers. 5:45 minutes.

POETRY

Collections

Becoming What I See: Poetry, 1985–1995. Submitted for publication.

1999

Brunnentür des Wunsches [*Well of Desire*]: *Gedichte, 1955–1995*. Munich, Germany: Verlag-Klaus Friedrich.

1981

Miniaturen [*Miniatures*]. German. Self-publication.

1976

Tönungen [*Soundings*] (1956–1968). German. Self-publication.

Individual poems

1998

"Northern German Garden." *Salamander* (Fall). Brookline, MA.

1993

"Eigenheim" ["Condominium"] and "Zurück" ["Native Tongue" (from *Miniaturen*)]. *Osiris* 37 (December). Deerfield, MA.

1992

"Morgen" ["Daybreak"], "Mistral" (from *Tönungen*). *Osiris* 35 (December). Deerfield, MA.

"Blue Light," "The Answer," "Fir Tree." *Atelier* 3(2) (December). Boston.

"Bitte" ["Supplication"], "Mischfarbe" ["Color Mix" (from *Tönungen*)]. *LOG Zeitschrift für internationale Literatur*. Ausgabe 55. Vienna, Austria.

"Ramada Inn." *NorthEastArts Magazine* 1(2). Boston.

"Abfahrt" ["Departure"], "Hand" ["Hand"], "Himmelsfarben" ["Sky Coloring"], "Wirklichkeit" ["Gap"] (from *Miniaturen*); "Engel" ["Angel"] (from *Tönungen*). *Rind & Schlegel* 23. Munich, Germany: Verlag-Klaus Friedrich.

"Härte" ["Severity"], "Irdische Landschaft" ["Earthly Scene"; from *Tönungen*]. *Osiris* 34 (July), Deerfield, MA.

1980
"Sirenes," "Angel," "Seafaring," "Flight," "Nightfall," "Winter Morning," "Black Angel," "Smile," "Farewell to Los Angeles." In K. Gaburo, ed. *ALLOS: 'Other' Language.* La Jolla, CA: Lingua Press.

1979
"Afternoon," "Black Angel," "Embrace," "Loss," "Seasons." *Five Laske Songs.* Music by Keith Thorp (BMI).

COGNITIVE SCIENCE AND THE ARTS

1997
"What Artistic Developmental Tells About Adult Development." In N. Zahler, ed. *Sixth Biennial Symposium for Arts and Technology.* Connecticut College, New London, CT., pp. 93–115.
"Four Uses of Self in Cognitive Science: The No-Man's Land Between Mindware and Mind." In P. Pylkkänen, P. Pylkkö, and A. Hautamäki, eds., *Brain, Mind, and Physics.* Amsterdam, The Netherlands: IOS Press. [Reprinted from In P. Pylkkänen and P. Pylkkö, eds. *Proceedings of the 1995 International Symposium on the New Directions of Cognitive Science.* Saariselkä, Finland. Hakapaino, Helsinki: Publications of the Finnish Artificial Intelligence Society.]

1996
"Knowledge Technology and the Arts: A Personal View." *Computers and Mathematics with Applications* 32(1):85–88. Special issue on mathematics, computers, and music, M. Witten, ed. [Also in *Proceedings of the 1993 SEAMUS Conference.* Austin, TX.]

1993
"Creativity: Where Do We Look For It?" Invited paper, National Conference on AI, Workshop on Creativity, Stanford University, Palo Alto, CA. In T. Dartnall, ed. *Creativity, Cognition, and Computation.* The AAAI/MIT Press, 1996.
"Mindware and Software: Can They Meet?: Observations on AI and the Arts." *Proceedings of the International Workshop on Knowledge Technology in the Arts.* Osaka, Japan, pp. 1–18. Keynote address.
"Understanding Music with AI." *Proceedings of the First International Conference on Cognitive Musicology.* Jyväskylä, Finland: University of Jyväskylä Department of Music, pp. 270–276.
"An Epistemic Approach to Musicology." In G. Haus, ed. *Music Processing.* Madison, WI: A-R Editions, Inc., pp. 109–118.
"In Search of a Generative Grammar for Music." In S. Schwanauer et al. eds. *Machine Models of Music.* Cambridge, MA: MIT Press. [Reprinted from *Per-*

spectives of New Music Fall/Winter 1973 and Spring/Summer 1974 (Double issue):351–378.]

"A Search for a Theory of Musicality." *Languages of Design—Formalisms for Word, Image and Sound* 1(3):209–228.

1992

Understanding Music with AI. M. Balaban, K. Ebcioglu, and O. Laske, eds. Menlo Park, CA: AAAI Press.

"AI and Music: A Cornerstone of Cognitive Musicology." In M. Balaban, K. Ebcioglu, and O. Laske, eds. *Understanding Music with AI.* Menlo Park, CA: AAAI Press, pp. 3–28.

"Foreword: A Conversation with Marvin Minsky." Foreword to *Understanding Music with AI.* Menlo Park, CA: The AAAI Press, pp. ix–xxx [Reprinted in *AI Magazine* 13(3):31–45.]

1991

"Understanding Music with AI." *Proceedings of the 1991 International Computer Music Conference.* Montreal, P.Q., Canada, McGill University: ICMA, pp. 188–191.

1989

"Introduction to Cognitive Musicology." *The Journal of Musicological Research* 9:1-22. [Reprinted from (1988) *Computer Music Journal* 12(1):43–57. Also in *Kognitiivinen musiikkitiede.* Jyväskylä, Finland: Jyväskylän yliopiston musiikkitieteen laitoksen julkaisusarja A: tutkielmia ja raportteja 8, 1992.]

"Composition as Hypothesis Formation: A Blackboard Model of Compositional Creativity." In V. Marik, ed. *Proceedings of AI 1989.* Prague, Czechoslovakia: Czechoslovakian Society for Cybernetics and the Prague University Department of Electrical Engineering, pp. 239–250. [Reprinted in *Knowledge-Based Systems* 3(1):36–41.]

1988

"Can We Formalize and Program Musical Knowledge?: An Inquiry into the Focus and Scope of Cognitive Musicology." In M. Boroda, ed. *Musikometrika I.* Bochum, Germany: Studienverlag N. Brockmeyer, pp. 257–280.

1986

"Editor's Introduction, Cognitive Musicology." *CC-AI* 3(3):159–183.

"On Competence and Performance Notions in Expert System Design." In J. Rault, ed., *Actes, Sixièmes Journées Internationales sur les Systèmes Experts and Leurs Applications.* Paris La Défense: Agence de l'Informatique, pp. 257–298.

1984

"Understanding Listening Procedurally." *Sonus* 5(1):61–71.

1983

Music and Mind: An Artificial Intelligence Perspective, vol. 1–2. Collected papers published 1971–1981. San Francisco, CA.: International Computer Music Association.

1979

"On Problems of Verification in Music Theory." *College Music Symposium* 19(2):129–139.

1977

"Musicology and Psychomusicology: Two Sciences of Music." *Journal of the Indian Musicological Society* 8(2):1–24.

"Introduction to Psychomusicology." *Journal of the Indian Musicological Society* 8(2):25–54.

Music, Memory, and Thought: Explorations in Cognitive Musicology. Ann Arbor, MI: University Micro Films International.

1975

"On Psychomusicology." *International Review of the Sociology & Aesthetics of Music* 6(2): 269–281.

"Toward a Theory of Musical Cognition." *Interface* 4(2):147–208.

1974

"Musical Semantics: A Procedural Point of View." In *Actes du congrès de sémiotique musicale.* Pesaro, Italy: Centro di iniziativa culturale, pp. 214–224.

"Toward a Center for Musical Intelligence Studies." *Numus West* 5:44–46.

"Musical Acoustics (Sonology): A Questionable Science Reconsidered." *Numus West* 6:35–40.

"The Information Processing Approach to Musical Cognition." *Interface* 3(2):109–136.

"On the Methodology and Implementation of a Procedural Theory of Music." *Proceedings of the International Conference on Computers in the Humanities.* St. Paul, MN (1973). Edinburgh, Scotland: Edinburgh University Press.

1973

"In Search of a Generative Grammar for Music." *Perspectives of New Music* Fall/Winter 1973 and Spring/Summer 1974 (Double issue):351–378.

Introduction to a Generative Theory of Music. Utrecht, The Netherlands: Institute of Sonology.

"Toward a Musical Intelligence System: OBSERVER." *Numus West* 4:11–16.

1972

"On Musical Strategies With a View to a Generative Grammar for Music." *Interface* 1(2):111–125.

On Problems of a Performance Model for Music. Utrecht, The Netherlands: Institute of Sonology.

1971

"An Acoulogical Performance Model for Music." *Electronic Music Reports 4.* Utrecht, The Netherlands: Institute of Sonology.

THE ARTS IN HUMAN DEVELOPMENT

1995

The Imaginative Self: Essays. West Medford, MA: Self-publication.

1994

"Creating Music as an Articulation of Pre-Linguistic Senses of Self." Invited lecture, Conference on "Technology and the Composer." Bibliothèque Nationale de Luxembourg and University of Maryland at College Park, MD. [Published for the first time as chapter 10 of this volume.]

"What Artistic Development Tells About Adult Development." Invited paper. Ninth Annual Adult Development Symposium. University of Massachusetts, Amherst.

1979

"Goal Synthesis and Goal Pursuit in a Musical Transformation Task for Children Between Seven and Twelve Years of Age." *Interface* 9(2):207–235.

1976

"On Some Developmental Problems of Auditory Imagery." *International Review of the Sociology and Aesthetics of Music* 7(1):77–82.

"Toward a Theory of Musical Instruction." *Interface* 5(3):125–148.

KNOWLEDGE ACQUISITION FOR KNOWLEDGE-BASED SYSTEMS

1993

"Technology Management as Action Research: Challenges for Organizational Re-Education." *CC-AI* 10(1):235–284.

1992

"The OBSERVER Tradition of Knowledge Acquisition." In M. Balaban, K. Ebcioglu, and O. Laske, eds. *Understanding Music with AI.* Menlo Park, CA: AAAI Press, pp. 258–289.

1990

"On the Acquisition of Compositional Knowledge in Music." In V. Marik, ed. *Proceedings of AI 1990.* Prague, Czechoslovakia: Czechoslovakian Society for Cybernetics and the Prague University Department of Electrical Engineering, pp. 278–298.

"A Course in Knowledge Management." Landsberg, Germany: WIC GmbH.

1989

"Articulating Musical Intuitions by Way of Rules." *Proceedings of the Second International Workshop on Artificial Intelligence and Music.* Detroit, MI. Menlo Park, CA: American Association for Artificial Intelligence, pp. 148–173.

DESIGN OF INTERFACES FOR COMPUTER MUSIC SYSTEMS

1985

"Considering Human Memory in Designing User Interfaces for Computer Music Systems." In C. Roads, ed. *Foundations of Computer Music.* Cambridge, MA:MIT Press, pp. 551–567. [Reprinted from (1978) *Computer Music Journal* 2(4):39–45.]

1978

"Understanding the Behavior of Users of Interactive Computer Music Systems." *Interface* 7(2):159–168.

1977

"Toward a Theory of User Interfaces for Computer Music Systems." *Computer Music Journal* 1(4):53–60.

THEORY OF MUSIC ANALYSIS AND LISTENING

1986

"Toward a Computational Theory of Musical Listening." In F. Vandamme, J. Broeckx, and H. Sabbe, eds. *Proceedings of the 1983 International Conference on Music, Reason, and Emotion.* In *Communication and Cognition* 18(4):363–392.

1984

"Keith: A Rule System for Making Music-Analytical Discoveries." In M. Baroni and L. Callegari, eds. *Proceedings of the 1982 International Conference on Musical Grammars and Computer Analysis.* Florence, Italy: Leo S. Olschki, pp. 165–200.

1980

"Toward an Explicit Theory of Musical Listening." *Computer Music Journal* 4(2):73–83.

1977

"Toward a Process Model of Musical Structures." *Proceedings of the International Workshop on the Cognitive Viewpoint.* Rijksuniversiteit Gent, Ghent, Belgium: Communication and Cognition, pp. 295–304.

THEORY OF COMPOSITION

1992

"*Furies and Voices*: Composition-Theoretical Observations." In D. Baggi, ed. *Readings in Computer-Generated Music.* Los Alamitos, CA: IEEE Press, pp. 181–197. [Also in *Proceedings of the Third Arts and Technology Symposium*, Connecticut College. New London, CT, pp. 180–192. Reprinted in this volume as chapter 9.]

1991

"Toward an Epistemology of Composition." *Interface* 20(3–4):235–269. (Otto Laske, ed.)

"Two Paradigms of Music Research: Composition and Listening." In B. Bel and B. Vecchione, eds. *Actes, Colloque Musique et assistance informatique.* Marseille, France: Laboratoire Musique et Informatique Marseille, pp. 179–185.

"Composition musicale et assistance informatique: Un exemple de composition interprétative." In B. Bel and B. Vecchione, eds. *Actes, séminaire créativité en art.* Université Aix-en-Provence: Centre de Recherche en Sciences de la Musique.

1990

"The Computer as the Artist's Alter Ego." *Leonardo* 23(1):53–66.

1989

"Composition Theory: An Enrichment of Music Theory." *Interface* 18(1–2):45–59. [Reprinted from *Proceedings of the Second Arts and Technology Symposium.* New London, CT: Connecticut College, pp. 101–119.]

"Composition Theory in Koenig's PROJECT 1 and PROJECT 2." In C. Roads, ed. *The Music Machine.* Cambridge, MA: MIT Press, pp. 119–130. [Reprinted from (1981) *Computer Music Journal* 5(4):54–65. Translated into Russian (1983).]

1987

"Verification and Sociological Interpretation in Musicology." *Series Music Theories.* Tokyo, Japan: Keiso, pp. 119–154. (Japanese). [Reprinted from (1977) *International Review of the Sociology & Aesthetics of Music* 8(1):212–236.]

1982

"A Definition of Computer Music." *Proceedings of the 1981 International Computer Music Conference.* San Francisco, CA: Computer Music Association, pp. 31–56.

"A Definition of Computer Music." *Feedback Papers* 27–28:8–24. Cologne, Germany: Feedback Studio Köln.

"L'informatica Musicale." In B. Barbini et al. eds. *Numero e Suono*: *Proceeding of La Biennale di Venezia.* Venice, Italy, pp. 45–48.

1981

"Subscore Manipulation as a Tool for Compositional and Sonic Design." *Proceedings of the 1980 International Computer Music Conference.* Flushing, NY. San Francisco, CA: Queens College and International Computer Music Association, pp. 2–21.

"Automated Composition/Composed Automation." (Translation from the French (G. Englert).) *Computer Music Journal* 5(4):30–35.

"Composition Theory: A New Discipline for Artificial Intelligence and Computer Music." In *Music and Mind*, vol. 2 [of collected papers published 1971-

1981]. San Francisco, CA: International Computer Music Association, pp. 157–196.

1980

"On Composition Theory as a Theory of Self-Reference." In K. Gaburo, ed. *Allos*. La Jolla, CA: Lingua Press, pp. 419–431.

PHILOSOPHY OF ART AND OF THE HUMANITIES

1992

"The Humanities as Sciences of the Artificial." *Interface* 21(3–4):239–255.

1991

"A propos du but projectif de la versification: L'esthétique de Charles Olson." In B. Bel and B. Vecchione, eds. *Actes, séminaire créativité en art*. Université Aix-en-Provence: Centre de Recherche en Sciences de la Musique.

1973

"On the Understanding and Design of Aesthetic Artifacts." *Musik und Verstehen*. Cologne, Germany: Arno Volk Verlag, pp. 189–216.

REVIEWS

1993

"Review of David Cope's Computers and Musical Style." *AI Magazine* 13(2).

1992

"About Vecchione's Musicological Research Today: Interrogations, Interdisciplines, Metamusicology." *Interface* 21(3–4):313–318.

1991

"Understanding Music with AI: An Introduction." *Proceedings of the 1991 International Computer Music Conference*. Montreal, Quebec, McGill University. San Francisco: International Computer Music Association.

1989

"Comments on the First Workshop on A.I. and Music, St. Paul, MN, 1988." *Perspectives of New Music* 27(2).

1987

Review by Marc Leman: "Otto Laske: Music, Memory, and Thought." *Computer Music Journal* 11(4):52–54.

1978

"The Tuning of the World. Review of Murray Schaefer's *Tuning of the World*." *Musical Quarterly* LXIV(3):394–397.

1977
"Toward a Musicology for the Twentieth Century. Review of J. Nattiez's *Fondements d'une sémiologie musicale.*" *Perspectives of New Music* 15:220–225.

SELECTED TEXTS IN GERMAN

1987
"Kurze Einführung in die Kognitive Musikwissenschaft: Die Folgen des Computers in der Musik." In G. Batel, ed. *Computermusik.* Laaber, Germany: Laaber Verlag, pp. 169–194.
"Memorandum zur Gründung eines Instituts für Musikalische Informatik." In G. Batel, ed. *Computermusik.* Laaber, Germany: Laaber Verlag, pp. 79–94.

1983
"Musik und Künstliche Intelligenz: Ein Forschungsüberblick." *Feedback Papers* 30:4–36. Cologne, Germany: Feedback Studio Köln.

1981-1982
"Computermusik und Musikalische Informatik." *Neuland* 2:209–213. [H. Henck, ed., Cologne, Germany.]

1966
"Über die Dialektik Platos und des frühen Hegel" [On the Dialectics of Plato and the Early Hegel]. Ph.D. diss., Goethe Universität, Munich, Germany.

UNPUBLISHED WRITINGS

In English

1990
"Two Approaches to Knowledge Acquisition in Music."

1989
"The Four Time Dimensions of Electro-Acoustic Music."
"The Jyväskylä Lectures on Cognitive Musicology."
"Design Paradigms in Artistic Composition."
"Three Prototypical Approaches in Artistic Composition."

1988
"Composition Theory as a Basis for Second-Generation Computer Music Systems."
"On Cognitive Musicology: Holding, Eliciting, and Modeling Musical Knowledge Observations about PROJECT 1."
"Observations about PROJECT 1."

1986
"Problems and Methods in Cognitive Musicology."

1985

"On Capturing Esoteric Knowledge for Use in Machines."

"On Purposive (or Semantic) Languages."

1984

"COMP1: An Expert System for Issuing Semantic Directives for Generating Musical Scores."

"COMPOSE: A Musical Story Generator."

"On Capturing Arcane and Idiosyncratic Knowledge for Machines."

1983

"AI Topics in Computer-Aided Composition: A Tutorial."

"Models of Musical Planning (NEWCOMP Tutorial in Composition Theory)."

1981

"An Information Processing Model of Melody Composition."

1980

"Preliminary High-Level Specification of a Computerized Music System."

"Requirements Analysis and Specification for a Computerized Music System."

1979

"Toward a Cognitive Theory of Musical Learning."

1978

"Musicology: A Perspective from Cognitive Science."

"On the Context Boundary Problem in Musicology."

"Music Analysis: A Cognitive Perspective."

"Empirical Data Representations for a Musical Process Model."

"Knowing Music, Making Music, and Interactive Computing."

1977

"Music Theory: A Cognitive Perspective."

1976

"A Conceptual Task Analysis of Monolinear Composition."

"GMPS: A General Problem Solver for Melody Composition."

"A Production System Model for OBSERV Protocols."

1975

"Problems in the Meta-Theory of Music."

"Music as a Topic of AI Research."

"Problems in Music Theory: Introduction to a Seminar."

"An Information Processing Model of Melodic Listening."

1974

"Toward an Explicit Model of Compositional Problem Solving."

"Short Report on Research Concerning a Performance Model for Music."

"Report on the Development of Tools for Procedural Research in Sound Systems."

"Real-Time Synthesis and Composition."

1973
"Toward a Science of Musical Problem Solving."

1971
"The Logic Structure of a Generative Grammar for Music."

1970
"A Methodological Inquiry into Computer Music Composition."

1969
"Basic Problems of Artistic and Ordinary Communication."

1968
"On Principles of Artistic Communication." (5 Lectures)
"Christoph Heinrich Koch: A Guide to Musical Composition."

1967
"Musical Time and the Concept of Composition."

In German (Publication in Preparation)

1990
"Zwei Ansätze zur musikalischen Wissensakquisition."

1989
"Die vier Zeitdimensionen der elektro-akustischen Musik."
"Die Integration neuer Technologien in die Denkweisen der Musiker."
"Kompositionstheorie: Ein neues Konzept musikalischer Theorie."

1988
"Karlsruher Masterclass in Computer Composition: Some Demonstrations of Rule-based Composition."

1987
"Das Zusammenwirken von moderner Technik und Kunst im Bereich der Musik: Rückblick und Ausblick" (Karlsruher Vorlesung).

1982
"Einführung in die Computermusik" (mit Martin Supper, Berlin, Germany).
"Begriffliche Grundlagen für das Arbeiten mit Computers in der musikalischen Komposition."

1981
"Einführung in die musikalische Informatik" (mit Martin Supper, Berlin, Germany).

1978
"Ein deutsches Computermusikzentrum."
"Computermusik."

1976
"Probleme kognitiver Musikwissenschaft."

(Utrecht Writings—1970–1974)

1974
"Zwei Ansätze zu einem expliziten Modell kompositorischen Problemlösens" (46 pages).

1973
"Auf dem Wege zu einer Wissenschaft musikalischen Problemlösens" (89 pages).

1972
"Über musikalische Strategien in Hinsicht auf eine generative Theorie der Musik" (22 pages).
"Die Logische Struktur einer generativen musikalischen Grammatik" (30 pages).

1971
"Eine methodologische Untersuchung der Komputerkomposition" (14 pages).
"Über Probleme eines musikalischen Vollzugsmodells" (62 S., übersetzt aus "On Problems of a Performance Model for Music").

1970
"Die logische Struktur einer generativen musikalischen Grammatik" (9 pages).

1966
"Zum Problem der Identität in der Dichtung von John Keats."

1965
"Hindemiths Unterweisung im Tonsatz: Eine methodologische Untersuchung."

1964
"Heinrich Schütz' Trauermotette für J. H. Schein (1630) und ihre Bearbeitung für die Geistliche Chormusik."

Index

About the Editor and Contributors

BERNARD BEL is a computer scientist with a background in electronics. In 1979 he began collaborating with anthropologists, musicologists, and musicians on a scientific study of North Indian melodic and rhythmic systems. In 1981 he designed and built the first accurate real-time melodic movement analyzer (MMA) for the analysis of raga music. He joined the French National Centre for Scientific Research (CNRS) in Marseille in 1986 to continue research on the rule-based modeling of training methods in traditional Indian drumming. Bel's research has been frequently published in journals such as *Anthropology Quarterly*, *Computers & Humanities*, *Leonardo Music Journal*, and the *Journal of New Music Research*. Books in which his writings appear include *Understanding Music With AI* (Balaban, Ebcioglu, and Laske [eds.], Menlo Park, CA: AAAI Press) and *Computer Representations and Models in Music* (Marsden and Pople [eds.], London: Academic Press). Having studied artificial intelligence under Alain Colmerauer, Bel graduated from Aix-Marseille III University with a Ph.D. in theoretical computer science in 1990.

Since 1994, Bel has been deputed to Centre de Sciences Humaines (CSH, New Delhi) to carry on projects in the fields of computational musicology and social-cultural anthropology. His present work is mainly focusing on innovative music forms: different ways of associating musical experience with information technology and questioning the usual modernity/tradition dichotomy outside western culture.

JOEL CHADABE is an internationally recognized pioneer in the development of interactive music systems. As a composer and performer, he has concertized worldwide with Jan Williams, percussionist, and other musicians since 1969. He is listed in the International *Who's Who of Musicians* and the *Who's Who in American Music*. His articles on electronic music have appeared in *Computer Music Journal*, *Contemporary Music Review*, *Electronic Musician*, *Perspectives of New Music*, *Electronic Music Review*, *Melos*, *Musique en Jeu*, and many other journals and magazines. Several of his articles have been anthologized in books by MIT Press, Routledge, and other publishers. His music is recorded on Deep Listening, CDCM, Centaur, Lovely Music, Opus One, CP2, and Folkways labels. He has received awards, fellowships, and grants from the National Endowment for the Arts, New York State Council on the Arts, Ford Foundation, Rockefeller Foundation, Fulbright Commission, SUNY Research Foundation, New York Foundation for the Arts, and other foundations. He has been president and chairman of Composers' Forum, Inc., in New York City. He is currently professor at State University of New York at Albany, and he teaches electronic music at Bennington College. He is president of Intelligent Music, a research and development company and founder and president of Electronic Music Foundation. Mr. Chadabe has a Bachelor of Arts degree from the University of North Carolina at Chapel Hill and a Master of Music degree from Yale University.

MICHAEL HAMMAN is a composer and researcher who develops software systems for music composition and auditory display. He is also investigating the impact data structures, interface metaphors, and other technological frameworks have on the performance of music composition and other problem-posing activities. His writings appear in such books and periodicals as *The Music of Morton Feldman* (Thomas DeLio [Ed.], Westport, CT: Greenwood Press), *Interface*, *Computer Music Journal*, and *Sonus*, for which he compiled and edited an issue on technology and music. His research has been presented at ICMC (1997, 1994, 1991), the Society of Composers Conference, International Conference on Auditory Display (ICAD, 1997), and the Contemporary Music Festival in Seoul, among others. Hamman's compositions and texts trace his research activities. Composed for solo instruments, instrumental ensembles, tape, and computer, his music has been performed and broadcast throughout Europe and North America and in Asia. His recent compositions, *topologies/surfaces/oblique angles/installed parameters* and *replâtrage* appear on the Neuma label's Electro Acoustic Music V and VI compact disks, respectively. Additionally, Hamman's work has brought him numerous fellowships and awards.

Hamman studied composition and theory at the New England Conservatory of Music, the University of Maryland at College Park, and the University of Illinois Urbana-Champaign where he received his doctorate in music composition. He currently lives in Urbana.

GOTTFRIED MICHAEL KOENIG was born in Magdeburg in 1926. He studied church music at the Staatsmusikschule in Braunschweig (1947–1948). From 1948 to 1950 he attended the Nordwestdeutsche Musikakademie in Detmold (where he studied composition, piano, analysis, and acoustics) and the Musikhochschule in Cologne (emphasizing technical aspects in music). He also studied computer structure and programming at the mathematical institute at Bonn University in 1963–1964.

From 1954 to 1964 Koenig worked in the electronic studio at Westdeutscher Rundfunk (WDR Radio) in Cologne. During this period he was an assistant in the radio drama workshop at the Musikhochschule in Cologne, teaching electronic music, composition, and analysis. In 1964, he was appointed artistic director of the electronic studio at Utrecht University (later known as the Institute of Sonology) in the Netherlands, in which country he had been giving annual courses since 1961 at the invitation of the Gaudeamus Foundation in Bilthoven. In 1966–1967 he taught composition and electronic music at the Rheinische Musikschule in Cologne. He has lectured extensively and participated in international congresses throughout Europe and in the United States and Canada.

In the 1960s Koenig developed compositional algorithms (realized in PROJECT 1 and 2) and a computer sound generation program (SSP), and in the

1980s, programs for computer graphics. When the Institute of Sonology moved to the Conservatory of Music at The Hague in 1986, Koenig elected to continue his work in the Netherlands as a freelance composer.

MARC LEMAN was born in Tielt, Belgium, in 1958. He received degrees in musicology (1980) and philosophy (1983), and a doctoral degree in musicology in 1991 from the University of Ghent, Belgium. He is currently research leader at the Fund for Scientific Research and professor in cognitive and systematic musicology at the Universities of Ghent and Leuven.

His research activities concern the epistemological and methodological foundations for computer modeling of music perception, in particular the search for new computational methods of representation and organization and processing of musical information based on pyschoacoustics, computer science, philosophy, music theory, and brain science. Marc Leman has organized several international workshops and conferences and is a founding member of the International Society for Systematic and Comparative Musicology. He is editor of *the Journal of New Music Research* (published by Swets and Zeitlinger), author of *Music and Schema Theory—Cognitive Foundations of Systematic Musicology* (Berlin, Heidelberg: Springer-Verlag, 1995), and editor of *Music, Gestalt, and Computing— Studies in Cognitive and Systematic Musicology* (Berlin, Heidelberg: Springer-Verlag, 1997).

JUKKA LOUHIVUORI received his doctorate at the University of Jyväskylä in 1988 where he conducted research leading to his manuscript entitled *Alternatives in Spiritual Folk Hymn Singing: Musical Distribution and Cognitive Processes*. He is one of the responsible coordinators of the research project, "Tacit Knowledge in Complex Mind-Environment Systems: Cross-Modal Temporal Behavior Modeled with Artificial Neural Network Societies," supported by the Finnish Academy of Science. He organized the First International Conference on Cognitive Musicology in Jyväskylä, Finland (1993). He is an advisory editor of the *Journal of New Music Research*, one of numerous journals in which his essays have been published.

Currently his scientific interest has been focused on modeling cognition with artificial neural networks. The aim of these studies is to understand and explain from a cognitive point of view variation found especially in folk music and oral traditions all over the world. Besides studies in musicology, he has pursued instrumental studies at Sibelius-Academy (Helsinki, Finland) and in Switzerland and the Netherlands specializing in early music and, presently, in Finnish folk music.

CURTIS ROADS is Visiting Associate Professor in the Department of Music at the University of California, Santa Barbara. He has taught at Naples, Harvard, Oberlin, Les Ateliers UPIC, and the University of Paris VIII, where he received his *Diploma d'Etudes Approfondies* in 1995. His composition *Clang-Tint* (1994) was commissioned by the Japan Ministry of Culture (Bunka-cho). Other compositions are available on compact discs produced by the MIT Media Laboratory and by Wergo Schallplatten. He has served as an editor of *Computer Music*

Journal since 1978. His writings include more than one hundred monographs, research articles, reports, and reviews. Some of these have been translated and printed in various languages. Recent books include: *The Computer Music Tutorial* (MIT Press, Cambridge, 1996), *Musical Signal Processing* (coeditor, Swets and Zeitlinger, Amsterdam, 1997), *Le son* (in press, Denki Daigaku Shuppan, Tokyo). A cofounder of the Computer Music Association, he was also cofounder of Newcomp with Otto Laske.

NICO SCHÜLER studied musicology, philosophy, and computer science at E. M. Arndt University (Greifswald, Germany) and A. Humboldt University (Berlin, Germany) and received the Master of Arts in 1995. He has also studied psychology and music education. His professional activities are diverse and include serving as chair of a study group (within the German Society for Music Research) concerned with methods in music research, editor of the series *Kammermusic Heute* [Chamber Music Today], and coeditor of the series *Greifswalder Beitraege sur Musikwissenshaft* [Greifswald Papers on Musicology]. He is author and editor of several published books on computer applications in music and twentieth-century music such as *Hanning Schroeder (1896–1987)* (Hamburg: von Bockel), *Festschrift Kurt Schwaen* (Frankfurt: Lang), and *Zum Problem und zu Methoden von Musicanalyse* (Hamburg: von Bockel, 1996). Nico Schüler is presently on leave from his teaching position at Greifswald University to complete his Ph.D. in music theory at Michigan State University in East Lansing, Michigan.

JERRY TABOR is assistant professor of music in the Department of Music at Salisbury State University (Salisbury, Maryland) where he coordinates and teaches in the composition, computer music, and theory programs. He has also taught courses in composition, electronic music, interdisciplinary arts, and creativity theories while on the faculties of Trinity College in Washington, D.C., and the University of Maryland, Baltimore County. His research and lecture activities include computer music, composition theory (a subdomain of cognitive musicology), and chaos theory and creativity theories as they apply to the compositional process. He has received numerous commissions, and his music is performed throughout the United States and is recorded on the Neuma label. He holds Doctor of Musical Arts and Master of Music degrees in composition from the University of Maryland at College Park where he studied theory and composition with the eminent Thomas DeLio.

BARRY TRUAX received his formal training in both the sciences (at Queen's University) and music (at the University of British Columbia). He has also studied at the Institute of Sonology in Utrecht with G. M. Koenig and Otto Laske. He is presently a professor in both the School of Communication and the School for the Contemporary Arts at Simon Fraser University (British Columbia, Canada) where he teaches courses in acoustic communication and electroacoustic music. He has worked with the World Soundscape Project, editing its *Handbook for Acoustic Ecology*, and has published a book, *Acoustic Communication*, dealing with all aspects of sound and technology. As a composer, Truax is best known for his work with the PODX computer music system which he has used for tape solo works and those which combine tape with live performers or computer graphics. A selection of these pieces may be heard on the recording *Sequence of Earlier Heaven*, and the Compact Discs *Digital Soundscapes, Pacific Rim*, and *Song of Songs*—all on the Cambridge Street Records label. In 1991, his work *Riverrun*, was awarded the Magisterium at the International Competition of Electroacoustic Music in Bourges, France, a category open only to eletroacoustic composers of twenty or more years experience.

ISBN 0-313-30632-X

90000>

HARDCOVER BAR CODE